TALES OF A TRAV

BY
BERNIE HOWGATE

**FOR MY DEAR MOTHER WHO GAVE ME THE
STRENGTH TO REACH FOR THE STARS AND
MY FATHER WHO PUT FIRE IN MY BELLY**

*Go for it David
from one cyclist to another
happy trails
Bernie Howgate*

The Travelling Man
Enterprises

TALES OF A TRAVELLING MAN
First Edition

WRITTEN AND EDITED
Bernie Howgate

COVER, MAPS, ILLUSTRATIONS
AND PHOTOGRAPHS
Bernie Howgate

PUBLISHED
The Travelling Man Enterprises
11 Andrews Avenue
Toronto
Ontario M6J 1S2
Canada

FIRST EDITION
1990

Printed in Canada

ISBN - 0 - 9694419 - 0 - 8

I SHOULD HAVE CHECKED MY BIKE MORE CLOSELY, BUT more important things than travel were on my mind. That morning I'd read and reread her letter, wearing out each word in turn. Eighteen months. Had it really been that long? I'd given up hope of ever seeing her again. Her last letter was from Sri Lanka where she was en route to Bombay and her flight home. In that letter she mentioned working in Greenland, now she was writing from Delhi. Until her letter, I'd planned to rest my bike and spend Christmas walking in the Himalayas, but the thought of her so close was like a magnet.

I started out from Kathmandu washed in the crisp cool of pre dawn dew, but my brain was in Delhi, still dancing with the thoughts of our meeting. Having, through travel, missed the kind of physical tenderness close relationships offer, pictures of our times together now drifted in and out of my mind.

We were in bed, I was holding her. I knew that was all she wanted, but something inside drove me to make love.

A truck passed, I braked, then the road cleared.

I watched her walk down the street towards me. I was always stealing glances. She would be ugly one minute then, some movement, expression of her face, made ugliness impossible. She was in my arms. Then, suddenly she was gone.

In front the road arced. I was drifting. Smells of oil mixed with rubber. Then silence. Slowly reality focused on a twisted bicycle frame, then pain. Oh God, the pain........

MAP ILLUSTRATIONS

CONTENTS

Every account of a journey celebrates an event that can no longer occur and mine is no different. I didn't find the missing link while I was away and women are still a mystery. I now have exchanged the fresh air of travel for Toronto's pollution count but I don't care. I am home. Once again street directions follow straight lines and there is no chance of getting lost!

Here I again make my way around the world but, this time, on paper. I trust my readers will skirt that obstacle called detail, long since altered, and offer me a ride on their imaginations.

Chapter 1:
On the Outside Looking In

I HAD THIS SUDDEN IMPULSE TO PACK MY BAGS AND GET away. Maybe it wasn't a question of escaping, but more of being released into my own custody. All through my 20's I'd been tied to relationships. Now I just wanted to stop running from one woman to the next.

Irena, my ex-wife from England, had supported me through immigration to Canada and, for the last eighteen months, Alison had been the other half of my life. Now she was gone too. I was now past the big Three-O and restless, or was it rudderless. All around my life seemed to be crumbling. I now felt squeezed between a love for freedom and that inner need for stability.

"Take time out." Tom had said.

He was a true friend. Squash partner, drinking buddy and confidant. We'd met in Toronto soon after my immigration from England to Canada in the early 70's and been a permanent fixture ever since.

"You've nothing to lose. Why don't you stand on your own two feet for once."

I spent one week buying equipment and another tuning my bike. I planned on a two month vacation. Time enough, I thought. It was the year the Golden Arches had reached the 50 billion mark. Little did I know then but the Big Mac would have surpassed 70 billion before my trip would end.

On my first day, I was already in panic. I had not wanted to start from Toronto on my bike; turning back would have been too easy, so I had bought a train ticket to Amherst, New Brunswick. Now I found myself on its platform, cycle bags in hand, but with no bike.

"Where's my bike?" I accosted the first uniform I saw.

"Steady on there, no bike came today."

Before he had even finished his sentence, I realized I had sent it the day before. Anticipating first day nerves, I had sent my bike on by train from Toronto.

I am not the most organized person you will meet, and if rushed, I panic easily. After I apologized for my mistake, the

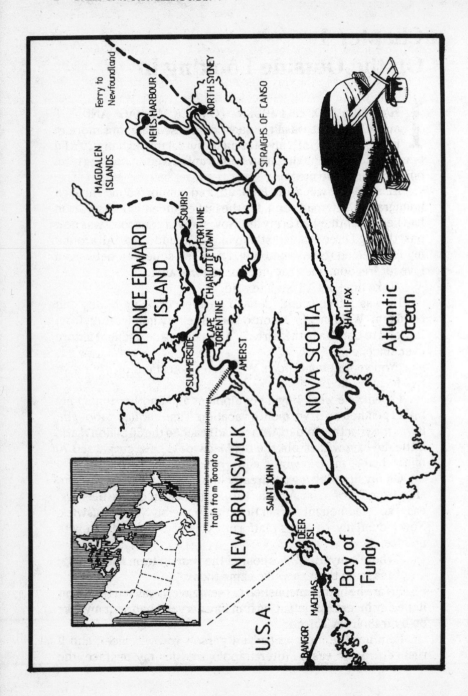

Ferry to Newfoundland

NEILS HARBOUR

NORTH SYDNEY

STRAIGHS OF CANSO

MAGDALEN ISLANDS

SOURIS

FORTUNE

PRINCE EDWARD ISLAND

CHARLOTTETOWN

CAPE TORENTINE

SUMMERSIDE

AMERST

Atlantic Ocean

HALIFAX

NOVA SCOTIA

train from Toronto

NEW BRUNSWICK

SAINT JOHN

DEER ISL.

Bay of Fundy

U.S.A.

MACHIAS

BANGOR

porter took me into the baggage room. There she was, propped up in a corner, looking for all the world like a long lost pup.

Having not practised putting on my saddle bags before leaving, I would be into my second week before finding the most practical packing arrangements. The front and rear saddle bags were comparatively easy to work out, if difficult to secure. The distribution of weight was the early problem. The sleeping bag was a heavy down type. I also carried a water-proofer which acted as a one man tent. A simple plastic half-moon rod arrangement fitted into the front, keeping the cover away from my face. Simple yes, but awkward to pack away. It was obvious from the start I had bought too many clothes, but being determined not to get cold and lacking any previous experience of cycling touring, I decided too much was infinitely better than too little. On the front of the bike, secured across the handle bars, hung my combined camera and map container. This clumsy looking piece of equipment proved to be my best investment.

I was surprised how soon I got the feel for the bike. The extra weight smoothed out the bumps in the road and also helped to steady the steering. My rear end was soon, however, to feel the discomfort of my not having listened to sound advice. It would not be until much later that I would change my plastic saddle for the comforts of a leather one.

By noon I had left Amherst station behind, en route to the Cape Tormentine Ferry to Prince Edward Island. I spent the first evening in a baptism of rain. My water-proofer leaked. Cycling through the rolling hills of the island's interior, the rain would follow me for the next few days. In the evenings I slept at Youth Hostels in Charlottetown and Midgel, before once again taking to the sea. From Souris I boarded the eight hour ferry to French speaking Magdelen Island only to find my arrival coincided with one of Canada's 'long weekends'.

These 'long weekends' (as if Canadians needed an excuse) are devoted almost entirely towards extended parties. Set aside for tribal get togethers in this land of many cultures, these mini-holidays were planned weeks in advance. Starting on a Friday night they would often continue unbroken until the early hours of Tuesday morning. Already the island was in festive spirits as many of its residents had already drunk and smoked themselves into a zombie-like state. This combination of drink and drugs acted as a catalyst, bridging the gap between the French/English antagonists, and was amusing to see.

I spent the first evening in Magdelen's only Hostel and on the second day struck up an immediate friendship with Carl, a small time film producer from New York. He was in his his mid-forties with a long grey beard and crew-cut hair and, like myself, had chosen cycling as a way of spending time alone. He told me of his experiences cycling in downtown Manhattan traffic, his arguments with Kamikaze taxi drivers, near misses with pedestrians and the inevitable over commercialization of bicycle clothes, the helmets, multi-coloured sweat shirts, and black padded knickers.

"You name it, they'll sell it", he said. "We'll all have to wear bloody helmets soon". His statement was humourous, but there was a vein of seriousness in it. "Why should I have to wear a helmet? If I'm going to be hit, I'm going to be hit. It's my problem, not the insurance man's. Before cyclist's in Manhattan started to complain, it was an unwritten law that cyclists gave way to cars, and cars, in turn, looked out for cyclists. Now it's open season on cyclists. Taxi drivers are pissed off with weekend cyclists and their government-backed lobby in Washington. Cyclists are getting too aggressive and their aggressions aren't always vented out on the roads. Soon pedestrians will have to wear helmets. The world's gone crazy. Just take my divorce. Lawyer tells me not to see my wife. I spent most of my life with her. Who is the best person to talk to her? Me or some anonymous lawyer working on a percentage? But I went along with it. Now she's getting less than I would have given her. That's lawyers for you. If I was to be hit by a taxi driver, it's probable that I'd never see him, only his lawyer. No-one gives a damn about your feelings, only your bank balance." I had a funny feeling he was right.

On Monday night the outgoing ferry to Prince Edward Island was full to overflowing. Magdelen's merry band of weekend rabble rousers were heading for the mainland and that unenviable Tuesday morning start at the office.

That afternoon the sun moved through a cloudless sky, I had not had one clear night since leaving Toronto so, taking advantage of the change in weather, turned off the main road at Fortune and headed down an unmarked track to the sea. Once on the beach I built a fire out of driftwood, then settled back to watch the sunset with a cigarette and a mug of coffee. One coffee led to another. I began to relax. Even the mosquitoes didn't bother me. By now the sky was royal blue and, as the first blushes of red streaked the horizon, I rearranged my sleeping bag nearer the fire and fell asleep.

Suddenly the air was full of violent noises. My legs were gripped. I half stood, then fell. Only yards away a black object was struggling to get away. Trapped in my sleeping bag I made a vain lunge towards it. A cloud of sand blinded me, then suddenly the struggle was over. It rose in the air. Taken for driftwood, I'd been an unwelcome landing sight. For a few moments it looked as if the Crane had lost its sense of direction, then circling the beach for a few minutes, it came to rest in a nearby tree. From his new vantage point he turned and glared at me. The feeling was mutual. It was then that I realized I was totally alone. I was miles from anywhere. Under normal circumstances I could have laughed off the incident, but this time there was no one to laugh with. I looked up. Above me the night sky was lit by the fluorescent curtain of 'northern lights' yet, as I lay back, even the rhythmic sounds of rushing water over pebbles couldn't take away the overwhelming feeling of loneliness that now crept over me.

The following morning my friend was still there. Was he guarding me? Or just intent in staring me out? Packing my saddle bags I left the beach under his watchful eye. Then, heading back to Fortune, I cycled straight into an invitation.

A farmer's breakfast is not for the weak stomached and what

the morning served up was to fill more than a little niche. Dominating the kitchen a stout wooden table seemed set for an army. In fact only four of us ate. Underfoot a bare wooden floor still bore evidence on previous feasts and, by the sights and sounds emanating from a large gas stove, would soon have another coating. First course consisted of an overflowing bowl of Cornflakes topped off with grated apple and, needless to say, I needed no prompting for seconds. Fresh air and exercise had given me an appetite and already my fuel tank was stretching to accommodate more food. First course slipped into the next. A large plate of 'standing room only' rashers of bacon was cleaned down to its pattern and when a dozen eggs appeared whatever semblance of table manners I had were forgotten. Sliced tomatos and beans and bread disappeared and when a large chunk of home made apple pie drowned in cream was put in front of me, I knew I was near the end.

After breakfast I was taken out into the barn to watch the milking, then, afterwards, I was introduced into the economics of barter. "Stick around Bernard, we're having lobster for dinner". The wily old farmer was exchanging excess milk for locally caught fish. Government quotas made little sense to this man. Seasons here were short and one year's surplus could easily lead to one year's loss. "Government turn a blind eye to our bartering, but that's as far as it goes. They take a much dimmer view towards our local stills." He took me behind the barn to an outbuilding.

"Like it?"

Inside I found an engineering feat of copper tube. Coils snaked everywhere and condensers secured precariously on top of odd shaped brackets gave it a 'hillbilly' look of home made industry.

"Only liquor outlet in these parts is over twenty miles away in Souris, so we make our own."

True to his word we had lobster for lunch and then in the afternoon, mostly to work off excess fuel, I helped bale the hay. In the evening he took me to the village dance hall, a converted chapel, where music was supplied by a small group of home bred musicians comprising drummer, accordionists, electric guitarist and fiddle player. The hall was small but bustling with people, but no sooner had the music begun then the men drifted outside. Inside there was no alcohol but it didn't matter. Everyone had brought his own supply and by 10:00 pm there was more action outside then in.

The following day I decided to leave and by late afternoon I was back on the mainland. Once again the weather broke. The wind changed direction and increased in strength all day, blowing the rain into my face. At one stage I was so frustrated I stopped riding and pushed the bike in an effort to calm myself down. Since Toronto I had cycled either with or under threat of wind and rain everyday and not only had it broken my momentum, but also my spirit. The weather was getting colder and wetter. I continually argued with myself, searching for reasons to continue. After two weeks, I was already in uncharted waters. This, so-called, break from work routine was turning into a survival course.

My frustrations boiled over into violent anger the day I approached the Cape Breton Causeway. I had drifted into the middle of the road, my concentration gone. The truck behind me had no option. It was a miracle he found space between me and the curb barrier. The first I realized there was anything wrong was when he came alongside. Then the force of the tail wind hit me. Handle bars jarred out of my grip. The road fell away, and I ended up in a ditch. I was enraged. The driver stopped and got out of his cab. Weeks of frustration were vented on him as I shouted one obscenity after another. He stood there for a moment without saying anything, then jerked one finger up at me, jumped into his cab and was gone.

Suddenly my whole body started shaking. Who was I fighting? Coming out of the bend, he must have seen me at the last moment and had he not been so alert they would be scraping me off the road right now. He had even stopped to help me. I had to pull myself together or next time I might not be so lucky.

Before I knew it I had crossed the short causeway over the Straight of Canso and entered Cape Breton. The accident left me in no mood to continue so, breaking old rules, I decided to stop in the first hotel I saw, no matter what the cost.

What a blissful feeling a warm bath can give when you're feeling low. The heat seeped through my skin. Aching muscles were soothed and after it I stood for quite some time in front of the full length mirror. The veins in my forearms were protruding, and biceps and leg muscles hardened from daily exercises were defined. My stomach was flat and hard. Gone were those earlier signs of city fat. My body was beginning to show the fruit of outdoor living and I felt good. My rear padding, so used to the comforts of office life, was also tight, but beginning to show those tell tale signs of wear and tear brought about by the plastic saddle. I had tried various methods to alleviate the pains. I had raised the saddle, lowered it, even tried to change my position from sitting at the very front to balancing at the very back. My latest idea had been to tie a towel over it, but this proved only a temporary measure. There was no secure way of tying a towel around the saddle and to some degree these setbacks made me resign myself to the inevitable. I had either to grow another layer of skin, or the one I had at present would have to become as hard as leather. Back pains were also a persistent irritation. Bent over the dropped handlebars for long periods was putting strains on untried areas of my body and this led to the experiment with raising and lowering the handle bars, even to the point of redistribution of weight. For days I would be continually repacking saddle bags in an effort to find the correct balance.

Despite the aching limbs, painful sores and irritating noises from the bike, I decided that only time would solve that problem. However there would be no more self-imposed daily mileages. I would have to learn to live without that particular goal. As for my body, only time would solve that problem.

In the morning the weather cleared and by noon I had joined the Cabot Trail. Cycling under clear blue skies I saw, in front of me, the impressive mountains of Cape Breton. Rising eerily out of the sea, with their tops shrouded in mist, they not only dominated my view, but my mind. Soon I was either cycling or pushing the bike up 1 in 4 gradients. At the top I was lost to the mist and freewheeling down, pockets of clear weather opened the window onto sights of wild, barren inlets. A hiss carried on the wind could suddenly turn into a deafening roar, as turning corners would often release more than a surprise view. That day the road would seldom stray from the coast and by late afternoon the sight of a secluded beach seduced me down to the sea.

My arrival in the small fishing village of Port Hood was washed with music. By now I was tired, too tired to investigate anything but the building that now faced me. A large hand-painted poster revealed the source of the music. I'd cycled straight into a village dance. I hadn't the patience to unpack my bags or the energy to camp. I had even lost my bicycle lock the previous week so, throwing all caution to the wind, I changed openly into my jeans and followed the music inside.

"What would you like?"

In front of me a make shift bar was flooded with the spillage of beer. I had stumbled into Port Hood's monthly dance and before I finished my first glass I had been introduced to nearly all the room's regulars and, spurred on by my third, was courting nearly all the local girls. The dance was in full swing and judging by my alcoholic state, both around and above me. Later in the evening I was approached by the chairman of the social club. He informed me in a polite, but authoritative manner that I would be billeted for the night in one of the regular's houses. He didn't want me to sleep on the beach. "There's thieves and muggers about, son."

By midnight the doors were locked, the women sent home, and the remaining men were gearing themselves up for a heavy night's drinking session. At sometime in the night I saw the chairman standing over me through a haze of smoke and light. He was definitely talking to me. His face had changed from that of laughter to that of a concerned friend. What was he saying? Suddenly he disappeared from my vision and was replaced by the cracks in the ceiling. Slowly the room started to move. The feeling was not an uncomfortable one, but when a biting chill hit me, nausea swept through my body in uncontrollable spasms.

"Don't worry, John Henry will see you home tonight. You'll find your bike in his house."

Again the ground moved. Then, weightlessness.

The next day I woke to the smells and crackling sounds of pork sausages cooking. I know people say the last thing you can stomach after a heavy night is greasy food, but that morning I surprised myself, eating a full plate of sausage, bacon, eggs and beans with relish and feeling none the worse for it either.

Only ten miles from North Sydney, my tyre exploded, shredding the inner tube. I hadn't considered tyre wear and consequently had no spares. I took the wheel off, then holding it in the air started thumbing. The ploy worked. I was only hitching for a matter of minutes before a pick-up truck stopped. Thirty minutes later I was dropped outside of North Sydney Youth Hostel. Then I spent the rest of the day downtown trying vainly to find a replacement tyre. Eventually I had to order one and, resigning

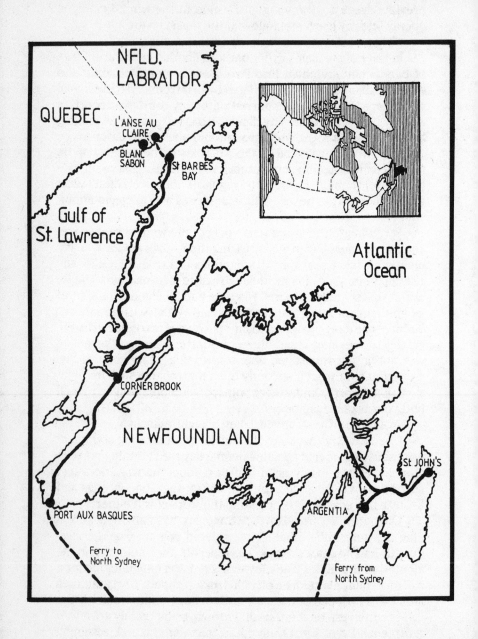

myself to a two week wait, I booked a passage on the ferry to Newfoundland for the following day.

That evening in the hostel I became engrossed in a long conversation with a group of American cyclists on a study trip of the Canadian Maritimes. They were all from various schools in the Boston area and ranged in ages from 14 to 16. The group leader, a school teacher, spoke of his pupils with the same concern a father has for his children. He impressed me with the way he instilled confidence and he also understood the need for good team spirit when taking his charges out.

"We ask the stronger cyclists to stay at the back to encourage the weaker ones. We also have a map reading section. Here we pair an academic student with a grasp of map reading with one that excels in streetwise survival. It doesn't always work, but it never gets boring. Last week many of the girls started doing more physical tasks, and the boys took over the cooking duties. It's an incredible turnabout, but I don't think it will last. Things haven't changed that much under the surface." He said it more as a joke than as a statement. "When we started we hadn't planned it this way, it's just evolved. We began by putting the emphasis on role expanding, sharing skills, not developing ones they have. We hope to make them more aware of their own needs and how to fit into group situations. All very philosophical," he laughed. "At least none of the girls are pregnant. We thought with bringing teenagers along that sex would be a major problem. But so far they all seem to be trying to impress each other with their maturity. I think it's the closeness of being around each other every day. Familiarity breeds contempt. Isn't that what you English say? The teachers are the ones with the problem." With a smile he pointed out one of the girls. " Just look at Kathy, she's bursting out all over."

It was a tiring crossing from North Sydney and to compound my frustration when the boat docked at Argentia Bay, I found no bus service.

"Come on lad. Want to share a taxi?"

It was the same group of singing Newfoundlanders who had kept me up all night, but once inside I soon began to melt to their humour and needed little persuasion to join them in a pub crawl of St John's watering holes. They had much in common with the people from the north of England; the Gaelic heritage ensures strong family ties, and wherever we went that evening, a tradition of large families was much in evidence. Their accents, dress and bluntness of speech were like a breath of fresh air and in their company I was introduced back into a life I hadn't experienced since my emigration to Canada. Tap rooms, darts, dominoes, and soccer were either played or talked about. I had only planned on an overnight stay in St John's, before pushing inland, but I ended up staying a week, and it was on one of those evenings drinking in the "Crown and Anchor" that I met Christa.

Christa, a German, was the kind of girl who took situations head on, having that economy of grace and style, that only the bluntest of women possess. Her courage (or was it naivete?) gave her the ability to tackle anything and, discovering that we were both heading in the same direction, she set about detailing not only our route, but the time it would take to cross Newfoundland, with the precision of a railway timetable.

"We need to start hitching before eight o'clock. We catch the Route 30 bus to the city limits and start there. I will organize breakfast and you can make sandwiches. If the weather is good we arrive Cornerbrook before eleven o'clock in the evening."

Amazingly, she was right on all accounts. She even kept a surprise for me. Weeks before, in Winnipeg, she had made arrangements with friends to arrive on this date, and when we eventually arrived they were, not only expecting her, but had anticipated her being with a partner. Beds were ready and a meal prepared within minutes.

Christa may have been a little overbearing at times, but I missed her organizational abilities the next day. Not only did I have to wait for over two hours for my first lift, but I also missed her knack for choosing the right ones. For the rest of the day I found myself leapfrogging from one village to the next; crawling up the coast to St Barbe's Bay en route to the Labrador ferry. Each lift dropped me off in the middle of nowhere with neither shelter nor the opportunity to buy food and, to make matters worse, I was reduced to wearing plastic garbage bags for protection against the ever increasing rain. So it was with great relief that I arrived in St Barbes Bay and, feeling cold and wet, I headed straight for its only hotel. First I enquired about the times of the ferry. Then:

"How much are the rooms?"

"Full up."

"Do you know where I can sleep then?"

"Don't know."

I couldn't believe his attitude. What did he expect me to do? Sleep out in the rain? By now it was dark outside; and the few street lights St Barbe's had were already veiled in sheets of rain. I was getting desperate and, spotting a light down by the wharf, made for the ferry. It was my last chance for shelter.

"Can I see the captain?"

"He's in the hotel."

"Would he let me sleep on board?"

"You'll have to ask him."

I turned to walk back to the hotel.

"Wait a minute lad. He's with a lady." A smile broke across his face. "He'll not like being disturbed."

By this time I was cold, wet and hungry and very, very tired. Nothing seemed to be going right. Then suddenly;

"Want a pot of tea?"

"Sure. Where did you come from?"

"Here, you're stood by the side of it." It was the diesel generator house that fuel the harbour. "I'm the night shift engineer. I overheard your conversation with the boat keeper. Stay here if you want. That's if you don't mind sleeping on the floor."

A dry floor sounded like paradise and I didn't have to be asked twice. Not only did I get a mug of tea, but half his pack sandwiches as well.

"You can hang up your clothes if you want." He pointed to the generator. The noise was deafening, but infinitely better than the sound of rain outside and, by the time I climbed into my sleeping bag, a third world war would not have stirred me.

In the morning all my clothes were dry and before leaving I was offered another mug of tea.

On the stroke of ten the old ferry left for Labrador. To say it was old was being kind. It still retained its original chrome/brass fittings and the smell of grease on polished woodwork stained the air. It looked solid and dependable, if a little on the slow side. On more than one occasion, great volumes of oil were jettisoned into the sea and the noises emanating from the engine room were not like any I'd heard on previous ferries. It was a venerable floating museum, as were many of its passengers, but worth the previous day's hardships just to experience.

The ferry landed at Blanc Sabon like an old lady would approach a railway crossing; precariously. First the engines prodded the old girl forward, then a splutter and a jerk announced reverse. A sharp command from the captain released a rope, and yet another extinguished the engines. The silence at first was beautiful, but when we started to drift away from the wharf, it became disturbing. Worried eyes followed an even more worried crew. Then a loud bang, lost in a cloud of smoke meant we'd landed. This was the cue for a spontaneous burst of applause. The ordeal was over, and when the gang plank was unceremoniously pushed over the side, no one wanted to stay a minute longer than was possible.

What made me come to this place? In front lay a ramshackle assortment of wooden houses and framed behind a bleak treeless wilderness smudged the town's backdrop in different shades of pale green. I turned to a fellow passenger.

"Could you direct me to the Youth Hostel please?"

"Parlez vous francais?"

With a name like Blanc Sabon I should have guessed I was in French speaking Quebec. I tried the little French I knew.

"J'aller Hostel de Jeunes. Direction, s'il vous plait?"

"Yes, it is in L'anse au Claire. Two miles north."

I'd found the key. Fumbling with my Beginner's French had opened the door to his excellent English.

I entered Blanc Sabon through a maze a dirt tracks and exited on the road north only moments later. The town had comprised two shops and a post office and, being lunchtime, all movement flowed towards its only bar. The road I now walked on was covered with a thin film of oil. I'd seen it before in remoter towns in the Yukon, a practise used to stop dust from blowing around during dry weather. Was this a good omen? I hoped it was.

The character of the inhabitants of L'anse au Claire had been moulded by its scenery. Bleak, windswept and made to last. Everyone I'd met since leaving the ferry had a natural tilt and, depending upon the prevailing wind, either glided with it or tacked against it. Obviously, there, beauty, as we know it, was not a priority. Excess fat, man's natural insulation against long, hard winters was much in evidence. A hand pointed the way to the Youth Hostel and in doing so blotted out the sun. Had the short ones been weeded out at birth? I asked myself. Then, moments later, the question was answered. Stepping off the boardwalk I was swallowed up waist deep in a sea of mud.

The Youth Hostel wasn't hard to find. Starved of variety, it doubled as the town's 'drop-in centre' and, within minutes of my entering, its willing residents had set about the tasks of doing my shopping and laundry. I was soon adopted into Labrador's life of the extended family. Invitations came thick and fast. I went fishing, hunting, and even turned out for the local baseball team. Well, that's what they called it.

Invited for lunch, you couldn't blame me for thinking the whole team was to be fed. "I can't remember all my children's names. I have to write them down". Having set the table for her fourteen children, she picked up a large cast iron bell, rang it loudly, then stepped back while the rush hour traffic of gnashing teeth filled her kitchen. In her house the food never had time to go cold and latecomers would find their helpings someone else's seconds.

I waited until my last night before taking advantage of one of Canada's many time zones. As luck would have it, this unique geological landmark cut straight between the towns of Blanc Sabon and L'anse au Claire. This unusual fact didn't go unnoticed by the locals and, to celebrate my last night, I was made to straddle this two hour time zone for, as the bars closed in Labrador we cross the two miles into Quebec, continuing our drinking until the early hours of the morning.

The following day I left for Newfoundland en route to North Sydney and my replacement tyre. Back at the Youth Hostel I received devastating news. A truck had spun out of control killing one of the teenage American cyclists and badly injuring the group leader I had spoken to. I remembered my own near escape and Carl's earlier warnings. I had to become more road conscious or I would end up under an eight wheeler as well.

Leaving North Sydney I followed the shore of Lake Bras D'or before again crossing the Straight of Canso to the mainland. From there I took the coastal road south to Halifax. I was now beginning to feel like a seasoned traveller and, having put earlier disappointments and cold weather behind me, no longer expected to make silly mistakes. I hadn't bothered with bike security since Port Hood, having by now acquired a sixth sense as to its safety. I even began to know when to expect trouble from strangers and had

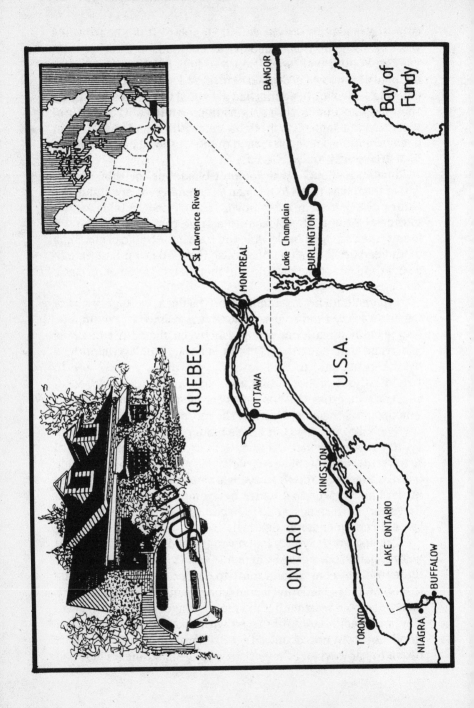

figured out how to defuse it. I also seemed to know what the trucks and cars were going to do before they did, and felt free to enjoy the scenery without too much distraction from the traffic.

The days were getting warmer and the nights clearer. More and more I found myself taking advantage of this break in the weather. Beaches again were slept on and fields, now stripped bare of their harvest and dried by the sun, were making welcoming beds so, on arriving in Halifax, I was in no mood to be reminded of city life and stayed only long enough to mail letters home. From Halifax I turned north and crossed through the interior of Nova Scotia in a frantic attempt to reach St John, New Brunswick before the weekend. I hadn't had any mail since leaving Toronto and my only post pickup, through an old working colleague, was c/o Xerox Canada Ltd. and its office in St John would be closed on Saturday.

The young girl on the reception was full of smiles.

"Forgotten our clothes this morning, sir?"

In my excitement, I'd jumped off the bike and dashed straight into St John's Xerox office without even changing. On the road I'd let common hygiene slip. Smartness now was a luxury I found hard to carry.

"Sorry love. My name's Bernard Howgate; have you my mail?"

Thankfully she had been warned of my arrival and, within minutes, was handing over a small file containing letters. I immediately opened the one from Alison. It read as I expected, but not as hoped for. She had left Canada for good. I'd cycled for two months with the thread of hope that she would return to Toronto from Europe. Now that I found her decision final, I left St John cocooned in questions I would have to answer on my return to Toronto.

Alison's letter had knocked my confidence sideways. I just wanted to finish. People and places now passed me without notice and each day found me sinking deeper and deeper into my problems. Then, entering Toronto, the sight of a roadside billboard shot me to the surface.

"TERRY FOX CANCER AGAIN"

Following a routine check-up, tests had proved positive. He had cancer. Three months before, news of this man's epic run had inspired me. If he could run Canada from coast to coast on one leg, I thought, then I could surely put up with the discomfort of cycling only half that distance. Now the realization that this young man would probably die of cancer put all my problems into perspective.

Two hours later I was cycling up Toronto's Queen Street, I was nearly home. I called in at the Balmy Beach Club hoping to see friends. It was empty. Then I went to the phone.

"Hi Tom. I'm back."

I had spent only two months away but already a gap had formed between me and my old environment. I now felt a degree of loneliness riding those busy streets that I had never felt before. Without an Alison to return to I felt adrift. My time away had solved nothing. I needed to set new goals. Then, entering City Square, I saw a picture of the Canadian Rockies. In that moment the die was cast and, even before Tom arrived to meet me, I had made up my mind to leave Toronto.

I left my saddest goodbye and hardest decision till last. We met in a restaurant. Irena looked stunning. We had separated in spirit long before Alison had entered my life and, now that I was leaving Toronto, I felt we should finally make it legal. All that week I had put off the inevitable meeting. Now we sat across a table from each other, sharing a bottle of wine. Our time apart had forced out a mature independence I'd not seen in her before. Irena had been part of my life for over seven years. We had met and married in England when I was a struggling draughtsman. Hard times together bonded us in a way that could be neither easily broken nor forgotten. Canada had led us to the easy life, gave us both the freedom we had not experienced before. Inevitably, this led to a rift and we drifted apart. This fact didn't make our decision to divorce any easier.

Within the week I'd said all my goodbyes. My new world now consisted of a change of clothes, toothbrush, car and bike. My plan was to move across Canada. I had no plans to work, no friends to visit. The real travel was just beginning and vulnerability to the unknown, as I was soon to find out, would be its main ingredient.

Chapter 2:
Burning Bridges

"**W**ILL YOU PLEASE PULL OVER SIR?"
Now cars had started talking to me. I'd never seen talking cars before, but then I knew you didn't mess around the Royal Canadian Mounted Police. Those words, "We always get our man", are not to be scoffed at. I was in Vancouver. It was my first day and I'd been out celebrating. Not drunk. Not sober either. I stopped the car, stepped out and slipped. Guilty. I didn't hear it, but I felt it.

"Did you know you were riding the double yellow line sir?"

It was a combination of drink and his emphasis on the words "double yellow line". I tried to suppress a smile but failed miserably.

"Sorry officer. Just arrived from Toronto. Was out celebrating."

"Don't they have drinking and driving laws in Toronto, or maybe you were just checking us out?"

He asked for my driver's licence and while he conveyed the information back to base, his partner gave my car the full check-up treatment.

"Could you get into your car please?"

"What is your licence plate number sir?"

I gave it.

"Can you depress your brake pedal sir?"

"Left indicator please? Right indicator? Thank-you."

"Could you engage reverse now sir? Thank-you."

"Have you in your possession any illegal drugs, or alcohol sir?"

"No officer."

It seemed like an eternity before he finished. If I wasn't sober before, I sure was now. His partner came over to join us.

"We have to advise you sir, that in the event you drive away in your car, we shall be forced to act upon our suspicions. It is your first day in our city. We don't want to spoil it. For your own safety, we advise you to leave your car here and walk to your place of residence."

Where is your place of residence sir?"
"I was on my way to the Youth Hostel."
It wasn't to end there.
"Hop in. We will give you a lift."
I couldn't believe in my luck. The boys in blue did themselves proud that evening. Had it been my English accent? My naivety? Or were the Gods smiling on me? "Welcome to Vancouver."

I stayed two weeks. Initial euphoria evaporated quickly. I spent hours walking aimlessly through a maze of city streets. Window displays went unnoticed and street noises didn't register. Disillusionment set in quickly and I began to feel trapped by the city and its people. Soon I was retreating from the hustle of street life. Unable to join in or enjoy, I now found myself searching for open spaces. Eventually I decided on a day out from the city as a tonic.

I only meant to see the mountains. "Back by teatime," I told the warden at the Youth Hostel. But I wasn't. I stopped to pick up a hitch-hiker just outside Vancouver and by nightfall I was sleeping in the car in a roadside park, somewhere in the province of Alberta.

Calgary, Canada's answer to Dallas. "Who killed J.R.?", was only weeks away, and John Lennon was about to take his last walk. The advertisement informing visitors: "Calgary is the fastest-growing city in North America", could be a little misleading to the casual visitor. The density of new high-rises gave one the overall impression of a young boy outgrowing his clothes. True, all downtown buildings were new, but some of its busier streets were either gravel or still under construction.

For some people, living within its boundaries was not enough. They had to own a piece of its most costly real estate. Here, oil was the name of the game. Men were men and women were expensive and it was compulsory to wear the Stetson Hat during Stampede Week. Rough diamonds, they may have looked, swaggering down the streets in their cowboy outfits but, given the chance, they showed a surprising warmth that I felt was lacking in their more cosmopolitan counterparts in the East. Set apart from the rest of Canada, (the Rocky Mountains to the West and the vast Prairie to the East) in Calgary there were less pressures on people to conform. There was a sense of freedom which ran through their veins, a cast back to the old Klondike days when men ruled the tides of change and the pioneering spirit was strong. It took people with a certain steel-like quality to live within these concrete and glass towers.

Later that week I took a ride out into the foothills. Looking down from this new vantage point, Calgary took on a new perspective. Concrete towers rose like great phallic symbols stretching towards the heavens. I wondered what shape architecture would take if women held the powers of change. Would every thing be of circular design with soft smooth surface.

I spent the next month alternating between sleeping in the car and Calgary's Y.M.C.A. With unlimited time on my hands I began to look over my shoulder back to Toronto. Then, passing a travel agency cured me of all thoughts of returning. I saw a picture of a Boomerang and a Koala Bear. It was as easy as that. Thirty minutes later I had, in my hands, a open ticket to Australia and by the end of the week I had sold my car, put my house in Toronto up for sale and had signed over all my life's savings into the care of a Toronto lawyer. I'd burned my last bridge.

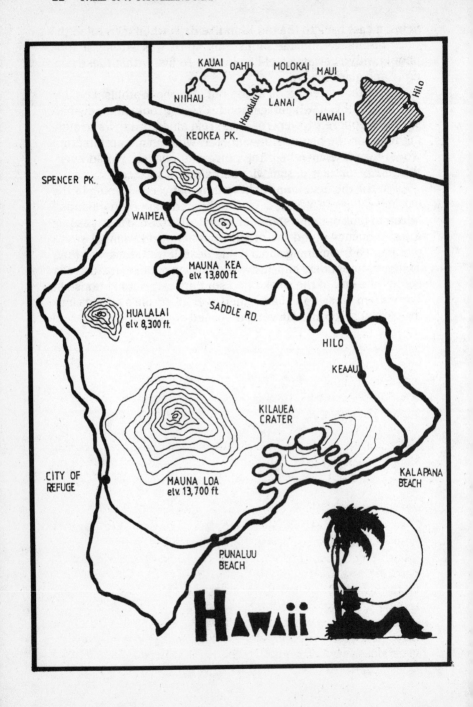

KAUAI OAHU MOLOKAI MAUI
NIIHAU Honolulu LANAI HAWAII Hilo

KEOKEA PK.

SPENCER PK.

WAIMEA

MAUNA KEA
elv. 13,800 ft.

SADDLE RD.

HUALALAI
elv. 8,300 ft.

HILO

KEAAU

KILAUEA
CRATER

CITY OF
REFUGE

MAUNA LOA
elv. 13,700 ft.

KALAPANA
BEACH

PUNALUU
BEACH

Hawaii

Chapter 3:
Fire, Wind and Water

I T ALL STARTED INNOCENTLY ENOUGH, AFTER A CON-
versation with a fellow flight passenger en route to Honolulu.
We were discussing recent outbreaks of violence in Malibu. In
Canada, the papers had been full of headlines, "Girl Raped",
"Violence, and Intimidation", "Police step up action against Beach
Boys." Not exactly a good advertisement for Hawaii.

Travelling by bike leaves you exposed and these reports only
enhanced my fears of travelling alone. Hawaii was not on my
itinerary. I even inquired about on-going flights before leaving
Calgary. Anticipating only an overnight stay in Honolulu, I made
no further plans, but this man was about to give me a different
idea.

"You don't have to visit Maui or Oahu," he told me. "These are
the places with the tourist beaches. That is where the trouble is.
Get off to Hawaii Island if it's peace and quiet you want. The
island's only attraction is Kilauea Crater. It hasn't any surf worth
mentioning, so there's no surfies; that means no girls, no beach
boys, no trouble."

So on the strength of one friendly Hawaiian I changed my
plans. Thoughts of being robbed still worried me but now the
dangers were different. Hawaii, I'd been told, was one of the few
places in the world where volcanic eruptions and earthquakes
happen with frequent regularity. Neither were very high on my
priority list, but "I may never pass this way again", I told myself.

Suddenly there was a loud crash. The ceiling moved.

"It's six o'clock. You'll have to hurry up if you want to catch
your morning flight." It was Gene, the airport's night security
guard. Some joke. He'd started the automatic baggage rack to
wake me up and in my fright I'd fallen off. Because I'd arrived late
in the evening, he had given me permission to sleep in the
airport's baggage collection area.

The flight from Honolulu to Hilo took less than thirty minutes.
En route we took a detour over Moni Island. Beneath me through
clear skies I saw a barren, scorched landscape dominated by an

impressive volcanic fault. Reds rimmed with vivid purples marked the spots of major eruptions, and small craters pitting the side of an immense rift, bore evidence of earlier ones. The plane was only over it for a matter of seconds, but I could not escape the feeling of its immense power and, as Moni's view drifted away, my excitement for Hawaii grew.

The beginning of my first day was a disaster. My bicycle chain broke and, with no tools to fix its link, I had to hitch a lift back to Hilo for repairs. By late afternoon I was on the road again. In Keaau I stopped at a police station to ask for a safe campsite.

"McKenzie Park is your closest sir."

I was still worried about the likelihood of violence, but the park was too far to reach before dark.

"I'm on a bicycle officer. I'll never make it before evening. Are there any other places ?"

"Have you tried the chapel ? They sometimes put up travellers for the night."

In Canada I had become accustomed to sleeping in churches. In some of the remoter towns, the local clergy were more than willing to let you sleep inside. Once, a pastor had even allowed me to sleep against the altar.

"Take advantage of its heating system," he'd said with a laugh. So the thought of asking for shelter in Hawaii didn't bother me, but I couldn't have anticipated either what was to follow.

"Peace stranger. All are welcome in God's eyes." I was met in the Chapel by a blond haired, green-eyed teenager. "My name is Charity."

She asked me to wait outside until her bible class had finished. Soon her sisters, Faith and Hope, (carbon copies) joined us. Then their parents arrived. They invited me to spend the evening at their home in Hilo. My bicycle was left in the Chapel, then I joined them together with half a dozen children in the back of their Volkswagon. The scene was straight out of the sixties, a throwback to the flower power era of peace and love. All the sisters had long blond hair, tanned skin and no make up. The Volkswagon had that well used look about it. Bible books and religious leaflets littered the interior and, while the girls kept up a lively conversation, the group of children started to sing.

The family was not living in splendor by normal American standards, but they were not poor either. Their house in Hilo stood in its own grounds and, from outside appearances, looked affluent, but the interior was a total contrast. I could not imagine this splendid colonial style building being so sparse and plain inside. The walls were bare and colourless. Floors were devoid of carpeting, shelves empty and curtains plain. The only colour in the living room came from a large display of flowers on the table. The overall effect was monotonous, but the colour of its inhabitants more than made up for it. I was immediately made to feel at home, and soon recruited to help prepare the evening meal. The food may have been bland vegetable-and-potato pie but, what it lacked in quality, it more than made up for in quantity. By supper time more people arrived. The table was set for ten. Before the meal we all held hands for grace. Then each in turn recited a verse from the Bible.

"Will you join us Bernard ?"

I was embarrassed at first. Saying grace before meals was not a part of my life. Grace in our family had only been practised till early childhood, then dropped. It wasn't their silent pressure to participate, that made me feel reluctant. I would gladly have done hand stands and balancing tricks for my supper, but obviously their belief was a stronger one. I didn't want to be a hypocrite, yet I didn't want to say no either.

"Take my bible." Charity came to the rescue.

I just opened it and read JOHN Chapter 8, verses 1-7.

After the meal, Charity's father told me of his travels and explained a little of their missionary work, the family's near escapes with death in Chile, persecution at the hands of the Military Junta after Allende's death, and their now quiet life in Hawaii. Although over seventy years old, it was obvious this man wasn't going to ease into his autumn years without a struggle, and going by his impish looks and sharp wit, didn't believe in stepping aside for youth either.

Then it was Charity's turn.

"Do you believe in the Revelations ? Have you heard of the coming Millenium and the Messiah's return ? Have you asked Jesus into your heart?"

I had never come into contact with Christian Fundamentalists before and, although I was a little taken back by her persistent conversion routine at first, it was refreshing to see people live their beliefs for a change. They weren't frightened to use the word love, or to touch either. They were always asking you how YOU felt and, if, in experiençing their lives, I had to share in their belief, then who was I to judge ? Charity might never experience the struggles of the material world, or its rewards for that matter. Her life was cushioned by blind faith and a reliance upon others within the sect. But what she may have lost in outer freedom, she more than made up for with inner warmth. There was a sparkle in her eyes that only a strong belief in the future could sustain. The whole family was refreshingly open, touching, smiling and hugging with no fear of embarrassment and I soon found myself joining in.

The following day I was driven back to their Chapel to pick up my bicycle. Promises were made to return and I knew I would. Then, heading out on Highway 130, I set off towards Kaimu. I had been told much of its unique black sands and I wasn't disappointed. Patient waves must have taken centuries to erode and polish the shattered fragments of lava into these fine black grains. I stayed there for some hours, fascinated by the colour. The fine black sands felt silky under foot and the dark blue backdrop of the Pacific Ocean only added to this beautiful sight.

From Kaimu the road followed the shore's contours, occasionally allowing views of drifting surf and rocky cliffs. On either side of the road, placed equi-distant, as if by royal command, were coconut trees. They deflected the sun's rays as I cycled past, casting dancing shadows in front of me. More than once I stopped to try and open a fallen coconut, but with no success, almost loosing fingers to my sharp knife in the process. At Kalapana I got my first clear view of Kilauea Crater. Rising majestically from the sea, it dominated the coast. Now the road would twist and wind its way to the summit four thousand feet above. From the rim, looking like great bleeding wounds, black streams of frozen lava flowed down its side and in places cut through by the road, opened up to depths of fifteen feet. Also earlier eruptions were clearly in evidence as seen by the roads many deviations from its original route.

I had just begun my ascent when I had to dismount. The four month absence from riding had left me with very few reserves to call upon. Only a few days ago, I had experienced the snows of wintery Canada; now, under clear blue skies I wilted. Common sense prevailed. This was not the time or the place for heroics. I hadn't seen a car since leaving Kalapana three hours before, and no water. The sun was fierce and the bush offered no shade. Then I made my first mistake. The lure of lava fields was too much and I spent over an hour, exploring its surface shapes and contrasting spongy and brittle textures. I underestimated the heat. I forgot how exposed I was. The inevitable happened. I collapsed. I remembered, as a youngster, putting my ear to the road and listening for oncoming traffic. The sounds I heard then brought back those memories. A distant rumble turned into a deafening roar, then stopped.

"What's happened ? You all right ?"

"I think it's sun stroke." My head was swimming.

"Haven't you any water or a hat ?"

"No, I didn't realize the sun was so strong."

He disappeared into his car, reappearing with two cokes.

"What you need is a good hit of sugar."

I drank them quickly and immediately began to feel better. The numbness started to disappear and my head cleared. Senses returned and with them a throbbing bump on my forehead.

"You'll have to be more careful in the future. Sea breezes have a habit of tricking people."

One hour later I'd reached the summit. The view was spectacular. Stepped down in layers, the Crater's many rims took on the form of scorched paddy fields and a road built with an eye on tourist dollars now took me to their very edges. Huge cliffs rose out of solid seas of lava and waves as if frozen on impact, clung in huge masses to their surface. The road at first skirted around Kilauea Fire Pit then, like a huge big dipper, dropped down a level onto a disc like plain dominated by Halemaumau Crater. Suddenly the Volcano flexed its muscles. The earth shook; belching roars gave ways to echoed thunder and toxic gases shot out like geysers. I left my bike to explore, but the combination of heat and fear allowed me to stray no further than the crater's rim. I spent all afternoon exploring its sights and sounds then, as evening came, I lay back to watch Kilauea Crater silhouetted against the backdrop of a blazing red sunset.

It was ten o'clock before I got up. My whole body was racked with aches and pains. Luckily the morning required no heavy cycling; I free wheeled the distance down to the sea which was exhilarating, and the previous day's trouble was soon forgotten. Turning off the main highway, I decided to visit Punaluu. The road swept down through a sugar plantation before paralleling the shore. Dominating the beach was a huge wooden building. Outside, a group of women sat talking and peeling potatoes. Some of the younger ones were filling large water containers from a tap on the side of the building. Its shape and size reminded me of old seaside shelters. Inside there were no divisional walls, just one large open area. It had built-in benches, a high ceiling and a concrete floor. I counted at least a dozen adults and twice that number of children inside. Sacks full of fruit and vegetables littered the entrance. Stacked high in the far corners were numerous blankets and pillows. Sleeping on the top of one heap were two babies and at the bottom of the other, almost lost in the bedding, was an old man asleep. Taking pride of place in the center of the room were the refreshments, crate upon crate of Coca-Cola and Beer. Huddled away in the only vacant corner were the men.

"Welcome Haole." (name for a white man)

Before I could reply, a can of beer was thrust into my hand.

"Want something to eat?"

The men facing me were huge, all looking like those grotesquely overweight wrestlers you see on T.V.

"Sure."

A young girl was called for, then sent for some food. Five minutes later a plate the size of a tray appeared overflowing with food: salads, beans, nuts, legs of chicken and the biggest fillet of fish I had ever seen. If that wasn't enough, I was given another can of beer.

"Why are you here?" I asked them but, instead of answering, they went straight into introductions. Customs and formalities obviously came first. I was introduced to all of them one by one. After these formalities had been observed. I was confronted with their ritual seating arrangements. A space had to be made for me. Each, in turn, had to move one place over. Arguments developed. No-one was willing to drop out. Positional placement towards the headman in the corner took on great importance. Soon the arguments spilled over into the children. It now became a jostling match as to who sat where, the circle changing many times before appearances had been kept and pride satisfied.

"Why are you living here?" I asked again.

"It's the tuna fishing season," the headman replied. "Our young men will be out fishing tonight."

"How long does it last?"

"For as long as it takes. While the tuna stays, so do we. Tuna comes twice a year," he went on. "It's custom, maybe you could call it a working holiday. Most people you see here work in local hotels. Everything stops when the tuna comes. It only lasts about ten days, but while it does, we stay."

"What about the building?"

"Before it was built, we all slept on the beach. In the evenings, our families had to go back to the village, but now they can stay with us."

I felt a certain romance in this type of freedom. Imagine the local industry in Canada shutting down for the duration of a salmon or moose hunting season. The mind boggled. I was glad they were different from what I'd heard. In Honolulu, Gene had forwarned me of the foreign influences. "Bloody Japs own all the commerce. People from the mainland own all the hotels. It's getting to where we can't afford to live in our own country. The only customs we have left are the ones we can sell." It was good to see that some customs had resisted the tides of change.

" You live off the land?" I said.

"It used to be like that. It's different now. The younger ones got caught up in the "American Dream" and wanted it for themselves. Most of our children work in the tourist resorts now on the other islands. It all started with "77 Sunset Strip". Then we had five glorious years of peace. Then came "Hawaii Five O". You could never believe how much television changed this place."

"Whatever happened to the 'hippies'?"

"They've gone underground. You can still see them on Maui. It's big business now to be a hippie. They still live in communes and own their own land. It was cheap in the sixties. They're the new generation of wheeler-dealers. Some on this island. Good group though. Laid back people. No problems here."

He went on to describe the differences between Hawaiian people and "mainlanders". His emphasis on the word, "mainlanders" spoke volumes. I'd often heard this word emphasized before and, in fact, Hawaiians didn't look or act like any other Americans I'd ever met. Hearing talk about the mainlander was the only time I found Hawaiians agreeing in unison on anything. Their dislike for "Big Brother" transcended all inter-island differences. It was obvious from their houses and cars that they liked the affluence statehood brought but, as I was hearing all too frequently, not the people who came with it.

Fresh beers and food flowed freely throughout the afternoon and for most of the day I was either eating or sleeping. Then, in the early evening, a young man produced a large bag of green leaves.

"We have the best stuff in America. Beats anything the mainlanders can produce."

Putting his hand into the plastic bag, he proceeded to pick out seeds, then crushed the leaves between the palms of his hand. He repeated this process several times before replacing the contents into the bag. He then carefully stuck four cigarette papers together, before filling it with the crushed leaves, making the biggest cone-shaped cigarette I had ever seen. "Want a toke friend?"

"What's that?" I asked.

What had I said wrong? They all turned and looked at me.

"You never smoked before?!"

"Oh, a joint...Yes...Sure...It's marijuana isn't it?"

I felt quite embarrassed. It was like teenage sex, every Canadian I knew said they had tried it, now I fell into the same lie.

No sooner was the first finished than a second was started. First I felt light headed. Red hot marijuana seeds were dropping out of the cone like sparklers. Reality was turning to jelly. Then, slowly, I slipped into a void of silence.

The next thing I remember it was dark. Time had fooled me and what remained of my memory was chasing its tail. There had been much coming and going and I now recognized no one. Feelings of paranoia gripped me. These new faces took on the appearance of prospective muggers. Were they talking about me? What were they planning? I tried to stand, but my legs didn't answer.

"Where are you going?"

I was on my feet and moving. "Want another drink?"

I didn't answer them.

"Why don't you stay overnight?"

A wall started to lean against me. My mind had only one view in sight and my feet weren't far behind. Suddenly the evening air chilled. I was outside. I found my bike where I'd left it, but before I'd gone two hundred yards, my front wheel hit a pot hole. Hands slipped, legs twisted and I fell off. I picked myself up, looked around and, seeing a low wall, threw myself and my bike over. I was still groggy, but somehow got my act together just long enought to pull out my sleeping bag and, within minutes, all I could hear was the hiss of my own breathing. I was dead to the world.

Sometime in the night I became aware of pattering noises. Water was peppering my sleeping bag... Where did the rain come from? The sky was full of stars. Slowly the noise ebbed away, only for it to return moments later. This time I was soaked. Looking around, I saw, not three yards from my head, the source of the showers. It was a sprinkler head, built into the ground. Two more sprinklers suddenly started up and I retreated back to the wall for shelter. I had stumbled, unknowingly, onto a golf course.

"Hi." The voice swung me around. "Got wet have you?" I recognized him immediately. We had smoked together earlier.

"I saw your accident. Didn't see you come over the wall though. Be back in a minute. I'll go turn the sprinklers off."

He disappeared on a golf cart, only to return five minutes later with a flask of coffee. He asked me why I didn't sleep in the hut. I was evasive at first, then told him.

"I felt intimidated by you all. I don't know why. I just had to leave."

"Don't worry, they're a good bunch. I know all of them. I think the young ones thought you were from the mainland. I think some mistook you for an American. If I was you though, I'd keep away from smoking joints in the future, pretty powerful stuff grows on these islands."

He left me his flask, then went back to the Clubhouse.

They were all surprised to see me the next morning at the hut, but soon it was as if I'd never left. I spent the day as before, eating and sleeping, but this time I followed advice and gave smoking a miss. I spent more time on the beach and in the evening slept by the hut, with the day's party still going on all around me. My earlier inhibitions had gone and, in the days to follow, I would have no fear of sleeping in exposed areas, spending nights on secluded beaches and in open fields, but I took no stupid risks either. One evening I was invited to sleep in someone's garden and another found me sleeping on a porch. From that day on Punaluu, Hawaii smiled on me. I followed beautiful coastal roads, climbed up the sides of extinct volcanos, and passed through miles of green coated coffee plantations. I spent one evening camped on a rocky cleft overlooking Spencer Park, then another taking in the magnificent vista of the "Seven Valley" from Polou Lookout Point. I climbed through the Kohala Mountains to Waimea. Strength returned to my legs and once again I started to revel in the physical exertion of mountain climbing. Every day I made climbs of over two thousand feet. My body, after its twelve week lay off in Calgary, regained its earlier toughness. Since I had arrived in Hawaii not a day had passed without someone offering me food or refreshment and, once again, those earlier feelings of freedom had returned.

From Waimea I crossed over to the west coast. Here the weather changed dramatically. The skies were overcast and I was caught in numerous showers. The scenery now reflected this change in the weather and from here to Hilo, it was like cycling through one continuous sugar plantation.

In Hilo I continued my friendship with Charity's family, then leaving all but my sleeping bag with them, set about climbing the six thousand foot high "Saddle Road". On the map it looked a piece of cake. Bisecting the island, the road rose from sea level, following a steep zig-zag course before levelling off between the lava flows of Hawaii's two largest volcanos, Mauna Kea and Mauna Loa, which must rank as one of the world's most unusual areas.   Isolated from the rest of Hawaii by its altitude and remoteness, it had an eerie atmosphere. The only sign of life was a warning poster by the side of the road: KEEP OUT — AMERICAN ARMED FORCES PROPERTY. (American astronauts took advantage of these strange lava surfaces to practise for their landing on the moon.)

Two days later I was back in Hilo.

It was eggs and toast for breakfast, then Charity's last chance to "witness" me. I was a lost cause and she gave up with a smile.

Surprise awaited me in Honolulu. Flights to Raratonga had been discontinued due to the cyclone season. I had to be rerouted on New Zealand Airways to Fiji.

"That will be fifty dollars, sir."

I was being asked for handling charges for my bicycle. I tried to bluff my way out of it.

"I'm writing articles for a cycle magazine. This won't look too good for your airline."

He wasn't impressed, so I tried a different approach. "Where does it say handling charges? I've never paid these before."

The next minutes saw me passed from one representative to another, eventually ending with the desk manager. By now they were making the final call for passengers to go to the boarding gate. Minutes stretched into half an hour before the manager finally reappeared and I was off the hook. Hidden away in the small print of their International Airways Charter were the words: HANDLING CHARGES ARE NOT INCLUDED FOR PASSENGER OWNERS OF HOLIDAY SPORTING EQUIPMENT, IF UNDER CHECK-IN WEIGHT. I was on my way.

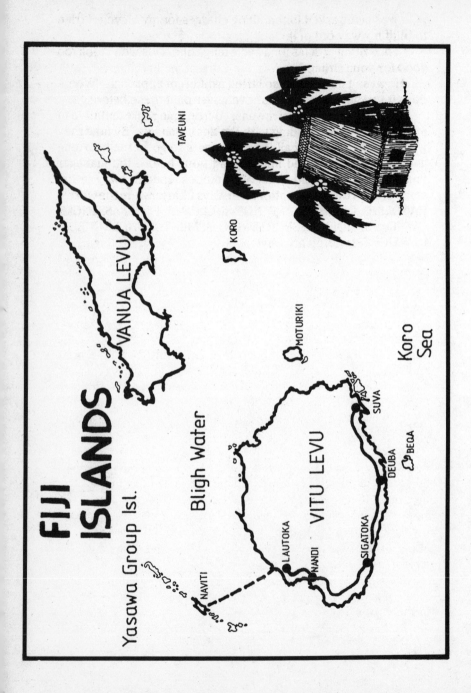

"**Y**OU'VE COME TO CYCLE OUR ISLAND, MR BERNARD?" At Fiji customs in Nandi Airport, it was all smiles. I'd arrived at six a.m. and already the atmosphere was hot and humid with more that just a threat of rain hanging in the air. At customs the officers were more interested in my bicycle than my passport, and it wasn't until I was out of the airport that I realized I had no entry stamp.

En route to Nandi, huge trees were uprooted, palm leaves and broken branches littered the roadside and a small, corrugated, iron shanty town, on the outskirts was devastated. High up in a tree, looking for all the world like a large umbrella, was a roof. A petrol station was gutted by fire and shop windows were boarded up. The pilot had warned us on landing and now I was seeing the after-effects of the cyclone at first hand.

Just before Nandi, I had spotted a likely advertisement; "Sunseekers-friendly atmosphere-dormitory accommodation-three and a half dollars incl. breakfast." It sounded good enough. I was reluctant to stay in hotels, but the price and increasing thoughts of a cool shower helped the decision along. Once inside, I was astounded by the variety of its guests. Ozzies, Kiwis, Americans, Japanese, and even Europeans. This was my first contact with long-distance travellers and, that evening, I was spell-bound by their tales of Asia. Listening to them opened up all kinds of new avenues in my mind. The germ of travel had been planted. Anything sounded possible.

One resident, just returned from an outlying island, intrigued me with her account of their earthy lifestyle.

"What island did you go to?"

"Naviti, it's six hours away from Vitu Levu by village boat." She went on to tell me how to negotiate for a boat in Lautoka harbour. "It only cost me ten dollars, but prepare yourself for some heavy bargaining. There's no set price, and get there early if you want to get a good place. There were at least fifty people aboard the boat I went on - it was incredible that none of us fell overboard."

"Any hotels on the island?"

"You must be joking. The captain got me a room with a family in the village, I stayed for nothing."

I couldn't believe it. I had always thought of Fiji as tourist haven. Then she added,

"Well I did bring some food, but I only meant to stay a few days. I didn't realize the boat only made the journey once every two weeks. There were a few shops, but they only sold tinned sardines, powdered milk and cigarettes. Most of their provisions are bought in Lautoka then, taken back to Naviti by boat and, until that cyclone, you didn't need much anyway. Bananas, papayas, oranges, they all grew on the island, and there was an incredible variety of fish you could catch before the floods stained the sea with topsoil.

"Were you there when the cyclone hit?"

"Yes. It was bloody awful. I don't want to go through that again. That's why I came back. They expect another. The biggest problem at the moment is water, they're boiling everything because they're scared of an epidemic, and flies are everywhere. If you can put up with all that, I reckon they'll be more than happy to see a white face." She then went on to explain about the visitor's permit. "They're trying to restrict visitors and their enterprising ways from spoiling their culture of living off the land or, for that matter, seducing their younger men with stories of bright city lights... Do you play rugby?"

"Well, I used to."

"You're in then. They're crazy about it, play it every night in the village. But, seriously, they need all the help they can get. There's a lot of rebuilding to be done."

Following her instructions, I went to Lautoka and arranged for a boat to Naviti, then to the Commissioner's Office to obtain written permission to visit the island. Back at the boat, I sent two crew members to the market with forty dollars and a list of provisions from flour and sugar, to tinned margarine, fruit and vegetables. Later in the afternoon I returned to Sunseekers and arranged for my bike to be stored and then, in the evening, I returned to Lautoka. The boat was to leave at sunrise the following morning, so I decided to sleep on the wharf that night with the passengers and crew.

Nothing could have prepared me for the scene I witnessed the next morning. I counted at least forty people on the boat. A complete suite of furniture took pride of place at the stern and two goats were tied up at the front end. Then just before the boat set off, an enormous, pregnant pig appeared with a similar sized owner. She was literally thrown onto the boat, then passed screaming and kicking over the heads of the passengers, before being tied up with the goats. If that wasn't enough, one of the crew set about syphoning off diesel into an open tank, with fumes from the spillage instilling not a trace of fear in the boat's numerous smokers.

"Come on, we're leaving." The captain was standing no nonsense and while I struggled to gain a footing between a mass of bodies on board, a dining room table bounced off my head.

"You sit here, Mr Bernard."

"You must be joking." I said. Before me, sitting in the couch, were three huge women. "There's not enough room."

The captain was having none of it, and after a few sharp words with the women a gap appeared. In unison they breathed in. I didn't want to upset the captain, or disappoint the expectant women, so I struggled in, and was immediately enveloped in flesh. To make matters worse they all started to laugh. The feeling was like being caught in a vibrating press. My head rested on one woman's shoulder, giving me an ample view of her bosom, while my elbow was lost in mounds of flesh of her neighbour. In front of me another woman was struggling to extricate a breast from the tight folds of her dress and, no sooner was it exposed, than her child clamped on it. Then I felt a momentary release of pressure and, like a piece of wet soap, squirted out, much to the amusement of every one aboard.

By now the sun was up and I dropped down into the hull for shade. At first I stumbled about while my eyes adjusted to the darkness. Suddenly a voice from above said,

"Up here Mr Bernard."

All I could see were these brilliant white teeth.

"Do you want something to eat ?" I recognized him as the captain's cousin. From my new elevation on top of the sacks, I saw half a dozen men eating rice and meat from banana leaves. A young boy made room for me and I entered the group.

"Have you a cigarette, Mr Bernard ?"

Maybe it was a mistake to hand them over so freely, but I did, and the consequences were inevitable. I would be asked for cigarettes continuously whenever I was seen smoking.

"What is your country of origin ?"

"Canada." I replied. English by birth, but Canadian by choice,

I thought.

"Is this an island like our Naviti ?"

He went on to ask about its population, my religion, employment, salary and politics.

"You speak good English Mr Bernard, for Canada."

"That is because I was born in England." Suddenly I had their whole attention.

"England!" His eyes lit up at the word. "This is glorious country, is it not ? We learned all about your Royal Family at school."

Then he offered up the question that would follow me half way round the globe, even into the remotest areas of Africa.

"HAVE YOU MET THE QUEEN ?"

All eyes were now on me. "I have not had the pleasure."

"I met her glorious personage twice." He then turned to face his friends."I have shaken her hand." The captain's cousin was beaming with pride and obviously enjoying center stage with his royal revelation. This high regard for the British way of life surprised me and if I mentioned anything negative about the Royal Family's privileged lifestyle, he unhesitatingly defended them. All heroes in their eyes were British and always the villains of the piece were portrayed as anti-British; even when I mentioned problems the British introduced, such as the Indian labourers brought in to work on the colonial sugar plantations, their disproportionate wealth and over population, (over half of Fiji's population are of Asian origin) he had answers.

"We are a lazy race. We only take from God's natural harvest what we need to live off. We do not take to working on the land easily. We like to live off it."

Every point of view, every argument, he saw through British eyes, even criticizing his own culture and I was beginning to realize why the authorities limited visits to these more remote islands. They even praised Christianity.

"It stopped cannibalism."

What lengths did we go to for conversion ? I tried to explain cannibalism to them in its ritual sense; the honouring of brave warriors killed in battle, and not of eating flesh, for flesh sake, but somehow it got lost in translation and I gave up.

The best came later. My passport. They all wanted to touch it. Was it blessed ? Maybe it held magical powers, Whatever it was, they treated it with a reverence I found both odd and amusing.

Amazing sights awaited me on my landing. Naviti's beach was a blaze of colour. Families gathered for greeting searched out loved ones with shouts, and others more anxious waded out waist-deep to help. Children swam out in races of excited sprays and teenagers, caught up in the occasion, paddled out in make-shift, wood-rope boats. On deck confusion reigned and while children fought in their excitement to get on, passengers either jumped, fell or dived into the sea. Soon the boat was rocking from greetings and when I was spotted, it nearly capsized. Instantly I was swallowed up by a swarm of scantily clad and naked children. Curiosity now reached out to touch and scream, to acknowledge. The boat never did make it ashore and while I was carried from boat to beach on the shoulder's of euphoria, the captain made arrangements for my baggage to be taken to his house, I was to stay with his family.

Once ashore, evidence of the recent hurricane was every-where. Coconuts like spilled bags of marbles littered the beach. A fallen tree blocked the footpath to the village and the surround-ing hills were scarred with landslides. The scenes that greeted me in the center of the village were reminiscent of the old Vietnam war newsreels. Many houses were roofless. Walls were splin-tered, roofs torn and twisted and smashed furniture was piled high ready for burning but, miraculously, no one had been badly injured.

Preparations at the captain's house were already well in hand when I arrived. I was given the only separated room with a bed. A mosquito net was donated by a neighbour, a chair by another and already their best crockery was laid out for a meal. For the duration of my stay the family would sleep on the living room's reed matted floor and, that first night, a call of nature found me stumbling over a dozen sleepy toes.

Familiar noises woke me the following morning. It was the pregnant pig. My bed lay directly above its living quarters under the house, and for the next six weeks its early morning grunting and screeching would wake me with the regularity of an alarm clock,

"Mr Bernard, you want wash ?"

Years of conditioning about bathing in private had left me self-conscious at being naked in front of others, and the very idea of communal bathing made me shudder. For the first week I'd been to timid to ask where they washed. I'd observed early morning movements, yet found no pattern to follow. Now watching the captain strip naked in the village lagoon, all my prudish feelings surfaced. Many men were already undressed and the longer I waited the more I felt their eyes on me. Was it adult curiosity or childhood fantasies? Call it what you like. I felt bloody embarrassed. Putting urges to stare any further to the back of my mind, I stripped off underwater and started washing. I waited waist deep for fifteen minutes hoping they'd go, but always sideways glances told a different story. Slowly I gave in to the game and stood. Suddenly I became aware of laughter. There were women bathing at the far side of the lagoon in full view, and while their laughter bounced around in my head, I melted back into the water. Some how I managed to put on my shorts and make a dignified exit.

"They laugh at your white bottom, Mr Bernard," someone explained, but the words made me feel only marginally better and to make matters worse, from that day on, Mr Bernard would now be exchanged for Mr White Bum, by the children. Wherever I went its call would announce my arrival to roars of laughter.

From the outset I was determined, as much as I could, to live life through their eyes. I declined seats, choosing to battle with the pains of sitting cross-legged. I ate, slept and bathed with them and, by the second week, I began to blend into their simple life. I enlisted enthusiastically into the rebuilding of the village. "Slow down Mr Bernard," I was repeatedly told. I found no urgency in their work. The men spent hours drinking 'yagona' (a traditional drink made from powdered pepper root) and sleeping. One day drifted into another, and soon all sense of time was lost. The pig still woke me, the captain's wife still fed me and layers of village life were still to be explored. In short, I was not bored.

In my third week the ever present closeness of children disappeared and I was no longer the oddity. Accepted into village life, men took me fishing. Swimming in my first coral reef was unforgettable. The contrasting colours and the amazing variety of fish was overwhelming and I indulged my fascination whenever possible. I was taught how to climb coconut trees and soon developed a second layer of skin on both knees. The great prize had lost its worth, like overpriced stock. Earlier jealousies which arose due to friendly invites from the captain's neighbours were no longer politely refused. The captain's status as 'Mr Bernard's host' was secure.

It was obvious even to the casual visitor that village life depended on full co-operation of its members. Trapped, as they were, on the island, all decisions were collective. A meeting of elders took place twice a week. Responsibility for child care was discussed, fish catches and coconut sales were equally shared. Families whose homes had been destroyed were allocated temporary housing, sometimes even doubling up with neighbouring families or relatives and, at one meeting, I also was on the agenda. Someone had been seen swimming on Sunday, thus breaking one of their customs. "Sunday is a rest day, Mr Bernard." I was told politely, but sternly, not to do it again, and I didn't.

Rains preceeding the hurricane had gone by the forth week and the evenings were now cloudless. The full moon came and went and stars hung in the skies like light bulbs. One evening, the captain gave me a bucket and lantern. "We go crab hunting." Was it the full moon, their mating season perhaps, or just a change in weather ? Crabs were everywhere, hundreds of them. It was impossible to walk the full length of the village without standing on one. That night was punctuated by screams of excitement and multitudes of dancing lantern lights, as groups of children played games of hide and seek with the crabs, and by the end of the evening we had caught over a dozen.

It was near the end of my fourth week before a local girl was hinted at. "She makes good cook, man without woman is not right." My refusal confused them and I had to make a tactical retreat with a white lie. "I am promised to a woman." Nothing more was said about the incident until I returned to Lautoka with the village boat for extra provisions. That night I got drunk while the crew drank Coca Cola and it was while I was making one of my frequent visits to the bar that the crew introduced me to the local prostitute. "She good strong girl. Yes? " It was a favour I found hard to refuse. Why were they always thinking I needed a woman? I tried to explain again, then thought better of it. Maybe they knew something I didn't. I'd never had a prostitute. I'd once got one for a friend, for his twenty-first. "Break him in gently," I'd told her jokingly. It had cost me fifty dollars, now the reverse was happening. Well, what the hell, now was as good a time as any, I thought.

She took me back to her room, bathed me and then put me to bed.
"Goodnight, Mr Bernard." She left! Here I was, already for my first
paid professional sex, and she'd left me with a teased erection.
Didn't my friends, the crew, pay her enough? Was I to pay?

In the morning I was met with embarrassed looks at the wharf.

"Why did she leave me last night, wasn't she with me for sex?"
I wasn't angry with the crew or the girl, I just wanted to understand.

"She wanted extra money? The captain's cousin took up the
mantle of spokesman.

"Why?"

"She says you have large prick?" He made a measurement
with his hands, then turned to his friends for support.

She'd obviously tricked them. I didn't want to sound modest.
Maybe they meant it as a compliment. Anyway, on the journey
back to Naviti, I made no attempt to confirm or deny their stories.
Ignorance is bliss sometimes, but it didn't last for long. At the
lagoon the next morning, they were all waiting for me to bathe.

"Are you disappointed...? I didn't have to ask the question
allowed, but could tell the answer from their looks on their faces.

Into the fifth week I got bored with the repetitious diet of rice
and fish.

"Can I cook a curry today?"

I was going against tradition again, but my determination
prevailed and the captain's wife reluctantly gave me permission.

Using spices bought in Lautoka, I cooked a pan full of vegetables to boiling point in the outside kitchen. Food smells attracted the pig, precipitating my decision to remove the pan and
its contents back inside the house out of her reaches. Surrounded
by an open fire, flames enveloped the pan's surface, making it to
hot to handle so, using my t-shirt for insulation, I gripped the pan
by its rim, picking it out of the flames. But entering the house I
slipped and instinctively my hand went out in search of support.
The t-shirt's protective guard was now stripped out of my grip,
sending burning pains shooting through bare flesh into my hand.

Suddenly the room flashed. Shock waves jolted my body, skin
felt torn apart and contracting muscles catapulted me across the
room. I screamed but heard no sounds. I screamed again and
again, then breathlessness silenced me. Muscles fused solid by
heat only moments before melted. I began to crawl, but all

movement drained me. Shock had blurred the memory, but the
sight of steaming curry brought it back and, with it, the pain. I was
badly burned. Already the spilled curried sauce was solidifying
on my thigh and the slightest movement exploded with pain.

"Mr Bernard...Mr Bernard...Mr Bernard."

Using the wall for support, I looked back towards the entrance. Shadows of noise filled the doorway and slowly my eyes
began to focus through the mist of tears. Wide-eyed children
bobbled about in the diffused sunlight, laughing nervously. Then
I recognized the captain.

"Mr Bernard, help come. Please no move."

He came over, knelt down, then putting his huge hands on
either side of my neck started to massage me. By now I had
reached thresholds of pain I'd never experienced before. Nightmare thoughts flashed through my mind. Infection, gangrene,
amputation. There was no doctor on the island, no medication
and the village boat wouldn't be back for another day.

What was this ? A young child was putting her hands on my
thigh. Protective instincts took over. I struck out my leg, knocking
her backwards.

"What the hell's she doing ?" The pain had come flooding
back. Was this the help he promised ? The captain didn't answer
me. He began applying more pressure with his fingers and soon
the rhythmic movements of massage had soothed the pains in my
head. I started to plead with him.

"Don't you have any sunburn ointments, creams, anything.
God don't you have anything, you stupid primitives ?"

Again I got no reply. The young girl was still there. She looked
scared, but made no attempt to leave. Earlier feelings of acute
pain were now replaced with deep pulsating sensations. I now felt
powerless and submitted like a baby to the strange events that
followed. The captain spoke to the young girl again. The look of
fright my earlier actions had given her had disappeared, again
she approached me.

"Please Mr Bernard, no fear."

The captain continued speaking, but by now I was slowly
sinking into my own deep fear. The young girl again placed her
hands over the burned area of my thigh. Only an intangible
confidence in this child now sustained me. I looked directly into
her eyes, her pupils dilated and beads of perspiration appeared

on her forehead. Soon her whole face was bathed in sweat.

Maybe the experience of intense pain sent my mind into shock. Trying to recollect this experience now is like trying to untangle the web of one's dreams. Time had no barriers, the girl's face remains that of a non-person, unrecognizable. The whole episode could have lasted seconds, minutes or even hours. I can only remember the feeling of contentment and weightlessness that bathed my body afterwards; like a boxer having fought a good fight and won, I felt no pain.

After, the captain helped me back to my bed. My sleep was deep and long lasting until the following afternoon and, besides a peculiar tightness in my skin, I could only find one purple swelling the size of a nickel where a badly burned thigh should have been. Did I dream yesterday's events. My experience with the young girl left me with no explanation and returning to Vitu Levu, I took the first opportunity to visit friends in Suva in search of answers.

"From what you told me Bernard," he said, "the girl's age, not into puberty, what she did and the circumstances you found yourself in, all fit into a pattern. Her family probably originated from Beqa Island. People there have the gift of fire walking. It's a big tourist attraction in Fiji. I'm told that children are chosen, then trained by their families to use their gifts for healing purposes. It's said they have the powers to transfer heat from other bodies through their own. Somehow they manage to dissipate heat quicker than us mere mortals. You have to believe, or it doesn't work. You obviously did."

Chapter 4:
Whiter Shade of Pale

"**A** RAVE FROM THE GRAVE, FOLKS," THE RADIO D.J. said as he announced a song by Procal Harlem which instantly transported me back into the sixties. Having left England for self imposed exile in '74, seeing bottles of milk, left sided traffic and Morris Minors again only added to the romantic memories of my youth. My first evening was spent eating fish and chips from newspapers, and drinking in the atmosphere of English style pubs. Even Auckland's Youth Hostel reminded me of the inflexible British rules. "Lights out by 11:00 pm." Gone was the freer approach of North America, but all these changes was like music to my ears.

My arrival coincided with an impending diplomatic break with close neighbour and arch rival, Australia. The cause, I found, was not a trivial matter of invasion or an embargo on New Zealand lamb but a cricket match. A cricket game, like rugby, held no less attraction than a mass religious festival did in Latin America. If an impending visit of South Africa's Rugby touring team split the country, then cricket united it. Overnight this sleepy outpost of western civilization was whipped up into nationalistic fever, placing it on a platform of world attention in a way New Zealand sheep could never do.

Needing the maximum six runs off the final delivery to secure a victory, Australia committed the worst kind of sin, and bowled a "GRUBBER". A grubber is a ball bowled with underarm action, fast along the ground, making it impossible for a batsman to strike the ball in the air, making the six runs needed impossible to make. The New Zealand papers were full of it. "Cheats, Unsportsmanlike, The sweaty armpit delivery." Even Prime Minister Muldoon got into the act. Speaking in Parliament, he made reference to the "canary" disposition of their opponents. "They were wearing the right colours." Although the incident had happened some weeks previously, it still commanded a great deal of press coverage and was still the center of many heated discussions.

"It's not enough they take all our best women, they even want to cheat us out of a cricket victory."

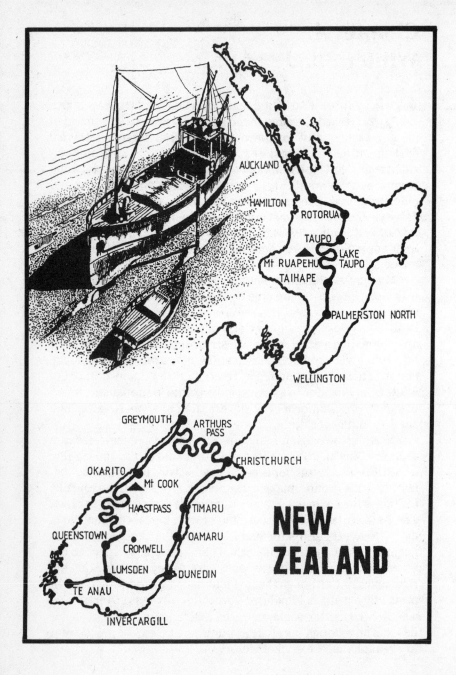

New Zealand's similarities didn't stop only at the visual, for it was also familiar for its attitudes of good humoured complaining. I became the butt of several winging-British grumbles.

"Look what you introduced into our country. First it was rabbits. A mistake you tell us. To cover up this mistake you introduced weasels to get rid of them. All they did was to kill off our Kiwi birds. Then you introduced foxes to kill off the weasels, and if that wasn't enough you introduced hounds to keep the foxes down. Then, when you got fed up with chasing foxes, you introduced deer. Now we're overrun with them. Best thing you lot ever did was to bring in a rugby ball, and you Brits aren't very good at chasing that either."

I stayed in Auckland only long enough to be asked to leave. I did not see eye to eye with the warden of the Youth Hostel.

"Rules are made by some to be broken by others." I said.

The warden was not impressed by my joke and, in the morning, I was given a ridiculous amount of duties to do. Being neither in the mood to argue or succumb to his authority, I left, avoiding both.

Heading South, I was forever climbing hills. Maybe there was some truth in the rumor I had heard in Auckland.

"All New Zealand's population is in this city. It has caused a definite geological tilt in our land mass. You'll find a gradual gradient all the way up to Invercargill in the South Island.

Soon I was cycling in rural country. Sheep and cattle abounded in all directions, so, seeing a ram chained up by the side of the road wasn't surprising. Having confronted two keenly territorial farm dogs only minutes earlier, I sped up, not sure what to expect.

The ram's speed from a standing start would have been the envy of any sprinter, and the way it recovered from the chain's neck yanking would have amazed the most experienced of hang men, but its next course of action left me little doubt that it had gone through all this before. Picking itself up it changed direction quickly and running across the road, it cunningly swept round the back of me, then headed down the road in the opposite direction. I had watched these events in the false belief I was safe. Suddenly the chain cut in front of my wheel, jerking me over the handle bars and, before I had time to recover my senses, I was hit again with the force of a Mack Truck. The next thing I saw was the blue sky through an unseasonable snow storm. From the bottom of the ditch I watched in dazed silence. The ram, having made his point, was already grazing again. Not wanting to precipitate a further confrontation, I walked away, cautiously approaching my bike from the far side of the road. Once out of reach I started to count the cost. Peddle bent, handle bars twisted, camera lens and radio smashed. A passer-by stopped on his bicycle to give me a hand.

"It tried it on me mate." He looked at me sympathetically. "I've told the farmer about it but she takes no notice."

At this moment a middle aged woman twice the size of my friend appeared and soon I was caught in a cross fire of Dutch obscenities. She grabbed the chain, picked up a large piece of wood and smashed it over the rams's head. The ram, fully grown, and now giving little resistance, was hoisted up and thrown over the fence in a single movement.

"Let a little thing like a ram bother you," she said with a smile. Then climbing over the fence, she grabbed the chain, belted it one more time, dragged it across the field and tied it up at a stake.

By mid day, I reached Maramarua and stopped for a bite to eat. Ordering egg and chips, I sat down. Opposite, dressed in baggy, corduroy trousers, sleeveless shirt and knee length Wellington boots, was a typical farmer. His face had that rugged, ageless look about it. His hands bore all the signs of manual labour, both in their size and shape. His biceps seemed to pop out every time his fork moved, and with his deep, reddy-brown tan, looked every inch an outdoor worker.

"Never seen a farmer before?" he said with a laugh.

"Sorry, I didn't mean to stare."

"Where did you come from mate ?"

"Canada."

"What did you do out there ?"

"Freelance engineer."

"What's one of them ?"

He surprised me with his friendly interrogation, but spent the next thirty minutes discussing my job, my reasons for travelling and, most importantly for him, sport.

"Where are you going from here ?"

"I'm looking for a place for the night. I had an accident with a ram just down the road, and I want to repair the bike."

"So you're the one."

"News travels fast around here."

"About the only thing that does. If you're still looking for a place for the night I have a trailer in the yard. My wife will be glad to see a new face. What about it ?"

His land rover was full of farming equipment but somehow we managed to secure my bike and were soon bouncing down gravel roads en route to his farm. Then after yet another meal, he asked if I wanted to help with the milking.

Thirty minutes later I was down in a pit, putting lubricated teats on cows' udders. Above my head a cow's tail rose slowly into the air.

"Look out."

Suddenly a jet of hot fluid hit me.

"I thought you said you'd been on a farm before," he said laughingly. "When you see a tail rise, then you know shits" gonna fall."

Back at the house I changed into overalls. Then he put me back to work on the tractor. "Driven one of these before, Bernard?"

"Something very similar." In Canada I'd helped a friend bring in the harvest, but his machine was far less complicated then the one being offered me now, and climbing aboard I was immediately lost in a confusion of instruments.

"All you have to do is keep the line of the previous cut at that point."

He pointed to a small mark at the front of the engine. First he took me for a trial run around the field, cutting down the grass in long straight furrows.

"Think you can do it?"

I didn't want to say no. "Sure, no problem.?

Then he left to go back to the house, saying he would come back later.

In front of me rabbits and mice darted about from their protective world of long grass. Hawks swooped down in attempts to catch them. I watched in amazement at the speed and accuracy of the attacks and, before long, their persistence was rewarded. An owl flying low over the high grass struck a rabbit only feet from cover. Then, without warning, while I watched it rise into the air, I hit a patch of swampy ground and got bogged down. Changing down a gear, I stalled. I started again, changed, stalled. Soon I was axle deep in mud. Changing up a gear, I surged free. Now travelling noticeably faster, I changed down and stalled again. I repeated this mistake many times more round the field, and as I looked back, evidence of my progress could be traced in wave-like cuts in the grass.

"Not going to win any prizes for neatness." The farmer was back. "An aerial view would confuse anyone."

I was glad he had a sense of humour, and before the sunset, with a little more tuition, I'd got the hang of it. That night he repaired my bike, his wife, my stomach and their heavy down sheets, my aching joints. Sadly the following morning looked like rain, and with no work to be done in the fields I left reluctantly, unable to practise my new skills.

The day continued to be overcast with intermittent showers but, due to the north island's semi-tropical climate, not cold. By Matamata, the skies had cleared. The winter's sun was now low over the horizon. I soon got cold. If I stopped sweat turned to chill. In one hour the sun would set. I wasn't relishing the idea of setting up camp in damp conditions but, with no tent to shut out the elements, I had no choice. To save space and weight on my bicycle I'd bought a sleeping bag water-proofer in Canada in lieu of a tent and, although adequate protection against the heaviest downpours, it allowed neither privacy nor flexibility. Once in, I had to zip up. It was too light to sleep and too early for the restaurants to be open.

Wet and cold, I cycled around the town looking for a suitable place to change clothes then, spotting a police station, left the bike outside and went in. Fifteen minutes later, feeling refreshed from a hot mug of tea, and sound advice, I headed off for the cinema.

"There's no restaurants here sir." The desk sergeant told me."We only have a Chinese fish and chip shop. That won't open till eight. Why don't you have a word with the cinema manager? I'm sure he'll let you leave your bike and bags in the foyer for safety. The show starts at seven, so you don't have to wait long."

I followed his advice more in an effort to warm up than for any entertainment and after the film, I called in the local chippy before making camp in a small playground in the center of town. Then, from within my sleeping bag, ate fish and chips while under the startled gaze of late night strollers.

"Been queuing all night have you?" I was woken by an early

morning jogger. Escaping a sudden thunderstorm, I had been forced out from my camp under a tree, for the relative safety and dry atmosphere of a concrete bus shelter.

That day's cycling to Lake Taupo turned into a carbon copy of the day before but this time my sleeping quarters were influenced by a camp superintendent. "No tent, lad. Well you can use the floor of the television room." At eight o'clock the room filled up.

"Coronation Street (Britain's longest running soap), used to be our most popular programme," the superintendent said." "Even showed it three times a week to catch up with you pomms. Now everyone goes crazy about Dallas."

By five past nine the room had emptied and while the news reader weaved his way around world news, I fell asleep.

Climbing above Lake Taupo's morning mist I was treated to a spectacular view of Mt Ruapehu and while the sun burned pockets of desolate landscape, my resources for the rest of that day were taxed to the limit. Aptly named 'desert road', it wound steeply through Tongariro National Park, before levelling off at four thousand feet and, by mid-day, I was cycling under clear skies for the first time since arriving in New Zealand. At this elevation the sun's rays burned into my skin, and when the clouds obscured them, I was chilled to the bone. Reaching the top of rises exposed an empty road ahead, where its progress could be traced in the miles of snake like bends, before disappearing over the edge of Tongariro's plateau. The wind by now had picked up strongly, and as the sun changed direction, the wind followed it. For one hour it blew constantly in my face, filtering out all noise behind me. Then suddenly a horn blew. The silence was broken and with the waving hands of its passengers, so was the days tension. By late afternoon I'd slipped over the plateau and left the park.

"Your shout, mate." It was my round for the beers. Having stopped for a drink in Taihape I had found myself surrounded by a group of Maori farm workers out for a good time. Since early childhood I had always dreamed of working on the land. I was never happier than when getting my hands dirty. Now, in thick of a conversation about seasonal farm work, I found the opening to ask that all important question.

"Any farm work around here ?"

"See Sonny." A friendly finger pointed in the direction of a table filled with empty beer glasses. "If there's any jobs going around here he'll know about them."

I found Sonny at the center of a heated argument.

"I'm the best fucking sheep shearer in these parts. You young ones talk as much wind as a sheep's fucking ass."

My introduction to his circle cost me another round and my memory of the evening's events is distorted more by beer consumption than by any time lapse, as both Sonny and his fiends refused to leave the pub until the night's rounds had been evened up. The next thing I remembered was waking up on the floor of Sonny's house which was to be my usual sleeping place for the duration of my stay. Appetites were now gained from digging ditches, mending fences and daylong roustabouts. I had got my wish of farm work and within the week I gained muscles and suffered aching limbs where I never thought were possible. A typical day started with Sonny collecting the sheep dogs from their kennels and his rough handling of them at first was a constant irritation.

"Do you have to treat them like that Sonny ?" He picked one up by the scruff of the neck and threw it into the back of his Land Rover. "They're not pets. They're here to work like we all are," was his answer.

My job was to patrol the high ground on horseback while Sonny worked the sheep dogs in the valley. Riding ridge tops afforded me unimpeded views of Mt. Ruapehu and, combined with the effects of fresh air and horse flesh under saddle, was just the tonic I needed from travel. I soon got the hang of my new work and with a sure footed horse to help me, these peaceful periods allowed me the time to reflect on the realities of my new life.

"Live for the day, Bernard." The cycle of life and death on the farm was reflected in Sonny's attitude. Don't worry about the future. Look at the sheep. They don't know what they're been bred for, couldn't do anything about it if they did. We all have to die sometime."

His hands were often bloodied from animal butchery, and he would smile with childish delight at his work. His behaviour paralleled that of his charges, and his treatment of animals lacked that sensitivity of a bystander. To him farming was not a gentlemen's pastime, but a way of life. His earthiness and ability to read both human and animal character more than compensated for his vulgarity and occasional outbursts of sheer brutality, but I doubted that I could live with such traits for long.

I learned that, in his youth, Sonny had been the best sheep shearer and roust-about in the valley, forever riding that thin line between people's admiration of his achievements and tolerance of his boastings, both as a shearer and with the ladies. Always at his best when challenged, our visit to the shearing sheds, one day, gave him all the excuses needed to show off his skills.

"Still think you're a better shearer than me ?" Sonny said.

"Ah, stop 'whinging', you're full of shit, Sonny," the young lad with us replied.

Squaring off like a fighter, Sonny bit at the challenge. Both combatants started to check their equipment. News of the challenge spread like wild fire and soon the shed was overflowing with good humored farm hands. Sonny was ready for combat first, and stood center stage, chiding his younger challenger, and taking every opportunity to milk the crowd's enthusiasm.

"Eh son, your slip's showing. Taught your father all he ever knew about shearing...I've forgotten more than you'll ever fucking learn."

Equipment now checked, seconds posted and sheep readied, they were off. The young lad's nerves got the better of him during the early stages, as Sonny continually taunted him. After thirty minutes Sonny was already three sheep ahead. Feeling confident, he stopped to drink a beer, while offering sarcastic advice to his younger rival.

"Better get your mates to give you a hand son. You don't look strong enough to hold 'em. You're not supposed to be milking 'em you know."

At the half way stage Sonny was clearly dominating the contest. Then striking up a rhythm for the first time, his youthful challenger gained rapidly on a visibly tiring Sonny and the tables were turned. Rival sympathies were split evenly between the old champion and his younger challenger.

"He's finished."

"No, he's not, he's only playing with him."

Then Sonny's head dropped. Anticipating an upset, silence fell in the shed. But driven on more by instinct, Sonny dug deep into unseen reserves, while pure adrenalin drove on his challenger.

"What's all the excitement about ?" The shed owner had arrived.

"A young lad challenged Sonny to a shearing contest."

"Who won?" Both contestants lay slumped in the corner, arms around each other.

"Sonny. You have to give him credit. If anything's going to beat him someday, age will."

After the contest we all went into Taihape to celebrate. Talk now revolved around the Valley Sports Day, and old times.

"Valley communities were bustling with life in the old days. Local fairs and sports days were the highlights of our year. There was no television then, we made our own entertainment. Taihape was too far away. We came here once a month to go shopping and twice a year for dances." In the valley, Sonny's neighbours often got together to celebrate marriages, and even a funeral could turn into a party. "Met my wife at one," Sonny said with a laugh. He then went on to explain the changes in his valley. Farm owners were becoming a thing of the past. New generations of farm children were being seduced away from the land in ever increasing numbers. "Young ones can't put up with the rigours of farm life these days, don't want to get their hands dirty. They're all off to Ozzie. It's the excitement of something different I suppose. Can't blame 'em. Not much around here anymore. Not even money." Even I could see in my short stay that small family farms were either being run down or amalgamated with larger ones and local schools reflected this change. Larger farms required fewer hands and the new style farm managers were childless. "We have a new breed of farmers these days. University educated some of 'em. All theory and no fucking sense," and on that note I buried all thoughts of becoming a farmer in New Zealand.

My final week ended with the annual village cricket match, held at the culmination of the Valley Sport's Day. People had come from miles around to take part. Men, some with their wives and girl friends, split into two different teams.

My introduction to the crease was marked with two consecutive bouncers.

"Eh, pomm's good at ducking."

My third and fourth deliveries were gifts to get off the mark, and were struck to the boundary.

"He's been in long enough." The shout came from the beer tent. "Want a rest pomm?"

I never saw it coming. The next ball uprooted my middle and off stumps, before I even had time to move.

"Next one please ," the bowler shouted.

A stout young girl strutted out to the crease. Dressed only in an oversized rugby shirt, her ample chest and thigh measurements bore evidence of a power greater than mine. After only one over she had surpassed my total and seemed set for a high score. Knocking up thirty runs in double quick time, an argument developed between herself and the bowler. In a fit of temper she knocked over the stumps. Then to the cheers of all, picked one up and chased the bowler round the field and was given out for unsportswomanly conduct. We now sent in our best batsman and they countered by changing the bowler.

"Come on Terry, you show 'em how to bowl."

"Dirty tricks," shouted Sonny. "She's going to disturb our lad's concentration."

Terry turned out to be a dark haired beauty and peeling off her sweater, soon had the beer tent rocking with cheers and whistles. Our innings only lasted three more overs. Terry had stripped to bra and panties, Sonny had made a streak and the beer tent had collapsed on the rumour of no more beers.

After our innings we took to the field. Estimates of our score varied wildly. Our scorer adjudged us to have made one hundred and forty, theirs only eighty five, and after a good humored debate in the beer tent, we compromised at one hundred. In the field I was given third man boundary duty and, sitting back under a shady tree, spent the rest of the afternoon eating barbecued mutton, drinking beer and practicing my courting techniques on Terry before leaving the following day.

After one night spent under the skies in Palmerston North, I arrived in the port of Wellington. Hoping for a quiet night, I made no allowances for it being St. Patrick's Day and, having celebrated my thirty second birthday on the farm only a few days before, I was in no mood for a repeat performance of hangovers and excesses of spending and, if that wasn't a good excuse, my funds were running low again. Calling in at the Youth Hostel, I found it full of British, in party spirit."

"Come on Bernard, no excuses."

Two 'green' beers later, (coloured with mineral water for the occasion) all resistance had diluted. During the night I somehow separated from the Brits, and found myself in the company of a group of local students on a pub crawl to end all pub crawls. Having exhausted all their local watering spots, we piled into the back of an old Ford Anglia, before spending the next twenty four hours gate crashing one student party after another, testing my capacities for drink, conversation and women to the limit.

Back at the Youth Hostel I spent a whole day in bed. Penance for past indulgences had to be served, and no amount of persuasion from the Hostel's warden could pry me from between my welcoming bed sheets. Feeling refreshed the next day, I felt able to cope with making arrangements to go to the South Island. I'd been looking forward to travelling on New Zealand's Legendary Inter-Island Ferry, but as luck would have it, it was on strike so, reluctantly, I booked a flight on to Christchurch.

Arrival in the South Island heralded the oncoming of winter. Temperatures had plummeted below 50 deg. F. Freezing cold winds and driving rain welcomed me at the airport and, to make matters worse, I overheard a weather forecast that mentioned snow. Everywhere, trees were in their final flush of autumn colour. Fields were bare of harvest and roadside stalls were selling the last of their apples. Only two hundred and fifty miles closer to the South Pole than Wellington, this short distance had made all the difference in the world. I did not want to visit Christchurch, so I had a chance to get around the South Island before winter set in. I headed south en route to a pre-arranged meeting with friends. I had met six months earlier in Canada.

I had met Alan, a law student from Dunedin, while both of us worked as waiters in Calgary. Listening to his stories of high mountains, deep fjords, remote beaches and active volcanos had fueled my imagination for this far flung country. Now looking forward to seeing familiar faces and, with the added bonus of mail, (I was using Alan's parents address) I wasted no time in making Oamaru to collect it, before continuing south to Dunedin and my meeting with Alan.

On my way down I stopped off in Moeraki, to see their famous 'round rock beach'.

Legend has it that the Sun of God breathed fire one evening

after a large spicy meal, I had been told. The resultant heat wave fused the universe together. Later that night he had a call of nature and, being a prude at heart and not wanting his father to see him, chose the remotest part of the universe for his ablutions. Here on Moeraki beach you'll find what remains of that monumental discharge. From those overly large global and fossilized forms, science will eventually prove the origins of the universe, and hence the beginnings of time as we know it. The Vatican, I've heard, wanted them displayed in Rome, but that's only a wild rumor.

Anyone could be excused for mistaking Dunedin, with its dour looking Victorian stone buildings, narrow, winding streets and Gaelic looking features, for a part of Scotland. Lacking the smoother features and daring dress sense of their neighbours to the north, Dunedin's inhabitants, with the help of Alan soon won me over with their sheer warmth, good humour and unhurried approach to life.

In the days following I saturated myself with world news and could be found every night glued to the television screen then, on my last night, gave in to insistent invitations to the pub, and it will suffice to say that alcohol levels in my body were enough to insulate me against the following day's cold and wet cycling after which I spent the night as a guest of Clinton Junior School's headmaster before continuing to Lumsden, fortified with a free breakfast of bacon, beans and egg. Two days later I found myself trapped in Te Anu waiting for the weather to break.

To even the most naive and untutored traveller, that morning bore all the signs of an oncoming storm. Muffled sounds of thunder broke the dawn silence and in the distance, banks of black clouds hung like great sacks over the horizon. With no trace of air movement to alleviate a hot humid atmosphere, I was bathed in sweat and, more than anything that morning, took to my bike from Te Anu for fresh air.

After only six miles I was caught in a futile race against time. Protective walls of trees were soon being punctured by gushing winds, ear piercing claps of thunder exploded in clouds above and the heavens opened with driving rain which bit into my face like grains of sand. Within minutes the low lying road from Te Anu was awash in water. Such was the storm's force that soon it had penetrated the protective lining of my clothes. Then, without warning, the wind changed direction catching my water proof poncho and ballooning it up over my face before tearing it in two. By now my toes and fingers were numb and without waterproof protection, I was soon soaked to the skin. My only warmth now came from the continued energy burned up from cycling and, steadily, I began to lose the battle to replenish my stocks as wind stripped away heat faster than my body could produce it. Climbing onto higher ground, hail replaced the rain and soon a thin film of snow covered the road. I had to find shelter and it didn't come soon enough.

The pot of tea's life giving heat flowed through my body and I hungrily devoured a plate full of egg and chips and ordered again. My saviour had come in the form of a roadside transport cafe in Mossburn. I changed into dry clothes, hanging the wet ones over air convectors in the forlorn hope they would dry before I left then, from within the cafe's secure environment, I watched and listened to the hail beating down.

"Will these help?"

The owner handed me two plastic garbage bags.

"I heard you say your poncho was ruined. You can use these as windbreakers."

She had already cut out holes for my arms and head. Her idea turned out to be a life saver. Although allowing rain in through the cut outs, it kept the wind out, and when I reached Lumsden I was soaked more in sweat than rain.

I was now travelling through the heart of rugby union country, Southlands. Here, spurned from within its tiny village communities, is the backbone of New Zealand's famous All Black Forward Pack. Legend has it in these parts that they don't just beat British Lions Touring Team but, bury them; for although Britons are welcome visitors, suppressed emotions have a tendency of bubbling to the surface during these games, turning them into battles where no quarter is given. White posts erected like church steeples marked the pilgrim's way to these holy battle grounds, where names like Colin Meeds and Sid Going were deemed saints in their own life times.

Queenstown came and went and from Lake Wanaka I started my ascent of Haast Pass. Banked on either side by mountain ranges, I followed the Makarora River on a steep course upwards and was in sight of its two thousand foot summit when I hit a road hold up. Heavy rains had washed away a large portion of gravel road here and at the Gates of Haast on the downward side of the pass. On both occasions road crews allowed me through after long waits. Throwing caution to the winds I hardly touched my brakes on the down side's dangerous switchbacks, trying to make up for lost time. Having left Wanaka at dawn I stood little chance of reaching Haast River village before night fall and, when the sun set during my descent, I found myself cycling in the ever decreasing light of dusk, setting courses between dark shades of trees with only a partially illuminated center line for guidance. Concentrating on darkened roads and attempting to sustain any kind of speed tired me out. Glow worms lit up and started out at me from surrounding bush. Sharp twists in the road disoriented me and large trees blocking out the stars swallowed me in darkness. Suddenly the road dropped. There was a thunderous roar and I found myself frozen at the very lip of an unseen river. I'd missed the road's single lane bridge. Unnerved, I sat down by the roadside, lit up a cigarette and waited. At 10:00 pm a pick-up truck stopped and minutes later I was relaxing in the smoke filled environment of Haast River's only pub.

The following morning my coastal skyline was dominated by a huge tidal wave of rock and forest. It was my first sight of the Southern Alps. Rising steeply to heights over twelve thousand feet, they effectively isolated Westland Country from the rest of the island. Again I started to climb into the mountains. By late afternoon I'd passed Franz Josef Glacier and Mount Cook and, on reaching Whataroa, I turned onto a dirt track road leading to the sea. Hidden, five miles off the highway was the remote fishing village of Okarito. For Youth Hostel buffs, New Zealand offers some of the most intimate places to stay. I'd been told of its happy go lucky atmosphere and one dollar a night cost in Lumsden, and had decided to make it a definite rest-up spot. Okarito had one main street, and comprised less than a dozen houses, one store and an old wooden school house.

"Do you know where the Youth Hostel is?"

I'd gone up and down the street looking for any Y.H.A. signs without success.

"You've just passed it," the store keeper replied. "It's the old school house. They've converted it, well let's say they've taken out the desks and chairs. There's no electricity or running water either."

That night I had to cook on an open wooden fire, get water from the well, and as darkness fell, I sat back to enjoy my first night in the company of a crackling wooden fire, complete with coffee and diary by candlelight.

A sign posted on the door greeted me in the morning.

"Didn't want to wake you. Store is closed today. If you want any supplies I go into Whataroa this afternoon. If you want anything before then come down to the house. It's the last one before the beach. Richard."

Richard was like no warden I'd ever met and, arriving at his house, I was immediately invited in for a drink.

"Have you any food?" he asked me.

"No, I've written a list out for you."

"Had breakfast?"

My answer opened his larder and, before leaving, he'd given me a bottle of milk, some eggs and a freshly caught fish.

"That should keep you going. " Then, as an afterthought, he asked, "Do you want any beers?" Before leaving he lent me a fishing line, advised me where to fish, how to get bait and where to look for mussels. The next two days were spent in idyllic isolation. Low tides bared a rich harvest of mussels and deep lagoons, their fish. Then, on the third day, I was joined by a group of 'alternative' people, (I use their words).

"Are you a vegetarian, Bernard?" We were to share cooking duties.

"No", I replied, none to sure what a vegetarian was.

I was then given a short lecture on the advantages of vegetarianism, and after our meal the scene was set for an evangelical conversion. A stack of leaflets from Ecology to Zen Buddhism appeared on the table and soon I found myself in the unenviable position of defending engineering. They'd obviously been battle hardened against better answers then those I could offer. Facts and figures were thrown at me from all directions, proving a never ending cycle of imbalances against nature, caused by the inventions of modern technology.

"What's wrong with you people?" I asked. "If it weren't for engineering, I couldn't be here listening to you lot talk. It's paid for my trip. I didn't have a choice until now to be 'alternative' as you put it. Engineering was a means to an end." I felt intimidated more by their educated grasp of words than their life-saving formulas.

Nuclear holocausts, chemical waste and acid rain either demanded agreement with their views or alternative answers. Their surface arguments were as smooth as silk, but when I offered reality in defense, they lost me behind smoke screens of philosophical clap-trap, using words I couldn't understand, let alone spell. It was as if we spoke two different languages.

"Bernard, you're too close to the subject, try and see it from a wider perspective." Common sense just wasn't in their vocabulary and to dip under their intellectual dictionary meant not to exist.

"Look I'm here on a holiday. Let's just drop the subject. I don't mind hearing someone else's point of view, in fact that's why I started travelling. But if all you're into is converting, forget it." The night's arguments were both exhausting and frustrating. Okarito's spell was broken.

When I woke the following morning they were gone. Their questions were still there, but it was a relief to see the back of them. Two weeks later I was in Christchurch and ready for the final leg on my air ticket.

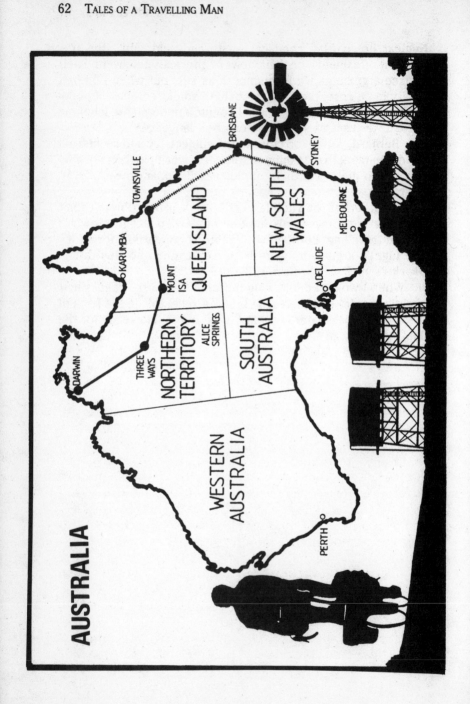

Chapter 5:
The Land of Oz

"HI POM. BROUGHT YOUR OWN TRANSPORT THEN?"
How stereotyped can you get, but those were the
first words I heard at Sydney Airport. Sydney itself
was a surprise to me. I'd boarded what I thought was a flight to
Melbourne and, not until mid-flight did I realize the mistake. My
ticket was for Christchurch - Melbourne - Sydney. Somehow
things had gone wrong again. But it could have been worse.

I'd already been acquainted with the Australians' over-zeal-
ous approach towards their own country. Just as it can be said
that Americans talk of their country in terms of size, so it can be
said Australians talk in terms of venom and from Vancouver to Fiji
I had been continually warned about their wild life, especially the
poisonous variety. The infamous red back spider - check the
toilet seat, whip snakes - check its direction, scorpion - don't pick
up stones, centipede - empty your shoes, sea snakes - don't go
swimming, and the deadly man-o-war jelly fish - don't walk on the
beach. The list was endless and, like their warnings, held no
bounds. Although I took their warnings with a pinch of salt I
adopted a cautious approach, deciding there was no smoke
without fire and invested in a one man tent before leaving Sydney
so I wasn't surprised to encounter all but the redback spider in
the following months, and most of the sea creatures as well. Soon
I would be accustomed to daily morning searches of boots, bags
and any opening which could house my poisonous friends. I
never forgot the fright of walking up one morning in Canada to
find a snake snuggling up to me in my sleeping bag. I learned my
lessons the hard way and in Australia searches became a daily
ritual.

After a short acclimatizing period in Sydney I made my way up
the east coast by train to Brisbane and, after a short visit,
continued onto Townsville in northern Queensland where, on
leaving the station, I met Gerrard.

Gerrard was young, fit and American, in that order and, like
myself, his year on the road had seasoned him to the rigours of
travel and its self imposed routines. He had a passion for order

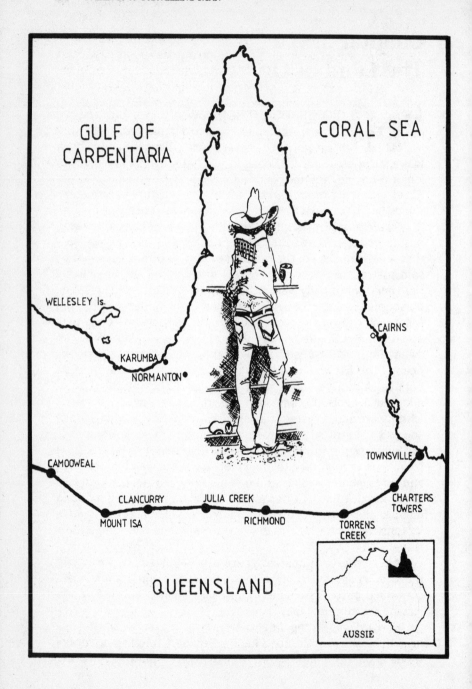

GULF OF
CARPENTARIA

CORAL SEA

WELLESLEY Is.

KARUMBA
NORMANTON

CAIRNS

CAMOOWEAL

CLANCURRY

JULIA CREEK

TOWNSVILLE

MOUNT ISA

RICHMOND

TORRENS
CREEK

CHARTERS
TOWERS

QUEENSLAND

AUSSIE

and planning, and his knowledge of bicycles was unquestioned. His attitude was in complete contrast to my easy going approach and this made us a good match. During the following weeks we would guard each other's freedoms like fighting cocks, coming together only in the evenings to share the load of setting up camp and cooking. Although it was never said, we both knew we were free to continue on our own but, if the occasion necessitated help it would be given without question. This was the first time in a year that I'd travelled in company and, although I'd come to view people as an intrusion, I soon began to revel in the security of my new companion.

From the outset our conversations were punctuated by long silences. Gerrard would often drift off in mid sentence, then suddenly continue the conversation like a runner missing a lap that didn't matter. At first it irritated me but then, at nineteen years of age, I could only imagine what influences had effected him. Still it left an uncomfortable gap between us. The first few days were uneventful. On the third day, we were invited to spend the evening in Marathon's Railway Encampment. After eating a meal with the crew we went to the games room to unwind.

At 11:00 pm. the television came to life and I was suddenly transported back to England

"Presented for your late night entertainment, we bring you live coverage from Wembly Stadium in London, England, coverage of the English F.A. Cup Final, between Tottenham Hotspur and Manchester City."

I spent almost the entire game answering Gerrard's questions. To him a corner was where two walls met; free kicks should be paid for and throwins were a waste of time. But when he heard the commentator say dead-ball, it was just too much. That evening broke the ice between us and by the end the occasion had gripped him.

From Marathon we left the hills of the Great Divide behind and, dropping down onto the plains with a strong tail wind behind us, had no difficulty covering the one hundred and thirty miles to Julia Creek. The following day we made Cloncurry and on day seven we reached the mining town of Mt. Isa, making camp under its shadow on waste land adjacent to the mine That evening we were treated to a surrealistic lighting display set against the backdrop of the Southern Cross. How ugly the mine looked in the light of day but, wearing its evening display, it took on the form of a Disney fantasy.

The next day started badly. We encountered numerous cattle grids on the road, resulting in frustrating stops on long flat runs. I decided to ride over one too many. A spoke snapped setting off a chain reaction and, within a few miles, pinging noises of snapping back wheel spokes had reduced my progress to a walking pace and, by Camooweal, I was nursing a shaking bike around the slightest bump.

That evening Gerrard set about proving his worth. Not only did he strip and replace the broken spokes, but cleaned and greased the bearings. Due to Gerrard's insistence, I had bought spare spokes in Mt. Isa. He had been amazed at my lack of preparation. I didn't even own a puncture repair kit and now, less than twenty four hours later, the spokes were being put to use. Due to the different makes and sizes of our bikes, his metric, mine imperial, the removal of my rear cog was a problem. Adjustable spanners, wrenches and cloth packing were used. With nothing to do but watch I found myself hovering around the scene like an expectant father and when asked to go find an extended wrench, jumped at the chance to feel useful. Clearly he was relishing this chance to show off his improvisational skills and I was amazed to find he had finished before I'd returned. Then like any good craftsman, he took the bike for a short ride before making final adjustments. Having been used to taking things as they came, I had almost forgotten there might be other ways of coping and to my embarrassment what I learned that day is still all I know about bicycles.

Later that evening in the bar we were joined by a group of truckies. Set apart from the main stream of life, this strange breed of men ranked in most Australian's eyes with that of the Abo. To these men the term 'keep on trucking' meant endless stretches of wilderness and weeks away from home. In the city, camouflaged behind the every day dress of shirt and tie, you may have been forgiven in mistaking them for your neighbour but, once in control of their macho 'sixteen wheelers', they were a much different animal. Living by a code of reckless violence, honesty and good humour, they seemed to revel in this exclusiveness. Their gypsy life style, C.B. handles and foreign phrases bind them together like a race within a race. Just nights before I'd witnessed a group of truckies in a bar room brawl the center of which was a wild pig. Ownership was in question and fighting was the answer. During the ensuing brawl the pig broke loose, crashed through the bar's glass door and stopped the combatants as if between rounds. Picking themselves up they tore off together in hot pursuit, chasing it around the parking lot. Cornered, the pig had no option. It dropped dead, causing yet another argument, and the fight was on again.

Soon talk that night revolved around the Abos. "What makes them laze around all day?" I asked. We'd often seen Aborigines walking aimlessly around the small settlements we'd passed through.

"You've got a cheek mate." I knew I was in for it from the tone of his voice. "What you see around here is a whole lot of disillusionment and apathy. They're caught between the old and the new. You'll find Abo shanty towns attached like limpets to every settlement in the north. It's the bright lights, a taste of the good life. No one forces them to come."

"That's putting it a bit strong, isn't it ?"

"I'm not sticking up for them. You get what you ask for in this life, but these so called savages have been hounded ever since we arrived. Take that rock in Tennant Creek." This gigantic piece of rock, together with the Ayres Rock dingo killing, was headline news at the time. "What would you feel like if someone stole you mother's tombstone and erected it as a bloody tourist attraction?" The Tennant Creek Rock had been taken without permission from a disputed Aborigine burial ground. "I personally don't give a damn about its significance, but if they feel so strongly about it, the government should return it from where they found it. You wait, we'll follow the Yanks yet. Ayres Rock will be transplanted into Sydney Harbour. It will make the biggest tourist attraction in the world." He paused, then a smile creased his face. "Then 'Packer' will get his cricket teams play on it and he'll have the biggest mass media event in history.

That evening only enhanced my respect for truckies and we left them in the early hours of the morning, still full of life and good humour.

Since leaving Mt. Isa we'd entered a vast semi-arid wilderness. By now, all hints of green had turned into a rusty brown. Endless horizons soaked up noises like a sponge and I was caught out riding the center line on more than one occasion by fast moving cars. The road was now as straight as a ruler and with no land marks to break up the view, distances were impossible to judge. For hours I could put myself on automatic then suddenly, for no apparent reason, I would have to turn. Maybe the bend was there to break up the monotony, if so many drivers had been caught out, as marking each turn like a graveyard, I saw upturned and burned out cars.

Nearing Soudan Station I surprised a herd of cattle. An enraged bull took exception and having seen me off, stood by the roadside in wait of my partner. I watched with mixed feelings. Gerrard at first didn't notice it, neither did he hear my shouts. Then the bull let out a roar and charged. Gerrard was a fast cyclist, but the bull was gaining. A bag fell off his bike. He stopped. The bull bucked with excitement and changed direction. Just before Gerrard disappeared in a cloud of dust, there was a loud peal of horns. Roaring down the road like some metallic beast, a trucky had come to his rescue. Two more blasts followed for good measure and as the truck passed Gerrard I could see the bull turning off into the bush.

Arriving in Soudan we made camp down by the dried out Ranken river. Dusk heralded our evening's entertainment. First we were treated to the night calls from a flock of pink cockatoos. Later two emus came searching for water. After supper the sky turned brilliant shades of red, and as the evening shadows lengthened, the horizon lost itself to darkness. Then came the astounding hush. A full moon rose to the cries of a lone dingo before that too was swallowed up into the night's vacuum.

In the morning, silence was broken by a peal of rollicking laughter. It was the bush comedian himself, the kookaburra, and down by a water hole a lone wallaby drank nervously while keeping a watchful eye on the both of us.

We were now over half way to Darwin and the scenery had changed little since Mt. Isa. We'd cycled through places with names like Frewena, Threeways, Rannier Springs and Newcastle Waters, all conjuring up memories of goodbyes and pleasant evening's drinking. In between we often arrived at nameless clearings only to find their water holes dried up. With settlements separated by more than one hundred miles of waste land, water was becoming a major problem. Neither of us had experience

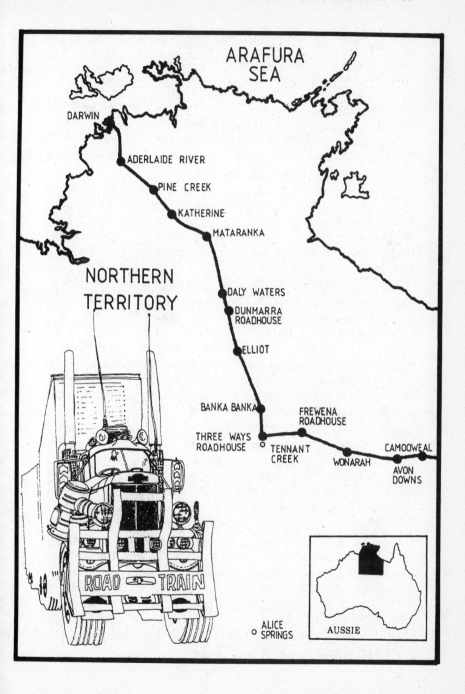

ARAFURA SEA

DARWIN

ADERLAIDE RIVER

PINE CREEK

KATHERINE

MATARANKA

NORTHERN TERRITORY

DALY WATERS

DUNMARRA ROADHOUSE

ELLIOT

BANKA BANKA

FREWENA ROADHOUSE

THREE WAYS ROADHOUSE

TENNANT CREEK

CAMOOWEAL

WONARAH

AVON DOWNS

ROAD TRAIN

ALICE SPRINGS

AUSSIE

cycling in hot conditions, and with only two four-litre water containers between us we now depended on the hospitality of fellow road users. Although not many vehicles were on the road, we never found flagging them down difficult. Sometimes we were offered cool beers. Sometimes sandwiches and even the odd chocolate bar. Since Townsville we'd not spent a dime on sleeping accommodation, usually having been invited to eat and sleep in the company of road crews and homesteaders and on more than one occasion I collapsed into sleep under the combined weight of the food and drink offered.

From Threeways we joined the Stuart Highway north to Darwin, and at Daly Waters, baked hard earth gave way to tropical vegetation. Dead snakes now littered the road. A problem at the best of times, early morning would find them lined up like sticks on the road drinking in the glaze of dew. Frequent checks of saddle bags and shoes followed and in the evening camp sites would be swept clean. At Mataranka our long awaited decision to take a rest was taken for us. Cycling in on a film set 'Land of the Never Never', we were immediately adopted by its film crew, and that evening found ourselves being wined and dined by its potpourri of stars, crew and assorted groupies. A construction 'site hut' doubled as canteen and no sooner had everyone squeezed in, when one after another impromptu performer leapt to the tables. Actors still dressed in period clothes slipped in and out of part as one split personality after another vied for the canteen's captive audience. Under the influence, technician mixed freely with producer and, as events slipped into overdrive, gossip soon overlapped that of argument. Ego after ego was punctured. Strained by long hard days under the sun, our arrival had given them an excuse to unwind with a party and tomorrow had been deemed a holiday. Everyone was letting their hair down and by midnight the whole scene had mellowed under a haze of smoke.

During the night it rained. We had cycled for days through humidity that you could have cut with a knife, now the weather had broken. It is said that when Ozzie awakes from its slumber, it does so on a grand scale and that night only added further weight to this saying. Within minutes the whole film set looked like it had been dropped into a lake. Forced to evacuate our tents, we took shelter in their film crew's games room and that night we slept in borrowed sheets on top of pool tables.

Fit and in good spirits we reached Katherine on day fifteen. By now routine daily mileages were easily covered, but only a short distance further on, our trip would take on a whole new meaning for Gerrard. Looking from the road at a giant termite nest, a loud explosion startled me. The tyre of a passing truck had exploded. Its rear wheels jack-knifed and in front the whole scene was enveloped in a great cloud of red dust. Miraculously the driver gained control, but Gerrard was missing.

"You're a lucky one mate". The last one took me over a week to scrape off the tyres."

I found a white faced Gerrard, standing by the trucky, only yards from a rimless wheel.

For the rest of the day, Gerrard was in a world of his own and in the evening he never spoke about the incident. He again withdrew behind the wall of silence I had taken so long to break down, and turning in for the night, I left him staring blankly into the night sky. The following morning his face looked drawn and pale and even his walk lacked that spring of youth I was so accustomed to. Like a player looking for the final whistle in a loosing match his heart wasn't in cycling anymore. On the outskirts of Darwin, a driver stopped to tell us of another cyclist behind. Suddenly Gerrard's competitive spirit returned. Maybe the thought of a stranger passing us so close to Darwin was an attack on his pride. The news was like giving him a blood transfusion. We set off like two sprinters, making the last twenty miles in double quick time. What a difference a quick surge of adrenalin can do to your outlook on life; but sadly it wore off, and Gerrard's state of euphoria at reaching Darwin would be only temporary.

'OH, DARWIN IS BEAUTIFUL WHEREVER YOU GO
AND THE RAIN IN SEPTEMBER
MAKES THE PALM TREES ALL GROW
OH HAPPY I AM TO BE AT THE TOP OF THIS LAND
WITH A DOZEN OF ME ESKIES AND ONE IN MY HAND.'

I'd heard this song in Sydney and it had already equipped me with a battery of frontier characters. It's girls I had been told were generally big, blond and brash and likewise, its males. Both I'd been told owned rapier tongues, that when blunted with alcohol tailed off like cuddly teddy bears. Isolation and lawlessness were the name of the game and any place where the ever present 'stubbie' was a way of life could not be called boring, so I wasn't surprised at my first experience.

Within sight of the town's center I was suddenly stopped in my tracks. A dog, tail between its legs shot across the road in front of me, Then no sooner had my eyes adjusted to its path when the object of its fright came into view. Chasing the dog down the street, I saw a four foot crocodile. Not a drop of beer had passed my lips and already I was hallucinating.

We parked our bikes in the center, walked into a bar and immediately set about celebrating our seventeen day cycle trip. Although it was only six o'clock, the place was packed and looked more like the beginnings of a cattle auction with its sawdust floors. Soon we were joined by a group of young men, all of whom seemed to be suffering phantom pregnancies. Like the Michelin Men you see in tyre adverts their massive rolls of flesh started at their bellies before tapering down in both directions, ending with the ever present stubbie attached like glue to one hand. As the evening drew on, our table overflowed with empty beer cans and by the end of the night we both found ourselves on the floor, counting butt ends. We decided to call it a day but, before leaving, found our decision overridden. The Michelin Men had attached themselves to us like only fellow drinkers can and they insisted on escorting us home. It was not so much a request as a command, and we were in no position to refuse. Plainly they wanted the party to continue, so a couple dozen beers were bought before we left. What a sight our overpowered escort of station wagons made. In true 'American Graffiti' style our guides crawled down the road at a funeral pace, sometimes weaving around imaginary objects and sometimes in short sharp sprints of burning rubber. Three abreast, the passengers would jump from one station wagon to the next, giving the whole scene the appearance of a motorized obstacle race.

Our intention was to spend what little remained of our money on a weekend between clean sheets, while waiting for the banks to open on Monday, but fate in the guise of a bank manager had other plans for us. There was no money in my bank and Gerrard's luck was no better. We then used up more precious resources making phone calls home. Gerrard's father would send money immediately, but it would take at least five working days to clear through the bank. I rang my lawyer, (who was handling my funds in Toronto) only to find he was on vacation. His secretary told me they had never received my telegram from Sydney and without his authority couldn't do anything about it. "Just a moment." Then she put me on hold. "I have the balance of your account, Mr Howgate if you want it?" I wanted to scream. Here I was, desperate for money and all she wanted to tell me was how much I couldn't touch. The only person in the world with access permission to my bank account was on vacation. I left a message, then walked round Darwin for a while. Without the cushion of my bank balance, and only fifteen dollars between us, the reality of our situation now slapped me across the face. I had to do something. I made another phone call.

"Hi Tom, how's the weather ?"

"Where are you calling from ?"

"Darwin, in Australia."

"Last I heard, you were on your way to New Zealand. What's the problem?"

"I've run out of money, Tom. Can you send me two hundred dollars ? I'll explain later."

The other end filled with laughter. "Haven't changed much Bernard, have you ?"

To conserve money we left the Youth Hostel, and spent the next few days bouncing from one address to another, looking up friends and friends of friends in an effort to find places to stay for free. Our first night was spent in religious indoctrination, but their constant bible reading and speaking in tongues was too much and we left two days later, to exchange the fanatically charged atmosphere of well meaning Moonies for the low-key life of Darwin's suburbia, to stay with Pat, a friend we had met at Daly Waters. On the fourth day Gerrard struck gold. He was offered a job on a building site with an immediate start and his spirits once again took an upswing. Since leaving the Moonies he'd fallen back into being silent. Religion had now entered his life and instead of bringing us together drove us apart. That evening he left to share a flat with his new work mates. It would be the last I saw of him. Months later Pat would describe his frightening behaviour and sudden departure for America.

Getting work myself was a big problem. Unlike Gerrard my visa did not include a work permit, so that cut possibilities down to casual work, where proof of visa was not important. My persistence however, was rewarded. I found a job as a barman. It lasted only two hours. A fight broke out in the bar. The owner told me to throw them out. I took one look at their size and stayed where I was. The owner took one look at mine and told me to leave. I don't know whether he fired me out of regard for my safety or to save himself the cost of paying my future hospitalization. The following morning I went to the harbour to enquire about work. I was offered the cook's job on board a prawn boat. History has a habit of repeating itself but I couldn't foresee it happening so quickly. A fight broke out onboard the boat. The crew went beserk and I ended up sleeping out on the wharf. In the morning I returned for my sleeping bag and saw the captain.

"Sorry about last night, mate. Fired the lot of them. I won't be setting off now until I get a new crew. That could take a few weeks. If you can't wait I have a friend who's looking for 'deckies'. He has a good boat, but he rules it with an iron fist. Tell him I sent you if you are interested. His boat's called the *Savo*".

Chapter 6:
King Prawn

"**W**HAT DO YOU MEAN SAVO'S A BAD BOAT TO WORK on ?", our engineer replied.
"You lot couldn't catch a prawn if one dropped in ya' lap."

A visiting crew had come on board for a party and no sooner had the drinks come out, then a stream of sarcastic baiting began. It had all started in the harbour with good humour, but now below deck weeks of suppressed anger spilled out into violent argument. Instinctively I found myself closing ranks behind the rest of the crew.

"Look, I didn't ask to stay on this boat for eight weeks, in fact I wanted off after two. We're not the best crew around, but we're not the worst either. I don't like the idea of you lot inviting yourselves onto our boat, drinking our beer and eating our food. If you can't think of anything better to say than to criticize us, I suggest you shut up and piss off back to your own boat." As soon as I'd finished the whole table fell silent, even the engineer had disbelief written on his face. What on earth was I saying? Why had I stood up for the engineer ? We'd been united in a running feud for the last six weeks. Arriving that morning at Karumba harbour, we'd spent the whole morning offloading two months' catch of prawns and now for the first time since leaving Darwin, we had time to relax and unwind. The last thing I wanted to hear was criticism, especially from outsiders. Suddenly the deckie I had spoken to sprang to his feet, but before he could hit me the engineer stopped him.

"You better leave, mates, before things get out of hand. You should know better than to talk like this. It was Bernard's first trip and he's still wound up. Give him a break. We'll see you all in the bar tonight."

It was all like some frightening nightmare. The argument had rekindled old fires of battle withstood alone at sea. Feelings of confused anger compelled me to seek refuge in the bunk cabin, and lying down I sought escape in my first unbroken sleep for over eight weeks.

To introduce the reader, our prawn boat's complement comprised seven people.

First and foremost was Carl, the captain. Younger and bulkier than myself, he was generously endowed with those two German obsessions of cleanliness and efficiency and together with his habit of looking out onto the deck from his elevated position on the bridge, gave the impression that he enjoyed a feeling of undisputed power.

Sue, the cook and occasional deckie, but most importantly the captain's moll, made her the most influential crew member next to the captain, but judging by Carl's almost constant bad moods, it was neither a secure nor enviable position. Never having been given the advantages of a girl's finishing school, she could be excused her continual lapses of unlady-like behaviour, but what she lacked in the finer arts of femininity, she more than made up for in her excellent cooking ability and topless entertainment.

Pete, of Malaysian descent, was first mate. Being the youngest member on board, his athletic prowess and youthful exhuberance could always be depended upon to raise even the lowest spirits and when called upon to mediate between captain and crew, he showed a strength of character which belied his youth. However, his calm demeanour was subject to short bursts of insanity, for whenever a 'hammerhead shark' got snarled in the nets, he would go completely berserk.

David, Ozzie through and through, was the ship's engineer. Too him a good bird was the type he could lay. On his own admission he was schooled in the libraries of western and war magazines. His heroes were John Wayne and James Dean, and his favourite regiment was the Green Berets. He suffered continually from recurring fantasies. In them he was a mercenary soldier fighting in the jungles of Central Africa, forever rescuing overendowed Janes from the hands of savages.

Chris, deckie and first timer at sea, epitomized one of Ozzie's typical nomadic urchins, forever bouncing from one job to the next. Young and naive, a born dreamer, he was the constant butt of everyone's frustration.

Len, deckie and also a first timer, took to it like a fish to water. He was the captain's favourite, but who could blame him with his long blond hair and deep blue eyes.

Bernard, yours truly, was the oldest and slowest worker on board, and an ever present thorn in the captain's side.

The first days at sea were spent learning the methods of casting away nets and the use of pulleys, winches and booms. We were taught knot tying and soon all those nautical terms like port and starboard were as familiar as our own names. The delegation of duties was at first dependent on ability, but gradually favoritism started to creep in. I began to learn the value of the word 'subservience'. To agree with Carl was a much better course of action than to disagree. Excused duties were used to play one deckie off against another and this tactic of divide and conquer soon began to work, as the captain tightened his grip on the crew.

Within two weeks we had been moulded into something more resembling the 'Mean Machine' than the smooth efficient robots Carl had hoped for. Central to our non co-operation was the captain's ever changing stories of what our trip entailed. All the crew felt deceived. We'd signed up for what was originally a two week fishing trip; sailing out and returning to Darwin. At sea, Carl immediately revised the schedule; the trips duration now depended on catching an allotted tonnage of prawns. Then when we were told we were moving into different fishing grounds in the Gulf of Carpentaria, and that we would not be returning to Darwin, but Karamba some fifteen hundred miles away, it was the last straw, and if that wasn't enough a near mutiny followed the news that we would have to work during the day on a boat refit. Carl fully intended to get his pound of flesh and not reading the small print in our contracts meant he could. It was usual practice to have refits between seasons, but time away from sea meant money. From sunrise to sunset, all rust spots would have to be painstakingly chipped off, carbonized, undercoated and then applied with a final coat of paint. Estimated time for this job was put at six weeks, and that only covered day time duties.

Night time duties officially began thirty minutes before sunset. Every night before the evening meal we cast away our nets for the first of our three, trawling sessions. By nine we were in bed. Fishing continued all night, in all weathers and sea sickness was not an adequate reason for excused duties. Nets were cast away and brought up every three hours and sustained sleep of any kind was impossible at first. This pattern of snatching two hours sleep between trawling sessions became a regular pattern of evening work, affecting everyone from deckie to captain and if anything went wrong, like broken equipment, one session would overlap the next. Eventually lack of sleep caused irrational behaviour, inevitably leading to short fused explosions of temper. The combined effects brought about through lack of sleep and heavy work load led to a marked deterioration in crew morale.

"The body can adapt to anything given time." These were the only words of comfort Carl offered. He seemed determined to break everyone.

On the deck, a huge black slate board dominated the sorting area. Used to chalk up the night's tonnage of pawns, it was always the talk of the breakfast table and with wages based on its percentage; was the focal point of our life at sea. Only Carl could write on it, and he often referred to its figures with the same mystique that Christains regard their saintly objects.

After one fraught night of broken equipment, we woke up to find a large 'zero' written opposite our night's catch. Carl had subtracted its tonnage and set it against the cost of new equipment. This precipitated my decision to leave, and the next morning Carl woke to find my resignation written in bold letters on his revered chalk board.

'REMEMBER 66 AND THE WORLD CUP'

He was a football fanatic and my words were a calculated insult. He got the message, but I didn't get the result I was hoping for. Until then I thought living in the gold fish bowl of boat life was only unnerving, but now Carl put all my movements under the microscope. From now on I had to be on my guard twenty four hours a day. The battle of wills was now public and to be seen to be Bernard's friend was to be translated into Carl's enemy.

I had timed my escape to coincide with our next fuel stop. My plan was to jump ship onto the fleet's fuel barge, then rest up till the mail boat came, but Carl had other ideas. The time of our rendezvous came and went. For one week Carl was strangely quiet. I should have known he wouldn't give in gracefully, but what happened next led to near bloodshed.

"All hands on deck."

Carl's voice boomed over the intercom. It was six o'clock in the morning. On deck I saw our sister ship alongside. I was still half asleep so the significance of its arrival hadn't registered, but when Carl asked me to pull in its fuel line, the penny dropped. He'd timed our sister ship's arrival superbly. It was now plain for everyone to see we wouldn't be making our scheduled call to the fuel barge, our sister ship had done that for us, and to rub salt into my wound, Carl gave me the responsibility of overseeing the fuel pumping and as our fuel gauge rose to maximum, I knew that I had lost the battle.

"Do you think any deckie worth his salt is going to work on a boat that's having its refit at sea?" Pete set about explaining Carl's reluctance to let me go. "I heard him ask for a replacement on the ship to shore radio, but everyone knows Carl. He's great to work with when the going's good, but no-one wants to touch him during a refit."

My chance had come and gone, and now I knew I was a virtual prisoner.

David was also frustrated. Due to our lack of experience, Carl had ordered him out of his privileged position in the engine room. Night after night he had to suffer the long hours sorting prawns with the rest of us and instead of venting off on Carl, he turned his anger on us. He soon became irritated by our sorting speed, and by the end of the week he'd picked fights with everyone except for myself, but I knew my time would come sooner rather than later.

A poisonous stone fish came down the conveyor right in the middle of some prize 'king prawns'. I gingerly picked one out, leaving the rest to be picked out by David further down the conveyor. Suddenly it stopped.

"What the hell are you doing?" By the look on David's face my time had come. "I've been picking out four prawns to your one all night. If you don't start pulling your weight. I'll shove 'em up your arse."

The conveyor started; then stopped again.

"Change places, you're bloody useless." David spat the words out only inches from my face. I"ll show you how its done."

In front of me he began picking out prawns off the conveyor like a man possessed. For five minutes not one prawn passed him. Then he missed one. My hands felt like lead weights. Helplessly I watched the prawn pass me, to the end of the conveyor before disappearing down the shoot and into the sea.

"You're a fucking fairy." David thrust his huge fist in front of my face. "I'm going to ram it down your throat. You did that on purpose."

I didn't move. It wasn't courage that rooted me, I just didn't care.

"You're a bloody coward, don't want to fight do you ?" He stood back jutting his chin out. "Think you're too good don't you?"

I took one step towards him. "I'm not going to stop you." I grabbed hold of his fist, hitting my face with it. "It's your answer for everything." He pulled his hand away, and I grabbed his other. "Go for it you bastard, what's stopping you ? It's your way not mine." Again he stepped back.

"You're crazy. Off your fucking head."

Due to our argument, everyone had forgotten the conveyor and by now the deck was littered with the night's catch. Suddenly Carl appeared on the bridge.

"What's going on ?"

"Nothing," said David.

"Well, bloody well get on with sorting, We haven't got all night."

The conveyor was shut off then, like maniacs, we shovelled up the spilled prawns. That night cleared the air. The chemistry between me and David changed. From that night he would never again wind me up or, for that matter, the others. Even Carl kept his distance and an unspoken truce was declared.

At last I was given space to enjoy my alien environment. I spent hours observing the sea. Whales passed over the horizon like drifting islands and closer to home, huge finned Marlins rose in arcs of slow motion, before crashing back into the sea. Dolphins were also a constant source of entertainment. Always on the scavenge during sorting periods, they would often go through their gymnastic paces as if in payment for a good feed. One night we caught a rare but harmless razor back shark in our nets and, like the sea turtles before we reverently returned it alive to the sea. On calm days, the water was always tempting, but refreshing swims were out, as sharks of every description appeared and disappeared in liquid shadows under the boat. My last memory was of a blazing red sunset over a silent mirrored sea.

"Come on Bernard. Wake up." It was Pete. "We're leaving today and you'll have to get off." His voice sparked me to life. "You slept the whole day and night away. Remember we're in Karumba."

Chapter 7:
No Turning Back

I WILL NEVER FORGET THE DAY I TRIED TO HITCHHIKE OUT of Karumba. In three hours not one vehicle passed me. By noon I was parched and calling it a day, I went back into the town for a drink.

"Looky here, we have a living Pommie in our midst." the bar man shouted. This was followed by loud cheers. There, unfolding before my eyes, recorded in brilliant technicolour was a pageant of events I thought I'd escaped years ago.

"He's got himself a real beauty there hasn't he?" The barman's remark was followed by an even louder cheer.

"Here, introduce the Pomm to our look-a-like." An embarrassed young girl was paraded in front of me, for my opinion.

I'd unknowingly stumbled onto the event of the year. Not since the heyday of Donald Bradman's heroic achievements in the 'old country' had all eyes been focussed on Britain. The day Charley and Lady Di married must rank as the best pro-British advertisement ever seen Down Under. All that surface anti-pommie feeling evaporated into a mass coast to coast drinking binge, as Ozzie drowned itself in nostalgia for lost roots. After all, Ozzie dearly wanted a history of its own, but the very fact it was wild and not trapped within a conformity of history appealed to me. Although not a monarchist, I couldn't help but get emotional with them. Not for the events unfolding on the screen, but for Ozzie's genuine warm hearted acceptance of the country of my birth.

My first job on my return to Darwin was to check on my bike.

"Hi Bernard, good to see you." It was Pat, I'd left all my personal belongings with her before leaving on the boat. Invited in, we sat down over a coffee, then conversation centered on my partner.

"Heard from Gerrard recently?"

"Yes, you've just missed him. He's gone back to America."

"I thought he was going to cycle through Asia. Why did he change his mind?"

She talked briefly about their meeting, his planned trip to Asia and then his sudden departure home.

"It started a month ago with a leaflet on mysticism. He met a religious group in the street. One week later he was round for his bike. He told me he was moving in with them. Religious sects are a dime a dozen in Darwin, so I wasn't worried. I didn't encourage him, but I didn't put him off either. Two days later he was back again, this time for money. He'd walked over and when I asked him about his bike, he told me he'd sold it."

"That bike meant everything to him, Pat."

"I know, I also knew he didn't need money. His father had sent him plenty, that's why he asked me to hold onto it, but what could I do. So you can imagine how I felt when I came home one evening last week to find him on my doorstep with only the clothes he stood up in, and penniless. I couldn't get anything out of him. I thought of calling the police, but I didn't know what I could tell them. At first I thought he was tripping on drugs then, when a friend knocked on the door, he made me promise not to mention his name and when the phone rang, he nearly jumped out of his skin. Whatever had happened was still out there and he was frightened. I stayed up with him all night. Then he came out and said it. "Don't let them know I'm here." It was his religious friends. He told me the commune would be after him."

"Why ?" This whole conversation on religious sects was outside my experience and I was struggling to understand what religion had to do with someone being frightened.

"All I can think of, Bernard, is that he had been too long on his own. Nineteen year olds don't exactly have a bank full of experiences from which to draw on and naivete can only be stretched so far before it snaps. In the morning I got him to telephone his parents in America. They made all the arrangements and paid for his flight home."

I spent the next few days walking around Darwin. I tried to piece together Gerrard's last two weeks, but was getting nowhere. I just wanted to know what had happened to him in the commune and, in searching for answers to Gerrard's return, began to question my own motives for continuing. My plans had ended with the flight tickets to Sydney. Now, one year into my travel, I felt straddled between two uncertainties. To go back now would leave the whole question of travel unanswered, yet to continue forward into Asia would not automatically open doors to a new life.

The question didn't stay unanswered for long. A quick visit to Darwin's Post Office gave me all the impetus I needed.

Getting news at any time is exciting, especially on the road. But, after six months without any, tinged with a little fear...

First, I opened two registered letters from Canada. In one was a copy of my Decree Absolute. My divorce from Irena was final. The second told me of my house sale. I now had a thirteen and a half thousand dollar cushion to travel on if needed. I then read half a dozen letters from my parents. All with the same underlying question: "When will you be back?" Then, inside a letter posted on from Alan's address in New Zealand was a letter from Alison. "Flying down to India for four months. If you're still travelling maybe we can meet there?"

There would be no turning back.

S.E. ASIA

Chapter 8:
Asia At Last

EARLY BLACK AND WHITE TELEVISION DOCUMENTARIES BY David Attenborough with sights of Pygmy tribes in the jungles of Central Africa and views of the Himalayas had fueled my imagination from an early age, but travel in those days took place only in my head. Now the prospect of bringing reality to these dreams filled me with excitement so, armed with only an open mind, I flew out of Darwin and, not wanting to spoil Asia's impact, arrived three hours later in Bali without a guide book.

Cycling from Tuban Airport was like stepping out of a time machine as picture frames of history came to life by the roadside. Bullocks bound together in pairs ploughed open paddy fields in clouds of dust. Further on I watched young women, calves deep in water, plant rice seedlings and when I was spotted they passed this news on in waves of recognition, like excited windmills. Soon these rural scenes were shut out by matted plantations of dark green foliage. All breeze was strangled and I experienced Asia's oppressive heat for the first time. Brilliant, coloured billboards shouted out to be read and, thirsty, I stopped at a restaurant stall only to gain an immediate taste for their clove-spiced tea. A young boy, dwarfed by his ancient looking bicycle, passed me and yet another, with a heavy box strapped precariously behind his saddle, waved me down.

"You buy ice cream,Johnny?" He said it almost apologetically. I smiled and said; "No." He smiled and said; "Goodbye."

Roadside activity was now increasing with every mile. Seeing a group of women spreading ash over freshly cut coconut, I stopped to watch. Immediately I was surrounded by smiling faces and before leaving I was offered a piece of their drying fruit. Another clearing offered screams of fright. I'd surprised a group of naked children washing by a well. A rickshaw full of laughing passengers passed. Then, without warning, I saw the sea.

I didn't so much as stop at Kuta, as be hypnotized by it. Streams of different colours, sounds and smells attracted me like a bee to pollen. Food stalls selling all kinds of exotic fruit lined the streets. Here, everything was guaranteed by touch. I squeezed,

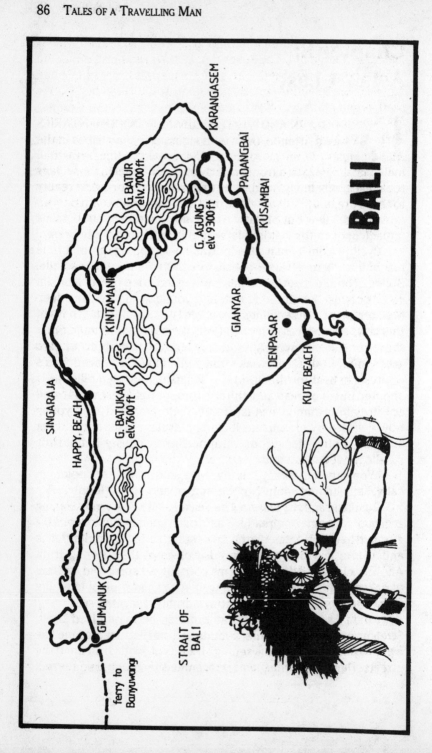

picked and plucked till I found the fruit I wanted. Then I tried to pay with a large bill. The seller laughed, waved her hand at me, gave back my money and, with a free pineapple in my saddle bag, I cycled on. Pseudo-western junk food was everywhere, I saw waffles and hamburgers sold and signs reading, "egg and chips", vied for prominence with that of "Denny's Steak House". New dishes like Nasi Goreng (fried rice and egg) and Gado Gado (salad and prawn in spicy peanut sauce), tantalized me with their unusual smells and enticed me with their names. Music with strange disjointed rhythms blasted out from roadside record shops only to be drowned out by the taped Beatles music from passing taxis. Having got used to Darwin's bland food and colourless street life, I was seduced into this potpourri of different cultures, as life spilled out into Kuta's streets.

The town itself was a complete mismatch, a planner's nightmare. One end catered to the jet set tourist with a view for hygiene, and the other end, in cheap "Losmens" for the third class traveller and his craving to go native. Intermixed between these extremes flowed Kuta's lifeblood. Clustered together, more out of family ties than for safety, were shanty-type houses of bamboo and corrugated sheeting. Open sewage stained the air and animals, kept more for their vocal ability than as household pets, roamed wild in packs. Everywhere there were children and home made signs, advertising everything from rooms for rent to personal massages, marking all intersections   like shop noticeboards.

On my first day I encountered an amazing cross-section of travellers.

"Bonjour", "Hi Mate", "Hello Lad", "Morgen".

Europeans travelling south and Australians, north, stopped me in the street. For all of us Bali, and especially Kuta, offered a stepping stone to and from a predictable west, a chance to acclimatize in this strange oasis of cross-cultures.

Those early days in Kuta were crazy times, and my letters home reflected this mood.

August '81
Kuta, Bali.
Dear Mum and Dad,
   Asia at last. Better than I imagined. There's so much to see

and do, I don't know where to start. Glad I kept the bike, it was worth all the hard times just to get here. Wonderful to ride it just for pleasure again without a load to carry. Can't beat it for getting around. Don't have the hassles of bus queues or taxis to contend with. So cheap to run as well. Can run on a tank full of tea for miles. The bike attracts almost as much attention as me outside towns. I can empty fields of workers, close down shops and create traffic jams within minutes of being spotted.

Let loose like a child in a candy store, I indulged in everything possible. I experimented with my first "Magic Mushrooms", gorged myself on new foods, visited topless beaches, permitted myself the luxury of an overall sun tan, and even went body surfing. In the evenings I went dancing and during the days I watched colourful festivals come to life but, everywhere there were "beach boys".

"Got dollars Mate? Good exchange?"

They were selling everything from cocaine to their sisters, but I wasn't interested, then...

"We have nice brothel, good clean girls. You come tonight, there's dance, no charge to look. " He said with a laugh.

That night I went along just out of curiosity. But the visit was depressing. The atmosphere intimidated. I watched Europeans of both sexes cruising, and dancing wasn't on the agenda. Prices were quoted openly, contracts argued over and partners chosen more out of size than colour or pedigree. Instead of being liberated by my freedom I now felt cornered by it.

At the bar I struck up a conversation with an Australian girl. That night we spent in emotionless action, and in the morning, I found her sleeping in the spare bed. Is that all we put into it? Seeing her in the spare bed cooled me to Kuta as quickly as I had been fired. I paid for my room and left that morning.

Soon the scent from exotic flowers was washing away all thoughts of the brothel and when I got my first sight of Agung Volcano, I had dispatched it to the past. In Padangbai I cycled straight into an Independence Day parade. Women were dressed in brilliant primary colours of red and yellow, and men, some carrying long bamboo branches trailing paper streamers like flags from their tops, wore eye catching black and white chequered sarongs. At the front, I heard music on strange looking instruments and when I was stopped by a member of the band, I jokingly swapped my bike for some fun. Soon I was beating away on the drums, much to everyone's amusement. I followed the parade to the sea then left to explore the miles of black, sandy beaches. Fish spread out on bamboo trays drying in the sun announced villages and men mending nets under the shade of palm trees gave way to an armada of multi-coloured catamaran style boats. Marooned on the natural dry dock of sand, I watched men apply strong smelling fish oils for waterproofing. What I saw next seemed pointless. For two hours I watched a man repeatedly carry water collected from the sea before spraying it onto the beach. This soaking and drying process continued for hours. Then it came to me... Salt!, All that effort just for salt. I couldn't believe the old man's patience or, for that matter, its reward.

Since Gianyar, the impressive Agung Volcano had dominated my skyline. Extinct for generations and covered in dense jungle, its shrouded top now beaconed my route inland. At Rendang I took a wrong turning and soon found myself cycling on a broken surface of volcanic ash as the road wound steeply through tiered paddy fields, only to lose itself at the top of Batur Volcano. It was still early so, leaving my bike in a village temple for safety, I climbed to the top of Batur. Half way up I noticed a figure following me. For three hours my shadow kept pace to the top.

"You drink coca?"

The young boy had watched me leave the village and followed in hope of business. I bought all he had, not out of any great thirst, but to make him go away. I wanted to be alone with my thought and his presence, no matter how innocent, disturbed me. I stood up. Below was a paradise called Bali. Bali was for lovers and, at that moment, I craved someone to share it with. The wind picked up and drowned my thoughts. These feelings of loneliness were always intense when morale was low and there had been many dips in the last year. In the past I had substituted beer for support. I had begun to think I wouldn't have got so far without it. In Darwin, after yet another heavy night's drinking session, I'd made a pact with myself, never to get drunk again on my trip. Maybe I was now suffering what alcoholics call withdrawal symptoms, yet mine seemed to be more emotional then physical.

My arrival at "Happy Beach" coincided with that of a young group of New Zealand student teachers on tour. Walking along the beach, I joined one of them for a swim.

"Look, it's a sea snake."

Automatically my words were drowned in spray. Seeing it in the water only inches away, she let out a loud scream and ran for the shore. Following the snake into shallow water, I picked it out by its tail, cracked it like a whip-lash, and watched its separated head arc into the air.

"Where did you learn that from?"

"Working on the prawn boats."

She was talking to me from the safety of the beach.

"We were always bringing them up in the nets. Usually they were dead but, sometimes, one or two would be a little frisky. It's better to be safe than sorry when you're working in bare feet."

She wasn't impressed with my catch and, on our way back to the hotel, she kept her distance. On arrival I was introduced to her friends.

"What's he got?"

One girl stepped forward for a better look.

"Hello. Who are you?" I said

"Janet. Who wants to know?"

Her introduction spoke volumes. Young, naive, arrogant and beautiful. Her tone slapped like a gauntlet. I rose to the challenge.

"Here, catch." I said, tossing her the sea snake.

To my surprise she did, holding it up like a prize. "Are you going to skin it?"

Unlike her travelling companions, in Janet I'd found a kindred spirit and, within minutes of our introduction, it showed.

Inhibited by her involvement with group activities, our relationship developed no further than the argumentative ease one finds between brother and sister. Small talk turned into heated debates, disagreements into out and out war, and always our meetings had that presence of stored up electricity, bristling with static. Her friends felt this and stayed at a safe distance whenever our paths crossed. We didn't so much ignite as explode every time we met. Teasing her was like putting a match to a fire cracker, and, although we only spent a total of twelve hours together, our parting smacked of the same irreverence as our meeting.

"See you, in Yogyakarta little sis."

"Bet you will wise owl. Are you sure your little old legs will get you there?" Her emphasis on little old legs set the mood. I was determined to arrive in Yogyakarta before she did.

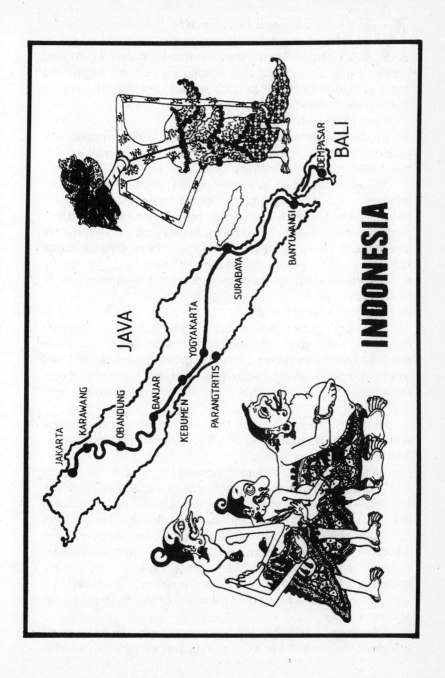

MY SAVIOUR CAME IN THE FORM OF A J.C. LOOK-ALIKE. Dressed in a native sarong, white shirt, and shoulder length hair, he had spotted me in the crowd. I had spent the last thirty-six hours either waiting for or travelling on the Strait of Bali ferry. Now, in Banyuwangi, my overland trip to Yogyakarta had come to a full stop.

"You have problem, yes?"

Producing a phrase book from his rucksack he proceeded to take command. Holding center stage, he soon translated the information I'd been stumbling over for hours.

"You need local bus." My long-haired apparition creased with laughter. Before me was a bus which had obviously seen better days. Seemingly only held together by a recent paint job, it was packed to overflowing. On the roof was everything from furniture to a basket full of chickens in various stages of asphyxiation. One side of the bus bore the signs of a direct hit and, on the front, both wings were dented. Spotting my apprehension, my rescuer offered reassurance.

"They all look like that."

Grabbing my arm, the bus driver guided me down the aisle over a maze of baggage and bodies to the front. A few curt words passed between my driver and a well dressed passenger seated by the window and it was vacated. I was given the prized seat next to the driver. I looked outside to my French companion.

"Where is my bike?"

"It is with the chickens on the roof. No extra cost." He said with a laugh. "The driver likes you. Not many tourists travel on his bus. Bon journey, mon ami."

He then disappeared into the crowd.

Left to my own devices, I felt childishly lost. So I was to be the bus driver's honoured guest. Some consolation. I looked down at my seat. It lacked any covers and had no back rest so I would have to sit sideways for support. Again the bus driver took over. A box was found and baggage was moved into the aisle to make room for it. An old lady pointed to my sleeping bag. I stepped out to make room for her which, after only a few minutes, she'd converted it into a small bed. I handed her some money. She smiled but accepted none.

I don't know whether the driver was trying to impress, or imagined himself to be in a Grand Prix, but whatever was on his mind, it certainly wasn't the road. My first impression of Javanese road behaviour was of survival of the biggest. He gave way to lorries, slowed down for buses, intimidated cars, and saw red when it came to cyclists. Watching bicycles forced off the road sent shudders of apprehension through me. That unseen bond felt for my fellow cyclists was being severely tested. I began to regret my front seat view, feeling more like an observer at someone else's execution than a sightseer. Like Moses, he parted seas of cyclists then, turning a sharp corner, we found ourselves in a showdown with an oncoming petrol tanker. His intoxication with power was short lived. Swerving to miss him, we hit the curb, brushed some cyclists into a roadside drain, skidded and came to a full stop. His success rate improved during the day and, on reaching Surabaya, he'd notched up victories against two motor bikes, a 'bemo' and even forced one 'express bus' off the road. Things didn't improve with a change in drivers either. Almost certainly he had given the replacement driver a pep talk as this one set about his night time duty with the same reckless verve as his day time colleague. Sleep was impossible during the night. Interruptions were frequent. Swerves, horn blasts, and unseen objects going bump in the night were a constant cause of alarm.

During the night the man I had dislodged from the front seat engaged me in conversation.

"Where do your family live?"

"England."

For the next thirty minutes our conversation revolved around his family and then, what was becoming an all too frequent topic, emigration.

"You come from very great country. We very poor..." He paused to draw me into comment, then, when I didn't bite, said in a whisper, "Is it possible to have your address?"

I answered as I always did to these questions, by telling him how expensive it was to live in England and Canada and how cold the weather was. Then, what never failed to confuse and frighten.....

"We don't look after our mothers and fathers like you do. Most people send their parents away into special homes when they get old."

"But this wrong!" He shouted. "For us it is a duty."

Shocked and hurt by this new revelation he changed the subject and, soon, the conversation had drifted on to America and Starsky and Hutch. "They have very good motor bicycles in America..."

By 4:00 a.m. we had reached Yogyakarta. My roller coaster ride from Banyuwangi had taken only eighteen hours, but in the process it had taken years off my life span. I said goodbye to my new friend. We did, after all, exchange addresses and parted on mutual accord.

Between Ji Malioboro and Ji Pasar Kembang (roads) I found Yogyakarta's network of cheap losmens. Interlinked by narrow passages they made perfect traveller's enclave and I booked into the first I came to. "Lucy Losmen" wasn't the best, but it wasn't the worst either, and with outside toilet, well water, open shower and mosquito bloodied walls, would be my home away from home for the next ten days.

Lucy Losmen, like all the travellers' rest houses before, had two things in common; friendly atmosphere and cheap. Hidden away in the poorer areas of cities they umbrellaed a multitude of sins and their distinctive architecture reflected past and present owners. For some of its more ancient colonial dwellings a major overhaul was urgently needed and for others anything was too late, as hundreds of years of accumulated whitewash and plaster would detach at the least movement. Unknowingly I'd slipped into this form of travel way back in Fiji and, by the time I searched out Sydney's "Happy Hour" hostel had hooked into a rich vein of shoe string accommodation. Not always secure, but never boring, their advantages for me, far out-weighed disadvantages. Never smothered in regulations, mixed dormitories were the norm and private cooking was never questions. Central to all, common areas both inside and out allowed one to mix freely and dominating their heart, pin boards, safer and faster than any post office 'post restante' relayed both private and public messages.

HEY JOHNNY LOSMEN
KUTA
May/82
Joe — gone to Jakarta for ten days.
If I don't see you when I return, all the best in Kathmandu.

Popular rest-up spots for the long distance traveller, late arrivals would never be turned away and often I would find make-shift beds on the roof. 'Newcomers' to travel used them for orientation and 'oldtimers' returning home, their last chance to solve the unsolvable questions travel threw up. To some their corridors were as familiar as home, yet for others their walls were as bleak as prisons. Revolution was schemed, partners seduced and religious and philosophical discussion often stretched through the night, and it was these conversations and its instant comradeship that attracted me to them.

Meeting Janet again was like a hurricane touch down. Her up-market hotel was in complete contrast to mine and, while I took my first bath since leaving Canada at her hotel in the morning, she revelled in the rigours of the 'have nots' of travel that evening in my losmen. We spent hours bartering in second hand silk markets, tried our hand at riding bicycle rickshaws, played street volley ball with students and visited out-of-the-way art shops. Our evenings were spent eating under paraffin lantern light in small canvas topped pavement restaurants and, generally, we kept to ourselves. For our last few days I talked her into renting a bicycle.

Less than twenty miles from Yogyakarta, Parangtritis held a kind of mystical attraction. Pete had talked about it on the prawn boat.

"The Goddess Kidu resides in the cliffs overlooking the beach. It is said she reflects your inner soul. She can make it the most beautiful, or the most deadly place in the world."

I had taken all Pete said with a pinch of salt. Two months at sea, and anyone could be excused the occasional fantasy.

"Have you ever been there ?" I asked.

"No, it's just what I've heard. But I believe it."

At sea, I had respected his judgement. As a friend, I found none better. I knew places held special meanings to him. After all, my own experience with faith healing in Fiji could not be explained away either, and he hadn't been skeptical about that.

When we got there, Janet stood in the dunes drinking in the view.

"It's unearthly."

A huge desert of unspoiled sand stretched west for miles down the coastline, and east, just as Pete had described them, huge cliff like fortress walls towered above the dense jungle.

"It's good for your soul." Janet was beside herself. "Can't you feel it, Bernard ?"

"Feel what ?"

"The beach, silly. You don't know what you're missing."

As usual I was left to look after the bikes and by the time I'd caught her up on the beach, she'd already staked her claim, unhooked her top and had started to read. Laying down by the side of her I felt strangely uncomfortable. Up til now our bodies had simply been vehicles we travelled in and the occasional nudity was accepted with the same familiarity as our own. I had broken that protective shell of predictability she had travelled in with her friends and now I felt an overwhelming responsibility towards her. The thought of making love only yesterday was incestuous. My conduct then had bordered on the priestly, but the freedom of the beach changed all that. My relationship in Kuta had been consummated before it had started. I had felt cheated. Now, with Janet, I felt guilty at the very thought. I wanted to touch, to please, but most of all to feel needed.

"Shit.." I jumped up.

"What's wrong, Bernard ?"

"I'm going for a cold shower."

I wasn't in the water long before I felt a strong undercurrent. I could still touch the bottom, then suddenly it opened. Water closed in and I was sucked under. Caught in a fast flowing rift, I was pulled quickly out to sea. Still less than one hundred yards from the shore, the strong current had swept me in an arc five hundred yards down beach from Janet. I beat the water with my arms, thrashed it with my legs, even shouted to attract attention. It was no use. Janet was only a speck on the beach and by now my legs and arms felt like lead. Exhaustion now drained me of all fear and as I slowly began to realize my fate, I lay back in the water to wait for it.

"Fuck if only...if only what ?" I started to struggle with my conscience. My trip to Asia, my bloody selfish trip. Me, me, me... Does the world have to revolve around me ? What about your parents, Bernard ? All those broken promises. Next year, always I'll visit next year... God my parents, not my parents. A telegram. A knock on the door. "I'm sorry Mr Howgate, your son has drowned..." Tears mixed with salt, and old memories flooded back. "You're always over stretching yourself." Irena would always say. She had never understood my nomadic longings.

"You're just a lone wolf, don't understand marriage, do you ?" Was marriage just another compromise ? An excuse against boredom ? Did I lack that special instinct to pair ? What about Alison? Didn't I throw that relationship away too ? I don't want to die, not now, not here.

Suddenly a mouth full of water and my survival instincts surfaced. Janet was less than thirty yards away and getting closer. The rift's current had brought me the full circle.

"Good thing you didn't fight it." She had been completely unaware of my struggle. "It would have sucked you under." She pointed to a deep gorge in the sand. "I thought you knew there was a rift on the beach."

Packing our things we returned to Yogyakarta. Facing death had left me on a peculiar high. Mundane chores were now done in overdrive, and for the first time in six months my bike was cleaned. The next morning Janet came over early to say goodbye.

"I'll be expecting a letter, wise owl." Then she was gone.

On the road by 7:00 am., I found myself hemmed in on all sides. The whole street had spotted me and now expressed its excitement with a chorus of ringing bells. Cyclists fought each other for a better look, and negotiating their near misses, I lost my way.

"Jakarta road, please? "

Stopping to check directions, I was quickly enveloped in a sea of bicycles.

"How much bicycle ? How many gears ? How fast you go ?" A continual barrage of questions were fired at me.

"No. Direction to Jakarta, please ?"

"Where you come from ?"

It was impossible. They weren't listening to me. Then; "I take you to road." It was a young student on his way to college. I followed him through a maze of back streets while, behind, my entourage kept pace. Suddenly an over-enthusiastic rickshaw driver pulled in front of me. Looking back, he hit the curb, arced in the air, then slowly completed the circle, depositing his customers like sacks of coal on the road. This accident acted like an unspoken signal and, after that, we were left alone.

On the outskirts of Kebumen I saw a group of boys playing badminton.

"You play, sir ?"

In and around Yogyakarta I often saw boys playing, usually on waste ground marked out with strips of bamboo staked to the ground.

"Yes." They were overjoyed, and immediately pressed me into a game. Soon word spread that there was a tourist in the village. Whole families poured out to see the action. Three deep in places round the court, some of the more daring climbed adjacent houses for a better look and others climbed up trees. Cheers followed my every shot, and after despatching my host in straight sets, the crowd's favourite took to the arena. Just a few exhibition shots into our warm up made the crowd ecstatic. Playing to a captive audience, I reacted by clowning around. Good humoured jeers followed my every point like a "Punch and Judy" show. Soon over confidence led to mistakes, and my new challenger got the better of me, much to the delight of the crowd. If, by losing, I thought my audition a failure, I was soon proved wrong. They begged for an encore, and I stayed for another game.

That afternoon taught me a valuable lesson. Not being able to speak their language I had searched for ways to communicate. Having discounted music and sketching, I had stumbled on what came so naturally to me: Sport. Like in Fiji, I noticed village life stopped at 4:00 pm. for a game of rugby. From now on whether it was volley ball, table tennis, cricket, badminton or soccer, I joined in whenever the opportunity presented itself.

From Banjar I left the flat coastal road and started my climb into the mountains en route to Obandung. I passed through small villages lined with fruit stalls. The air was heavy with the sweet smell of freshly cut pineapples. Every day is market day in Indonesia, and I was finding it increasingly difficult to resist their colourful selections. Up til now the bike had always hampered my movements and the narrow gaps between stalls didn't lend themselves to the passage of bicycles. Trailing it around was tiresome and the crowds it attracted detracted from my enjoyment. I had not locked it up since Canada, and my saddle bags would offer a rich bounty to any enterprising thief.

"Not touch."

Dressed in western clothes, a forceful looking man stepped forward waving his hands to the crowd. Not one word had passed between us, but he seemed to know instinctively what I wanted.

"No problem, I look after it."

Would he be able to control the crowd? I had to start trusting my judgement of people sometime. Unhooking my camera bag from the handle bars, I left my trip in the hands of a man I had never seen before, surrounded by a faceless crowd. How long should I trust him? Five minutes, ten minutes? I turned back, but he waved me on. Answers like these to unspoken calls, were becoming both unnerving, and an ever-present part of my trip. Gestures like this were God sends, and people like him, indispensable. Putting all fears out of my head, I gave myself to the market. After thirty minutes I returned. My man had the crown enthralled. Tracing his hands over the gears, he had no doubt made himself an authority on 'ten speeds'. Caught in this impromptu lecture, he stopped, embarrassed.

"I ride please?"

I couldn't deny him the pleasure. He'd earned it. Closely followed by his street audience, he shakily rode down the street.

Leaving Karawang on my last leg to Jakarta, I made a fundamental error of judgement. Communication at the best of times was difficult and misunderstandings due to language barriers inevitable. Arriving at a roundabout, I saw no road signs. Stopping a pedestrian I pointed in what I thought was the right direction.

"This way to Jakarta?"

I was answered with a likewise pointing of the finger, a nod of the head, and a bemused smile. It was not until I reached Cikampek fifteen miles down the road that I realized my mistake. I had pointed myself in the wrong direction. I don't know whether my street navigator didn't want to disagree, displease, or just couldn't understand my question; whatever the reason, this mistake of pointing in the wrong direction only to have it wrongly confirmed would repeat itself on more than one occasion.

Nearing Jakarta the traffic increased noticeably. Since leaving Toronto I'd lost the street wise survival technique called city cycling, and with my bus driver's callous attitude towards fellow road users still fresh in my mind, the prospect of cycling in Jakarta frightened the life out of me. Traffic speed and aggression now reflected that competitive edge so common in all cities, and, to make matters worse, the road surface had deteriorated badly. Large pot holes and cracks in the road forced me to swerve, precipitating screams of abuse and, on one occasion, a bottle of Coca Cola came flying my way, and not for consumption either.

For one hour I fought the tide of crazy taxis, thunderous super-tankers and the kill-on-sight bus drivers, and it wasn't until I could see Jakarta's high rise buildings poking through a thick haze of car fumes that the road dualed into a carriage-way. Immediately the fast moving traffic diluted.

The only memory I have of the city is of a deep longing to leave it. Having said that, I will always remember 'Jolan Jaksa Losmen' off Ji Keboh Sirih, for its happy go lucky atmosphere, which was enough to raise anyone's spirits. Evenings spent telling tales, imaginary or otherwise, kept alive my spirit of camaraderie, which I'd missed travelling on my own. Having spent one week on the road from Yogyakarta it felt nice to lose myself once again in a group of like minds.

The day I left for Singapore was almost a non-event. Not leaving myself enough time to cycle to the airport, I was reduced to making frantic phone calls for taxis. The first wouldn't even consider taking my bicycle. The next turned crazy over a small scratch my bike made on his car. Finally, an old battered Fiat accepted my load. Crashing down his boot, I heard the painful noise of grating metal.

Chapter 9:
Fallen Angel

ONCE AGAIN I ENTERED THE COMPLEX WORLD OF COMputerization. Rising above the early morning blanket of mist, Singapore's concrete and glass towers dominated my foreground like a huge glittering pyramid and, caught in its network of road arteries, I was soon drawn irresistibly to its heart. Marking road intersections like armless wardens, traffic lights danced in coloured unison and pedestrians, adjusting to predetermined road crossings, took on the form of a regimented army of ants. Sidewalk greenery was manicured to perfection. "NO SPITTING" signs and waste paper containers were everywhere, and the whole feel was one of antiseptic cleanliness. Unlike Jakarta's cosmetic approach of token adjustment Singapore personified western values to the core.

Following up an address I'd been given in Jolan Jaksa Losmen I found myself on Bencoolen Street, sleeping in a converted fifth floor office block. Earmarked for demolition, many of Bencoolen's deserted offices had been turned over to temporary accommodation, for in Singapore legality openly took a back seat to 'free enterprise'. Stripped bare of furnishings my home was now the spotlessly clean floor of an open plan office area and my bed a rolled up mattress. Security was no problem. A burly Asian vetted all callers and from his size and position by the door blocked all opposition.

On my first morning, I found myself in Singapore's famous or infamous 'Thieves Market'. Here shops overflowed with every conceivable electric gadget known to man. Street side restaurants offered Kung Fu video programmes like menus of the day and, for the evenings entertainment, was a continuous transvestite parade of male prostitutes.

Later I enjoyed a night of vulgar escapism in the Hyatt Regency's Victoria and Albert Restaurant. For once I could return to that power game of aloofness paying for the privilege of impersonal service from a gilded cage paid for in dollars. In my dreams my dinner date had long black hair and chocolate brown skin. For that one night Chandra, an old lover of my brother

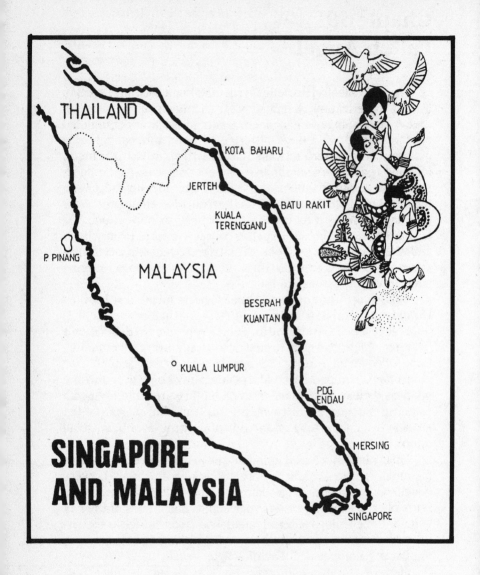

THAILAND

KOTA BAHARU

JERTEH

BATU RAKIT

KUALA
TERENGGANU

P. PINANG

MALAYSIA

BESERAH
KUANTAN

KUALA LUMPUR

PDG.
ENDAU

MERSING

SINGAPORE
AND MALAYSIA

SINGAPORE

played out the game like an indulgent elder sister. Drinking good wine in opulent surroundings I enjoyed every minute.

Life was running along smoothly. Adjustments to the city, although not entirely to my satisfaction, had compensations. Money transactions from Canada were completed swiftly. I had no trouble replacing worn out tyres, and even treated myself to a new 35mm lens. As an extra, in Xzera, I had found the ideal day time companion. We had been thrown together in the communal atmosphere of our shared fifth floor accommodation and I was glad of her company. For her part, having a distinctive multi-coloured hair style and outrageous punk clothes from England, she was relieved to get what little protection I afforded from the unkindly stares of a conservative street level audience.

By day five, freedom of the road beckoned me again. My transactions completed, the city held no further attraction for me. I took one last walk. I had accompanied Xzera up Robinson Road. Going our separate ways, we made arrangements to meet later at MacDonald's for lunch. She didn't turn up. Not feeling unduly worried by her absence, I went shopping before returning to Bencoolen Street.

She sat silently on the mattress.

"Where did you get to ?" I asked her.

Xzera half turned. Then putting her head between her knees, drew her arms tightly around her legs. I began to feel terribly uneasy. This wasn't like her. Maybe she'd been robbed. I slipped my arm over her shoulder and as I pulled her towards me, she burst into tears. She started to shiver; sobs turned to hysterical laughter; then a long silence. Slowly she raised her head.

"I've been raped."

The coolness of her reply unnerved me. I felt anger; repulsion. She'd only been going to the bank. How could it have happened in such a short space of time. Suddenly a pornographic picture burned into my eyes and for the next five minutes we were locked into an emotional roller coaster.

"What do you want me to do ?"

"I don't know ?"

"Let's go for a walk."

Oblivious to street surroundings, she recounted the events that led up to the rape.

"I think you should tell the police, even if it's only to discourage that bastard."

I honestly didn't know if my advice was good or bad. There would be police, publicity, court appearances. Her surface strength threw me off guard. I needed badly to see a fallen angel.

"Will you come with me?"

Before a rethink was possible, I'd flagged down a police car. The wheels of motion had started rolling and events, oscillating between black comedy and sheer humiliation, would unfold in the hours to follow.

Notified of our arrival, an elderly inspector was waiting at the reception desk.

"What relationship do you have with him?" The inspector was pointing at me. His emphasis on 'him' startled me. Xzera promptly came to my defence, and I was invited to join her in the interrogation room.

"Could I see your passport?"

The officer's manner towards Xzera wasn't exactly caring, but somehow his authoritative approach diffused the tension of the situation. "I'm sorry, but we have to fill in these forms first."

At regular intervals over the next thirty minutes questions were asked and answers methodically recorded. The wheels of bureaucracy were set in motion. The bureaucratic hunger had to be fed and, after what felt like hours, a file number was given.

"Where did the attack take place?"

Unable to follow her directions we returned with the inspector to the reception desk. Lost in a huddle of policemen, spasmodic arguments broke out. The inspector pointed to a green portion on the wall map, and two patrol men were singled out for a dressing down. Then our inspector retreated hurriedly back to his office.

"What's going on?"

My question was drowned in a hum of apologetic sighs and embarrassed looks.

"What the hell's going on?" I shouted again.

"We have brought you to the wrong police station. Very sorry." The desk sergeant then barked out a stream of commands and soon policemen were tripping over themselves to please.

"I've ordered a police car to take you to Robinson Road Police Station. Sergeant Raza - the young policewoman - will assist you."

Soon we were speeding through a congested network of backroads. Arriving at an intersection sparked off yet another argument. Messages were relayed back and forth on their radio. Puzzled looks followed. Then a map was spread out.

Sergeant Raza interpreted. "They try to find your Station."

"Are we lost ?"

"Yes."

Xzera burst out laughing. This human error united us all. Soon we were exchanging sweets and cigarettes. Xzera's aggressive manner towards Sergeant Raza softened. Small talk turned to fashion and boyfriends. This friendship blossomed, but ended on our arrival. The Sergeant was ordered back with the car.

Inside we were greeted by a young inspector. Trapped within his youth, his questions lacked the authority of experience and Xzera's forceful replies left him struggling to regain his composure. The flow of questions was continually interrupted by long silences. Soon he was drowning in a sea of embarrassment. Sensing this, Xzera became very uncooperative. At first she frustrated the inspector with vague replies, and rebuilding her trust required a great deal of patience. Then her diary of painful events unfolded.

"I met him coming out of the bank. I was hungry. He invited me for a meal. I know I was supposed to meet Bernard, but he was interesting. I would not have gone, but then a group of his friends joined us. They were all well dressed like businessmen. Anyway the restaurant was only next door. His friends only ordered drinks, and left before we had finished. Afterwards he insisted on paying. He ordered a taxi. Said he would drop me off at Bencoolen Street. On the way he suggested we stop off at his apartment. Had to change for a business meeting, he said. I had enjoyed his company. He was young, and anyway it was broad daylight. I was a little apprehensive. He wasn't insistent. Sitting on the landing was an old woman. Seeing her made me feel safe, so I went in. When we got to his apartment he left the door open. I could hear people talking in the corridor. The old lady I had seen downstairs put her head round the corner, smiled and left. He went into the bathroom to change. After about ten minutes he came out. Asked me if I wanted a drink. I said no, but didn't mind him having one. While he was pouring the drink I picked up a magazine. The next thing I remembered the door was closed and a record was playing. He started asking me about England. Poured himself another drink. Gave me another coke. Then he got up. I hadn't noticed the bed before. It was in the corner of the room. It was the way he was looking at me. 'What do you think I invited you back for?' He just said it like that. Before I could get to the door he had grabbed me. Then pushed a coke bottle in my face..."

Suddenly she broke down. Shocked had blotted out much of what happened next.

We took a short walk, then she returned to more questions. "Did he use force? Where did he put his penis? How many time? Why didn't you call for help? How did you escape?"

Then while she was still immersed in painful recollection, files of pictures were brought in for her to identify. Leaving Xzera with another officer, I joined the inspector outside. Then he went through the problems of bringing a successful case to court.

"If the man is caught, and that's improbable in the time she has here in Singapore, the case would take up to six months to get to court. She will have to return to Singapore at her own expense. Then there is the publicity. She will have to go through the humiliating experience again in court. Talk it over with her Mr Howgate. If she agrees to go ahead, we will need a specimen of semen. I will arrange for a car to take you to the hospital, if needed. Also we will have to try and identify the house she was raped in."

I knew Xzera would need time to make a decision, so after her statement was finished, we returned to Bencoolen Street

Do women have a telepathic understanding of each other? Christa was fantastic. A fellow traveller from Europe, she could empathize with Xzera in a way I could never manage. We met in the dormitory on our return from the Police Station and while Xzera washed and changed I went over to speak to her.

"Well, what is it?"

"She's been raped." The word took forever to form, but once shared, immediately bonded us.

When Xzera returned, I introduced them, and Christa willingly accompanied us to the hospital, where Sergeant Raza was already waiting. Thankfully she had paved the way by cutting through all time consuming formalities. A female doctor was notified of our arrival, and she took Xzera down the corridor. Ten minutes went by, then the muffled sounds of English voices filtered down the corridor. Just as I made out the word syringe, screams split the calm.

"You're not putting that thing up me."

A few more loud words were exchanged, then the doctor appeared. Sergeant Raza again acted as interpreter.

"She wont let the doctor use the syringe. We have to have a specimen."

Again words passed between Sergeant Raza and the doctor.

"I go speak to Xzera." Sergeant Raza was in no mood for compromises by now. After twenty minutes Xzera came out with the Sergeant.

"That's worse than the real thing."

By now we all felt very much involved, so no prompting was needed when the Sergeant asked Xzera to return to the Police Station for an identification parade. On the way we were to pass through an area where the police thought the rape took place.

"This is the street. Yes, I remember the painted wall sign."

The car stopped and Xzera jumped out.

"We think he bring you here." Sergeant Raza was leading Xzera back into the car. "Every house on this street, brothel. The woman you see, we believe Madame. Conversation in the corridor you hear, probably client. Man very clever, no frightened of noise you make. Very sorry."

It was 10:00 pm. when we reached the police station.

"I'll get some food."

The recipe of the days' events, its pressures and responsibilities had left me drained. Selfishly, I took the opportunity to be on my own but, returning with some food, I walked straight into a hornets' nest of activity.

"You fucking bastard."

The Sergeant was vainly trying to restrain a wild eyed Xzera, who was beating her fists against a wall of wire mesh.

"That's him." Christa pointed to a frightened man pinned behind the protective wall.

Later when the situation had calmed down, a story of unbelievable luck unfolded. Arrested on the street for being drunk and disorderly, he had been brought in to spend a sobering night in the cells. No sooner was he inside than Xzera recognized him. Pandemonium followed. Attacking from blind hate, her strength had surprised everyone. One hour later, statements and identification complete, we returned wearily home.

For the next two days both Christa and I never strayed far from Xzera's side. By the third day, confirmation of Xzera's boyfriend's arrival sealed my own departure. Now secure in the knowledge that Christa would bridge the gap until he came I said my goodbyes.

Chapter 10:
East Coast Travel

A RAPIDLY RISING SUN QUICKLY TURNED EARLY MORN-
ing pools of rain into clouds of steam. So high were
humidity levels in the morning that my only relief was in
the saddle, for to stop meant being immediately soaked in sweat.
By noon the heat was so intense I had resorted to bathing at
roadside wells. After the relatively breezy conditions of Singapore, I wasn't ready for the almost claustrophobic atmosphere
of mainland Asia. I had lost almost twenty pounds since leaving
Canada and I didn't relish the thought of losing any more to this
humidity.

Hemmed in on both sides by rubber tree plantations and
endless jungle, my isolation on the road was only broken by packs
of roadside monkeys. Seemingly undisturbed by what little traffic
shared our open corridor, they would scream at me whenever I
passed. At higher levels, brilliantly coloured birds filled the trees
like overcrowded buses and, at ground level, I saw the occasional
snake slithering off lazily into the undergrowth.

Twice, on the first day, I was caught in heavy downpours of
rain and, shivering with cold, I was forced to take shelter. When
I called in at roadside villages, the people displayed an overwhelming friendliness and curiosity towards my trip which was
remarkable.

"You write book ?"

"Why you come to our country ?"

"Do your government pay for your travel ?"

As if it was an everyday occurrence to have tourists as guests
they lost no time inviting me to stay, and I was soon adopted for
an evening. Home cooking was, without a doubt, the best way to
sample traditional foods and during my stays, I wasn't disappointed. Payment was made by taking family portraits, with a
promise to send them on later, a very good way of sampling local
customs. One evening, both to my surprise and initial embarrassment, a young girl came into my bedroom. First using sign
language then, a little cheek, and, finally, ending with a professional manner beyond her years, she stripped me, motioned me

on to my stomach, then slowly rubbed, nipped and knuckled my body, from toe to thigh, before leaving thirty minutes later having given me the best massage I've ever had.

It was now two weeks since I had left Singapore and five days since I'd crossed the border from Malaysia into Thailand. My legs were now pumping up and down like well greased pistons and covering long distances was no problem. Following my success staying with families I found a new chapter of travelling unfolding. Whenever possible I left myself open to village hospitality.

The day I left Hat Yai I was in good spirits. Routed through dense jungle, the road's emptiness suited my mood. Plans to reach Bangkok from Singapore in three weeks were now well in hand. What I'd seen in Malaysia and Thailand appealed to me but, due to my haste, I was unable to do them justice. I was still shedding weight at an alarming rate but, besides my occasional dizzy spells from the heat, I was functioning well physically. It had rained heavily that morning and under clear skies the air felt drier than usual and I hoped to make Thung Song before nightfall. In the last hour I had seen only two vehicles, both military jeeps. This scarcity was unusual even for this desolate stretch.

Suddenly I was startled. A loud whirling noise whipped up the air into a small tornado. Hovering above me like some obscene pregnant duck was an army helicopter. It tilted and I saw a frantic uniform in dark glasses pointing an angry finger in my direction. After making circular patterns above the adjacent jungle, my unwelcome intruder roared off at tree top level in the direction I'd just come from. No sooner had it disappeared than another approached. This time I was forced to take evasive action, ending up in a ditch.

"You bastard!" My shouts were drowned out by its noise.

He'd come down so low I could have jumped into the pilot's seat. Watching its process down the road I didn't see the shadow appear. There in front of me, in full battle fatigues, was a none to pleased soldier. He wasted no time in diplomacy, and I got the message quickly. He wanted me off the road. Still he wasn't pleased. I couldn't understand him. Panic took over. He put down his automatic rifle, took two steps towards my bicycle, then ripped my shirt out from underneath my bicycle's back support straps. What the hell was going on ?

Now I noticed a convoy of vehicles speeding towards us with

their headlights flashing. He shouted again. My shirt was being held out. I put it on, then he immediately turned his back on me. Yet another shout, this time with a measured tone, followed by a loud crash. The surrounding jungle disgorged soldiers from all directions. Earlier feelings of panic turned into terror. In Singapore, the British Embassy had warned me of guerilla fighting in Thailand. Their advice was to go by bus when near the Burmese border. "If they want your money give them it. They're not stupid. Dead tourists don't make good publicity, so no heroics please." Sound advice I thought, coming from the embassy, but this soldier wasn't asking for money; anyway, he looked too clean to be a guerrila. Could this be an ambush? Would I be caught in the cross fire? My first reaction was to throw myself on the ground, but I froze. Everything was happening at frightening speed. A loud command split the tension. Immediately soldiers whirled round to face the jungle. Another shout saw them at attention. Then yet another. It was like being on parade, except I wasn't in uniform. These authoritative commands helped me to gain my composure. Thank God for leaders. I'd have jumped into a barrel of shit to please them. Soldiers now stood in regimental order, lining both sides of the road at regular intervals, guns at the ready. I was now completely ignored. Then before I could react the first military jeep tore past me. Next, two army personnel carriers brimming with armed soldiers passed. Then yet another jeep, and when two black mercedes flashed past all my questions were answered. He was only framed in my vision for a second, but he was unmistakable. It was the King. Now all was clear, especially the need to put on my shirt.

Is it better to travel than arrive? I'd asked that question of myself every time a long run had ended. After twenty days' cycling from Singapore to Bangkok, the thought of swapping freedom of the road for the comforts of city life was small compensation. Pumped full of adrenalin, I was in no mood to gorge myself at the table of Bangkok's night scene. Sex and drugs weren't high on my agenda and for the first few days, Bangkok's title of 'Sin City' was one continuous yawn.

Safely housed in the Scout's Hostel, I looked down from the dormitory window, to find my first morning lost in choking fog. Attached to the National Stadium and within a large University

Physical Education complex, I soon took advantage of the University's subsidized canteen and sports facilities. Friends were made, games planned and, for the next ten days, every spare moment was spent playing pick-up games of soccer. In the evenings I took in Thai boxing, floating flea markets and inevitably, Patpong's red light district.

My reason for staying so long in Bangkok stemmed from my attempt to obtain a three week visa for Burma. To the untutored traveller, a three week visa was two weeks too long. For some reason known only to itself, this Socialist State restricted visits to its country to only seven days and, only through Rangoon. It was impossible to enter overland. With this in mind, I visited the British Embassy for advice.

"Publicize your cycle exploits. One man's trip of a lifetime. You know, give it a human angle. It might work, nothing lost trying."

I took that advice, and the following day found myself at the offices of the *Bangkok Post*, where they were more than willing accomplices.

BRITON'S ODYSSEY ON TWO WHEELS
Bangkok Post, Sunday October 4th 1981
   In June last year, 32 year old English engineer Bernard Howgate sold his house and property in Toronto, Canada to fulfil a childhood dream to travel round the world. And last Wednesday Howgate arrived in Bangkok on his ten speed Raleigh bicycle with an exhausted body but undeterred determination to pedal on..............

   It was a long story, but the reporter was sympathetic to my idea, and although the article read like a school report of the countries I'd visited, it was more than I had hoped for. Armed with a printed copy and borrowed clothes to impress, I visited the Burmese Embassy in hope of winning a three week visa.

   Burmese Officialdom treated the traveller with about the same mistrust as one would a valuable Panda given to mischief. On no account must any harm come to the animal, it must be closely watched at all times, housed in special accommodation, not seen too much, do too much, or influence local inhabitants with its strange behaviour. Their reluctance to sanction my proposed route from Rangoon to Mandalay and grant an extended visa was expressed in concern about the suitability of accommodation between the two cities, language difficulties and fear for my safety.

The first official I saw was greatly impressed with my portfolio of press cuttings and passport visas. I fostered this enthusiasm further by describing the hospitality I'd experienced in villages en route, dispelling his fears of my fitness to take adverse conditions and lack of language skills. I'd done my homework well and, like a good salesman, put forward a positive advertisement for Burmese hospitality. Slowly I climbed the ladder of seniority. Degrees of ministerial influence were reflected more in personal manner then dress, as each new person asked the same questions but with increasing tones of authority. My initial request for three weeks through delicate negotiation and compromise was now reduced to a twelve day visa. I'd anticipated this compromise and everything was going to plan. These five extra days were all I needed to cycle from Rangoon to Mandalay and more than I'd realistically expected. Then, suddenly an unexpected spanner jarred in the works.

"Why can he get an extended visa and us not ? "Grumblings from a small band of travellers following my progress surfaced.

"What right does he have that we haven't ?"

"We want the same."

Soon complaints turned into heated arguments, as the whole queue jumped on the band wagon of a twelve day visa. From the first dissenting voice I'd sensed my case slip away. I retreated from behind the counter in embarrassment. By now the official was under a great deal of pressure from these questions, and was visibly hurt by their aggressive behaviour.

"Mr Howgate, can I have your passport please ?" Harassed, the officer wanted any excuse to leave, then like a jury pressed into a popular verdict he returned five minutes later to offer a perverse judgement.

"We give you seven day visa, Mr Howgate. No exception. You take it or go now."

It was a bitter pill to swallow. But seeing my position was hopeless, I filled in the forms, flashed a threatening look at my fellow travellers, and left with a seven day visa.

Chapter 11:
A Whirlwind
Seven Day Courtship

I SHOULD HAVE BEEN CYCLING INTO RANGOON, BUT   instead I was going by taxi. What had happened to that cool Bernard, so used to non-involvement ? Why had well rehearsed lines been thrown away ?

Three hours before, I had been patiently going through the time consuming official details of customs entry with the air of a seasoned traveller. "Don't lose your temper whatever you do," I told myself. Sound advice, and it had been well tested and proven right on many occasions but this time my provocateur had bitten straight into my 'Achilles Heel'.

It started with a rigorous check of my passport. Then my bicycle was wheeled in and, besides its curiosity value, was just waiting to be collected

I don't know why I lost my temper. Maybe the attachment to my bicycle was greater than I'd realized or maybe it had never been tested. It wasn't his lack of concern for other people's property that sparked my anger but more the way he abused his position as customs officer. It was that counter, that invisible border which allowed his dominance of the situation. He was playing a childish game of bait the foreigner. First he started by playing with the bell, then when he got bored with that, he sat on the saddle, tried the brakes, and pulled and strained the cables to the point of snapping them. Next he decided it needed further testing and went about the gears with wild abandon. I had let people in far less responsible positions inspect and ride it in Asia, even out of view, without fear of loss or damage, but always by consent. I never refused when asked politely but this official was out to impress, without the slightest care for ownership.

I leapt for the counter and only the speed and strength of an American student stopped me from clearing it. My reaction surprised everyone and what happened next was inevitable. Maybe it was their intention all the time. I'd been warned and now it had happened. I was led away into a side room; given receipts in triplicate.

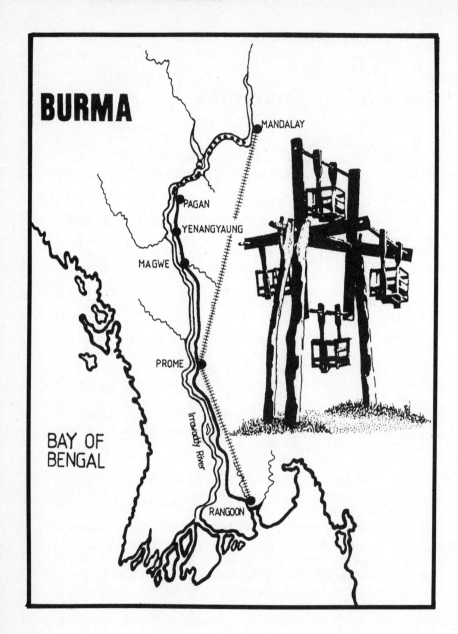

BURMA

MANDALAY

PAGAN

YENANGYAUNG

MAGWE

PROME

Irrawaddy River

BAY OF
BENGAL

RANGOON

"You have back when you leave the country." My bike was impounded.

Rangoon saw my lowest low. Without my bike I felt like a fish out of water. So far my trip was reading like an overdrawn bank balance or a mission without a meaning. Values that had sustained me for over thirty years had turned topsy-turvy. I needed an injection of good times, a reinvestment. I wasn't so much searching for a purpose, as motivation. I left the airport determined to stick my neck out and to hell with the consequences. It was to start with a train trip to Mandalay that evening and be succeeded by a whirlwind seven day courtship with Burma.

Travelling third class, hard wooden seating introduced me to the rigors of train travel. As if tourists were unwanted guests, the seating arrangements had grouped a small band of travellers at the compartment's rear. Isolated by government intent, we became the focal point of curious stares. Unable to sleep or to communicate with our fellow travellers, a perceptible tension enveloped the compartment. But gradually the courage born through innocence attracted tentative advances down the aisle and, stealing glances, children played games of touch the tourist. One, more daring than the rest, suddenly found his escape route cut off. Dashing between spread feet in the aisle, he fell into the outstretched arms of a seated tourist. This incident bridged the gap caused by our forced separation, and was the prelude to an enjoyable evening. Carrying the tearful child back to his parents, we soon found ourselves invited to share in their food and, before long, a bottle of our duty free whisky was opened. This spontaneous gesture from one of our band precipitated an exchange of T-shirts, lighters and cigarettes, as Burmese good will stretched deep into the night.

When empty, the whisky bottle became the center of arguments. Unknown to our group this bottle was of great importance. Used as a status symbol it would be filled with rice wine and the empty cigarette packets, which had been snapped up eagerly, would be filled with local brands. These items would be used at weddings and paraded in front of guests as prized possessions of western wealth.

We arrived in Mandalay just as the sun rose. With only six days left on my visa, I wasted no time in making for the Tourist

Burma Offices. These government branches, dotted all over
Burma, made off-limit travel almost impossible. It restricted all
accommodation to government approved hotels. Ticket pur-
chases to only authorized areas effectively shackled the tourist.
Mandatory currency forms - given on arrival to record all pur-
chases - also made travel an expensive proposition. Introduced
to keep the average person within the bounds of honesty, they
worked as a stick against the carrot of Rangoon's infinitely better
black market currency exchange rates. Wanting more to experience a journey down the Irrawaddy River than to visit any ancient
temples, I booked on the evening boat to Pagan.

With the whole day to fill, I took to the streets. What had been
a sleepy city on arrival was now alive with activity. Streets choked
with dust from horse-drawn tongas and bicycle rickshaws made
road crossings hazardous, and with no knowledge of road discipline, it was almost impossible to determine traffic regulations.
On either side, dilapidated colonial style buildings blended like a
finely shaded water colour with sun baked dirt roads and together with their layers of peeling plaster recorded the path of an
Empire's decline. At roof top level I saw a jungle of bushes and
guttering, once installed to carry monsoon rains, now housed un-
cultivated masses of weeds. At pavement level, missing flag
stones allowed the viewer into the very heart of a once great
engineering network of sewage channels. Any pedestrian out
after dark would certainly be courting disaster. A large hand
painted Coca Cola sign took prominent position, non-availability
of which was the best definition the amateur anthropologist
could give for an under-developed country- even overshadowing
that of Buddha in a shop devoid of the product. Street vendors
likewise sold Levis Jeans, their only discernible likeness being
their copied leather name tags, as both material and quality
didn't match. On seeing me, men carrying large boxes filled with
black market items, became instant salesmen, spilling out goods
of whisky and cigarettes onto the pavement in hope of purchase.
Continually bothered by these young steetwise racketeers, I
turned off into the back streets. Isolated from the mainstream
tourist routes, I got waylaid by a different type of person. A young
man invited me back to his home.

I was beginning to lose count of my invitations into family life,
and never wanting to disappoint, I soon found myself following

narrow passageways and jumping the streams of open sewage. The young man's home consisted of two rooms on top of a large building and, once inside, orders were given and accepted with a smooth balance that only centuries of unchallenged status quo and a well developed sense of family authority could achieve. A young child was sent for a chair, another for a radio, and his wife obediently retreated into the kitchen to prepare tea. By now my treatment as an honoured guest was becoming a natural off-shoot of my travel and I slipped into the part with the ease of Royalty. Soon uncles, cousins and neighbours were brought in front of me as if my presence imparted some kind of blessing for future good fortune.

A large, laughing, lady obviously not intimidated by our differences in cultures, looked me over with the same stern look of disapproval, as if she had been introduced to a future son-in-law. Smoking an enormous bamboo shoot cigar, she moved about the room totally unconcerned by the impact my presence had made on the rest. Later while I ate rice dishes from a table on borrowed stainless steel plates, the large family sat cross-legged on the floor eating small portions off an assortment of dried out banana leaves.

After the evening meal my host took me into the town where, as luck would have it, the "Festival of Light" (one of Asia's many full moon celebrations) was in full swing. By now flickering lamps mounted in doorways and widows bathed the street in dancing shadows, and I saw the amazing outline of Mandalay's main Pagoda. Attached in dazzling patterns, against a pitch black skyline, electric light bulbs burst out in blazes of red and yellow. An explosion swung me around, and yet another depth-charged our narrow street. Everywhere the air was thick with sulphur, as plumes of purple smoke from extinguished firecrackers drifted skywards. Spicy aromas led to street vendors, music-to-pavement entertainers and sellers, each trying to outperform his neighbour with magical acts and balancing tricks, thrusting balloons and toys in front of would-be buyers. A fire eater surrounded by an approving crowd gave way to a salesman selling cosmetics and, in competition on the opposite side of the street, a snake charmer likewise held the attention of another crowd, beating out rhythmic patterns of noise to baskets filled with Cobra snakes.

The heart of the free festivities centered in the streets surrounding the Pagoda. Barricaded off from the traffic, crowds of people streamed in from all directions generating a mass excitement not matched in innocence to any large gathering I'd experienced, and the equal of any pop festival in its appeal. At the end of the first street I saw a large make-shift screen. Its program of Black and White Key Stone Cop movies, transcending all language and cultural barriers, and judging by the crowds reaction, approval. Dominating the next street, a large stage devoted to a costume theatrical troupe played out a spectacle of royal intrigue. Another troupe, this time accompanied by music, played out a romantic story of young love with dance movements. Stick puppets drew yet another crowd, this time of cheering children, and its players acted out the age old battles of good versus evil.

Captured in the jostling crowd I was drawn into the Pagoda's walled compound. Going through its narrow gateway, I was confronted with the most extraordinary sight I'd ever seen. All of twenty feet high and, carrying as many people, was a large wooden 'ferris wheel'. Neither its size nor the ornate carvings which covered the wheel's two huge pillars, were the focal point of my amazement, but the ferris wheel's jerky rotational movement. Placed either side of the wheel, steps of wooden boxes were a major clue. The wheel's power didn't come from any electrical source, but was generated by people. Two men, one either side of the wheel continually climbed the steps of boxes. Then catching the underside of the chairs on their downward motion, they stepped off like circus acrobats letting their own weight pull the wheel round.

The festival's amazing assortment of entertainments left me exhausted and, with a full moon to light my way, I reluctantly left my host for the boat. Once aboard, I again found a group of tourists isolated from the rest. Erecting my mosquito net (bought in Bangkok and becoming an indispensable part of my travel) I spent the night sleeping on the open wooden deck, being interrupted by all kinds of alien noises before finally drifting off into a fitful sleep.

Awakening just after sunrise I found we were already under a full head of steam, with Mandalay only a smudge on the far shoreline. At first glance our steamer looked like it could have been second hand before its maiden voyage down the Irrawaddy River. It was a living monument to the British Empire and legacy of British Colonial days when 'Mem Sahib' travelled in style. It still bore many of its original trappings, now looking obscenely out of place, in what could only be called third class accommodation by today's standards. Brass name plates still directed the unread Burmese traveller to the genteel sounding Ladies and Gentlemen's toilets and we class conscious Brits had even managed to separate eating quarters by naming the first class "Dining Rooms" and second class "Restaurants".

Still able to cut a rare turn of speed, the old girl lazily displaced water in rhythmic waves, washing a shoreline some hundred yards away. Adjacent to my open sleeping quarters, a saffron-robed Buddhist monk was already giving his early morning discourse to a faithful band of followers. Not impressed by religious exercises, I decided on a more physical form, and set about to inspect my temporary home.

The boat comprised three levels, each having its own distinctive smells. We tourists shared first class and a select band of religious and business officials. A large Bhuddist deity surrounded by sweet smelling incense sticks took pride of place, between the obligatory framed portraits of stern looking government leaders, no doubt there to remind us all of our respective allegiances. Second class housed the majority of paying passengers, and already many of the women were preparing food on small cersean (paraffin) stoves in make-shift open kitchens on the deck. The lower level was packed full with sacks of sugar and grain and all kinds of houshold furnishings and supplies and one end was occupied with the same reason I slept badly. A small herd of cattle was silently munching on corn, while a dozen squealing pigs with their attendant children were being soundly beaten. Scattered around under the ceiling beams were hundreds of caged-up chickens, and standing silently, as if above all this commotion, was a horse.

During the dy, history drifted by on the wind. Large armadas of sailboats tacked silently up and down the river, cutting V-shaped courses in the almost still waters. Occasionally, one would stray across our path, igniting the captain's wrath, and blasts of his steam horn.

It was while drinking a poor excuse for tea that I was jarred out of my seat. Totally occupied in my history lesson, I'd forgotten that our boat made stops and the abruptness with which we rammed the shoreline shocked me. Within seconds a large wooden gangplank was secured from the second class level onto a muddy bank. A dozen women carrying baskets full of fruit to sell onboard competed with off-going passengers on the narrow gangplank, precipitating a near riot. A loud splash sent screaming children to the opposite end of the boat, where cattle and pigs were being unceremoniously dropped over the side and made to swim ashore. These stops against the river banks repeated themselves at regular intervals through the day and, in the evening, we found ourselves tied up for the night at a small town wharf where, once again, I joined in the continued festivities before returning to the boat in the early hours of the morning.

By noon the following day we reached Pagan. After a short visit to the ancient templed city I retired for the rest of the day, catching up on much needed rest. Determined to carry out my threat of off-limit travel, I spent most of the evening scheming and confidence-building for my planned off-limit return to Rangoon.

At first light I made my way down to Pagan's bus station, only to find there were no buses to Rangoon. I then tried the market and, after an hour, doing the rounds of trucks lined up by the roadside, I found one that was going to Prome where, I was told, in broken English, I could get a bus to Rangoon. Sacks of grain filled the rear and metal boxes, the sides and with only a wooden floor to stand on, I wasn't exactly looking forward to my little 'off-limit' adventure. The time set for our departure came and went, and it wasn't until ten, two hours overdue. When the truck was full to overflowing with passengers and baggage, that we set off. Soon my legs were like shock absorbers and only the tight packing of my fellow passengers kept me from falling over. After one hour the road left the river and climbed slowly into the surrounding hillsides and, to get a better view and escape the claustrophobic environment at the back of the truck, I exchanged my relatively safe canvas topped position for the roof of the driver's cab, where I had an unimpeded view of the surrounding countryside. Soon I could see why the government was so reluctant to allow tourists into this region. Miles of unattended tea and cash crop plantations spoiled the hillsides and derelict oil rigs lay idle, rusting under the sun, in what must have been a once highly productive oil field. When we stopped at an army check point, it was made abundantly clear I was an unwelcome intruder. They were bewildered to see my white face, and I wasn't sure if their initial laughter came from nerves or genuine amusement at my cheek for being there, but before a decision could be made either way, our impatient driver left them in a cloud of dust. By now evening was falling rapidly, and approaching Prome was like seeing a desert mirage grow before my eyes. Again I encountered embarrassed officials, but far from demanding explanations, they were overjoyed to see a foreign visitor and I found no difficulty purchasing a ticket to Rangoon on an overnight bus. Since arriving in Burma four days before, I'd only been able to snatch token sleep and, after a bumpy, sleepless bus journey, I went straight to the Tourist Burma Office in Rangoon, where I booked into a hotel and slept the clock around.

The following morning I was baptised by my first monsoon. The sky slowly went black, then burst. Sheets of rain deafened, gutters turned into cascading waterfalls and narrow passageways that only a few moments before echoed to the sounds of laughter, turned into dangerous rapids. Streets became instant rivers and pavements were lost to slow moving lakes. Whirlpools formed over open drains and swallowed street garbage like hungry beasts. Traffic frozen as if by picture and half submerged, now housed their passengers on their roofs. Nowhere was there panic and soon children, taking advantage of this natural watery playground, swam and splashed about with no care for hygiene, as gutter flotsam bubbled like a boiling spring under the sheer force of the rain. At its height visibility was reduced to the far side of the street and the thunder, felt more than heard. Its sudden start was only matched by its sudden end. Within minutes rushing water turned into trickling streams. The watery playground that only an hour before held the attention of screaming children, drained as if unplugged by a higher force and was soon scorched dry by the sun.

With only two days left before my departure, I did Rangoon full justice, spending hours exploring what once was called the "Pearl of the British Empire". Obviously the reality of economics made preservation a secondary issue to function. Many of its stately looking buildings had fallen into disrepair yet many more street dwellings had stood the time of change well. The spotlessly kept public toilets, with their still working coin operated, slot machine entrances and accompanying toilet attendants contrasted with the Olympic size swimming pool, once used by only the privileged few, through lack of adequate maintenance, was covered in a thick film of slime.

In stark contrast in this Socialist country was the Shwe Dagon Pagoda. Central point of Buddhist pilgrimage, it dominated the city like a golden goddess and, on my last day, I gave into its temptation. What a contrast it made to the rural Pagodas with their live-in festivals and informal behaviour. A monument to religious extravagance, it offered a fantasy lifestyle to a privileged group of academic philosophers and manicured Lamas. Lifeless in the extreme, it propagated a message of pay now for a better rebirth the next time around, with the same insensitivity a robber has for his victim. As I went up the famous steps to the Pagoda's entrance I had to run the gauntlet of high pressure sellers and, on entering the golden shrine, a spiral of light to the "All Seeing Buddha" lit up like a slot machine, as if on payment. Although my stay in Burma was blotted by the two extremes of religion and politics this in no way detracted from my love of the Burmese people. Never at any time during my seven days' travelling was I abused, accosted, short changed or, for that matter, indoctrinated. The old seemed content with their lot, dwelling nostalgically on the past glories of the British Raj as if talking about an indulgent, if not, tolerant aunt. The young, although staunchly anti-capitalist in their belief were, in general, more proud of their own brand of socialism then showing any revolutionary commitment to change the world. After signing my autograph as 'Round the World Cyclist' for airport customs officials, with more than a little humour. I left this unique country with fond memories.

Chapter 12:
Faith or Superstition

WITHIN HOURS OF ARRIVING IN CALCUTTA, I WAS swallowed up by India's seductive chaos. Faith or Superstition, at least here, God was not separated from the world, and His very presence was reflected in a country where religious practice was an everyday part of their life. Having experience Hindu roots in Bali and then in Burma, I would now slip into its philosophy with ease. Homeless, classless, and with neither a political ideology nor a religious belief to hold on to, I now felt open to anything, and looked forward to seeing how India would effect me.

Still within sight of Calcutta's Dum Dum Airport, I was seen. Behind me two cycle rickshaws overburdened with passengers crashed into each other; another so shocked, let out a scream, hit the curb, and ended up crashing into a roadside fruit stall. One cyclist, wife seated on the back support, child balance precariously on handle bars pedalled furiously to catch me. Another, on tireless wheels executed a U turn, and skidded. Falling, he put his hand out, hitting my pursuing family, sending the entwined mass of bodies careering off the road.

Soon, open patchwork of paddy fields gave way to Calcutta's sprawling suburbs. Having been brought up in England on the politics of the poor, seeing Calcutta's urban breeding ground of poverty didn't intimidate, and I sped into it with curious abandon. Turning off into Chandra Road, I entered the heart of Calcutta's teeming metropolis.

Approaching Sealhah Railway Station, my progress was blocked by a chanting funeral procession, centered by bearers carrying a bamboo trestle. Suddenly an ash coloured elbow appeared beneath its linen cover, then a whole arm exposed itself, followed quickly by the owner's shoulder and torso. Up till then no one had made any attempt to arrest its passage earthwards and slowly with the certainty of gravity the whole body emerged and slipped lifelessly onto the road. At first no one broke ranks. Then acting as if the incident was an every day accurance the bearers, in one swift movement, scooped up the body,

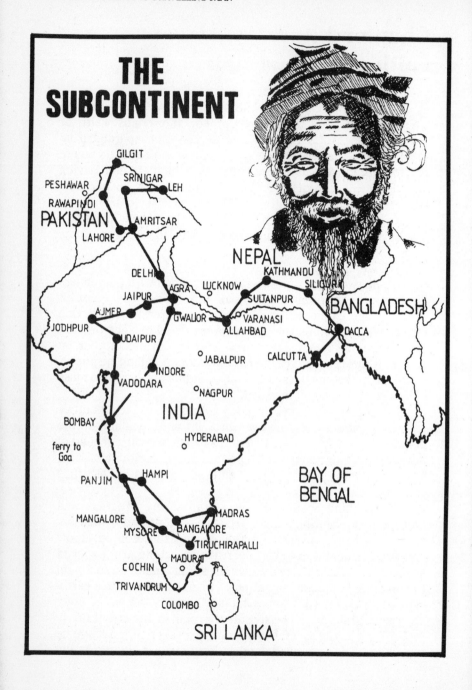

dumped it unceremoniously back onto its tressel and, before the flower petals had settled, they set off chanting down the road without batting an eyelid. Had I imagined it ? Rooted to the road, I exploded in laughter. India had welcomed me.

From humble origins, between Third Class Hotels and Street Shelters in Sudder Street, the 'Red Shield House' marked the beginning of my eighteen month love-hate relationship with the 'Salvation Army's unique brand of Christianity. 'The silent listener to every conversation'. These words, underneath an austere looking J.C. picture in the dining-room, spoke volumes for the Army's treatment of their sometimes non too welcome guests. Notices warning; 'Breakfast Times 7:30 - 8:30 am', and 'Lights Out by 10:00 pm.' were posted everywhere, and I was quickly to find out that these rules were not to be broken. At first this regime was hard to stomach but, in its defence, the institution's Mother-knows-best attitude, Praise the Lord, and toast and jam was to become a welcome oasis. A place to retreat to; a place to close the doors on the relentless pressure of an Indian Subcontinent where white skins expose love and hate on a grand scale, and from where there is little refuge.

At breakfast I encountered my first large groupings of travellers since Bali. In those early days I had been the baby of travel. I remembered that listening spellbound to tales of Asia and India had been its essential ingredient. Now, less than six months on, it was my turn. I was now the seasoned traveller and at breakfast travellers going in the opposite direction listened to my experiences. I now had a new confidence and didn't shrink away from them. I was beginning to feel proud of my mode of transport and there was no denying that a large part of that confidence also came from the fact that my expenses were being met from the fruits of my own labour.

"You sold up everything ?"

My story had all the ingredients of some romantic adventure novel, Man in search of himself and captured the imaginations of my breakfast audience.

"Why didn't your friends do it ?"

It was a question I'd asked myself also, but it didn't have any easy answer, if an answer at all. As much as my friends envied me, they were simply too absorbed in their own lives to want to leave them.

"We all live each other's dreams out. I travel. They father babies."

That morning's topics changed, reversed and took off, embracing subjects like mortgages and professional ambition and, for once, I found myself not having to defend my old way of life.

On the way back to my dormitory I stumbled into the wrong room, straight into another brand of Indian traveller. Sitting crosslegged in the center of the room was an orange-robed man. Face painted as if on the war path, he was deep in conversation with a small group of Europeans.

"Come in, Where are you from ?" someone asked.

"Canada."

"I'm from the States. Where in Canada ?"

"Toronto." I replied.

"Oh yeah, that concrete jungle. It's all about big business, profit margins and Indian slavery. Terrible place." His friends muttered in agreement, then continuing he added. "In my previous life I came from India, and you ?"

"Never given it much thought."

Was he joking ? I decided to play along and sat down.

"Here, give him the chillum."

A large cone-shaped pipe came into my hands.

"What's that ?" I asked.

"It's the path to Shiva man." The painted face then went on to describe the Circle of Destruction and Creation, the need to destroy evil and create good. "Hashish, man, food for the Gods, it flies you to higher levels, awakens your consciousness man." He was beginning to sound like a second rate 'B' Movie on California Flower Power. Then there was a tug at my shorts.

"It's love, can't you feel it." A young girl with flowing blond hair looked into my eyes. Not being one to turn down invitations from lovely blonds, I moved closer.

The chillum had passed along and already others in the group were smoking it. While watching its journey around, I took stock of my fellow travellers. Two, like myself, clean shaven and looking reasonably healthy, were listening to the young painted chieftain. Being new arrivals, restless to start our journey into India made us only too eager for information. The rest meanwhile inhaled and writhed in ecstasy, drinking his words in, as if there was no tomorrow. Krishna Consciousness, Energy Levels, Wheels of Life, all manner of phrases surfaced as the young chieftan held court over his small band of emaciated devotees.

"Science is leading us deeper and deeper into the possibilities of total annihilation." The words spilled from his mouth, as if speaking a great truth for the first time.

"How long have you been in India ?" I asked the young girl.

"Two years."

"What are you doing here ?"

"I am being." She answered

"Being what ?"

"Being. Getting in touch with my inner self. I left that messed up world of materialism behind me. My past never existed. My future is predetermined. Everything is an illusion, trappings, camouflages against your real self. I left home to break away from all that nonsense. Just allowing you into my space is mind blowing."

I was trying hard to stop myself from laughing, but the more serious she became, the more amusing she sounded.

"Why carn't you sit here and be with us ? Just BE man. Let our energies overlap without speaking. Let yourself go and feel it. It's beautiful."

"Hare Krishna, Hari Rahma." The chieftain started a slow chant.

"Do you feel it ?" another said.

All I felt was like getting out. I looked over to the two newcomers, by now staring blankly at the wall.

"Did you get that hit of energy ?" the chieftain asked.

There was a breakdown in communications. I looked at their shaggy excuse of a leader.

"What energy ?" I asked. He didn't look as if he had the energy to stand, let alone touch me with it. They quickly closed ranks, shutting me out of any further conversation.

"Seen Chrissy ?" A somewhat worried looking young man stopped me in the corridor outside. "Oh, she calls herself Shanti now." His description fitted the young girl I'd just left.

"She's in the dormitory at the end of the corridor."

"Was she with a long haired guy, in an orange robe ?"

"Yes."

"That's her Guru. We met him in Goa. She's been following him ever since. Once it was sex, drugs and rock and roll that ruled her life. Then she got religion. God she's boring now." Then as an afterthought he added. "Quality control pal, that's what's needed. Definitely should be some kind of quality control on Gurus. She's quite mad." he said with a laugh. "You wait till she gets pregnant. That'll do it. Nothing like a quick injection of reality, eh?" I wasn't sure if he was being serious or just being sarcastic. "That will do it. It always works," he said, as if speaking from past experience.

With the whole city my playground I set about that week, dusting off its layers of dirt, as if searching through a long forgotten attic.

Before breakfast the following day. I took an early morning walk in Victoria Gardens, where even the most disciplined health fanatic would have been impressed with what I saw. Men of all ages and sizes were grouped together in islands of excersize. One group, led by an elderly gentleman, legs disappeared behind his head, were going through their daily yoga exercises. Another group made up of energetic young men was engaged in body building, using large stones as weights instead of bar bells. Others more committed in individual pursuits jogged fully clothed around the park's perimeter in various stages of collapse and ablutions separated into opposite corners of parkland were performed openly.

Back on the pavement, safe behind invisible borders, women were now cooking their family breakfast on open fires, while further down the road, child beggars fought over strategic areas in hope of extracting pitiful sums from the thousands of early morning office workers. In one street, stolen cobblestones had been used to build pavement shelters, resulting in a deep wound in the road's surface, which years of monsoon rains had opened up to depths big enough to swallow cars. Off Tagore Street make-shift shanty towns attached themselves like limpets to waste ground providing accommodation for Calcutta's floating refugee population, while down by Hoogly River, in the daily mountains of garbage, children searched like scavenging packs of dogs, recycling waste, not out of any ecological desire, but out of everyday need. A bus, weighed down by its load, jettisoned a wheel into the air. Sparks flew, but the driver continued, only stopping when the steering became impossible. Two manpowered rickshaw wallhas collided and argued with the ferocity of boxers over a fare, exchanging insults and hand gestures to a growing gallery of on-lookers. At a road crossing, an impeccably dressed policeman majestically conducted road traffic with a whistle and baton, performing splendidly without an audience, as traffic laws were regulated more by size than law. The bigger the vehicle the more the respect it was accorded, and pedestrians crossed at their own peril. A cattle stampede of India's none to 'holy cows' ploughed through rickshaws and pedestrians alike. Up-turned loads caused sudden traffic detours, yet the masses passed by without thought to plunder.

No visit to Calcutta could be complete without taking in Howrah Bridge. Rising hideously above the city's sky line, this engineering masterpiece to the British Army Corps. of Engineers was a living monument and often I would sit on its steel structure watching the world go by. Another landmark, no less visited, was the Queen Victoria Marble Statue. Stern in features she personified a different aspect of the British Empire, and invited the city pigeons.

That evening the sun dropped into a smoke filled haze, immediately shattering its outline into millions of diffused fragments. A torch had been put to the sky and its red cloud hung over the city like an apocalyptic fire until it set. Overpowering smells of urine now gave way to the sweet scents of burning insence sticks, as street vendors went through ritual pugareers (holy services) to a many faceted God before opening for the night's trade. I stayed ten days. It could easily have been ten years. This was the India I had come to see, the human wallpaper of everyday life. I left Calcutta knowing I'd only just scratched its surface.

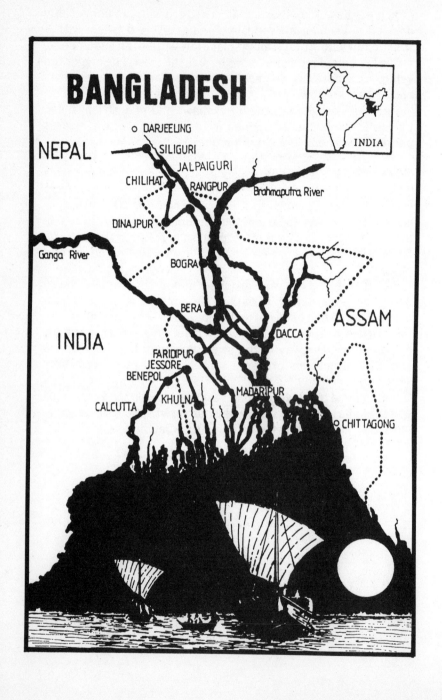

Chapter 13:
Ajit, Son of Baidya

THE BRITISH LEFT MANY VISITING CARDS BEHIND IN India and none could have a more powerful pull on the imagination than the symbolic Lion and the Unicorn. Symbol of British permanency and commonly called the British Passport, it intimidated the handler whenever touched. Its power to move mountains, solve the unsolvable, and open doors that only the privileged few Indians could enter were legendary and, in the process, could and did make any fellow traveller green with envy.

I arrived to find the Bangaon customs yard in a ferment of activity. Piles of open suitcases containing sarees, blankets and an assortment of electrical items were being guarded or argued over between men dressed in every kind of robe and headware and army officials from immaculately dressed Sikh Officers, down to the crumpled khaki Private.

Spotted by the Private, I was waved to the front of the queue and on seeing my passport, his eyes immediately stood to attention.

"Please follow me."

Holding my hand like a little child he took me into a rundown concrete bunker where a small huddle of officers pointed to my bicycle.

"You cycle from Calcutta ?"

"Yes." I replied.

More and more questions totally unrelated to my exit followed.

"How many gears ? How many miles do you travel in a day ? Where you put air ?"

By now I felt as if I'd entered a lottery, with first prize being my exit. Suddenly everyone stood. A distinguished looking Sikh Major appeared, bedecked in all manner of decorations and coloured braid.

"Can I offer you tea ?"

With a glass of milky tea, deliciously spiced with cardamom, I sat back to enjoy this man's pronounced public school accent. Educated at Sandhurst in the arts of warfare and good manners, he spoke with ease slipping into that educated aloofness I was becoming accustomed to seeing in British educated Indians.

"My father and my father's father fought alongside the British in many campaigns and I have nothing but the greatest respect for your Queen and Country."

He spent the next twenty minutes taking me on a verbal tour of Indian monuments.

"You must visit Amritsar when you return to India. The Golden Temple is a most wonderful place."

A second cup of tea was followed by biscuits. Then with an authoritive bluntness, he terminated the conversation.

"I shall go now. I leave you with this officer. If you require any further assistance, please do not hesitate to ask for me."

My private audience at an end, I passed down the chain of command, finishing, as I started, with the private bringing back my bicycle.

A no man's land between the borders bore out much evidence of the '72 Indo/Pak war, where make-shift bridges, adjacent to their original bombed out foundations held up precariously under the mass confusion riding them. Railway lines ended abruptly and large, half- destroyed houses gave way to smaller outcroppings like a cancerous growth. This nameless, stateless shanty town born from free, if not illegal enterprise, housed a thriving black market and, travelling at a walking pace, I needed mountains of discipline to ignore it. India had sucked nearly all my luck that day, now in Bangladesh, Benopol's custom's would finish it off.

The manner in which I was ushered into the customs office bore all the signs of oncoming disaster. I was made to wait on a low seat so that regarding my interrogator was like looking up the barrel of a gun. Being at eye level, my attention rested on a rather large pyramid of books on his desk, concerning student dissidents, undesirable citizens and counter revolutionists.

"Your passport." His look was venomous and I gave it to him with maximum submission.

He zeroed in on my visa quickly. "Where is your bicycle permit ?"

"I wasn't told I needed one." I honestly couldn't remember, but this wasn't the time for honesty.

"You were wrong."

I swallowed hard. "I told them all about my bicycle." My heart was pounding. "They didn't say anything about a special permit."

"They are wrong. Where are you going ?"

"Dacca."

"Why ?" I hurriedly showed him some cuttings from the Bangkok Post, hoping confirmation of my trip's importance would lend sympathy to my plight, then set about explaining its reasons as if my future depended on it, stressing its educational value, the photographs I hoped to take, and the school children back home I hoped to show them to.

"You have camera ?"

"Yes."

"Why didn't you tell us ? You have to declare everything."

Taking out my box full of slides taken in New Zealand, I handed them to him.

"Look they are for children. Hold them up to the light, you can see better."

His face now reflected a change in attitude and, while he continued to look at the pictures, I was given some forms to fill in.

"You were wrong in Calcutta," he repeated. "Next time be correct."

"I'm allowed to go ?"

"We cannot ignore formalities. After all, we learned them from you British. This time we shall overlook your bicycle permit."

My ordeal over, I breathed a noisy sigh of relief and before leaving, my name was registered with incredible formality into his enormous ledger.

"You can go."

"Thank you."

He looked surprised. "Thank me for what ?"

"I always thank everybody. We British are very polite."

He burst into laughter, then looking up added with special emphasis. "Can I help you further ?"

I fumbled automatically to my pocket, then decided against it.

"I'll change my money in Jessore," I said firmly.

His face broke into a big smile. "Banks closed."

What the hell. I took out my remaining dollar bills kept for emergency and changed half of what I had left.

"Can I have a receipt please ?"

"Receipt." He smiled, then dissappeared into his office. I wanted to say something, but thought better of it, and left empty handed.

After the hills of South East Asia, Bangladesh, with its tapestry of paddy fields was like a pancake. From Benopol long stretches of road, badly holed and broken, detoured into adjacent fields; collapsed bridges into make-shift slip-ways and, at some points, even gave way to village footpaths. I was soon lost in a maze of narrow passageways, as snaking through one coconut plantation after another, I would only have the distant rumblings of occasional trucks for guidance. This pattern repeated itself the following day en route to Khuna, and later these unmarked detours would prove a major part of my trip, as to shock people off the beaten track was a unique antidote to boredom and I was beginning to revel in the power effected by my white skin.

From Khuna I boarded the aptly named Rocket Steamer (a left over paddle boat from the British Days of the Raj) on its thirty hour journey through the Ganges Delta to Dacca. Like during the trip down the Irrawaddy, every type of animal shared my passage.

Dacca meant exit visa and little else and, while waiting, I shared my dormitory accommodation at the Y.M.C.A. with its overflowing population of thirsty mosquitoes. Because the Y.M.C.A.'s coffee lounge was one of the few cultural points open to Dacca's students, it was a natural environment in which to meet foreigners and exchange views, and it was here I met Ajit and his friends. All Catholic, they had been drawn together by winning individual scholarships, and it was during one of our breakfast exchanges that I was press-ganged into refereeing a soccer match. Someone had definitely forgotten to tell them that being British didn't automatically make one an authority on soccer. They wouldn't take no for an answer so, four hours later, I found myself center field with a whistle and little else to back up my on-pitch duties, in front of a packed local stadium. The field sloped, dipped and was pitted with ruts, but there was no denying the team's enthusiasm or, for that matter, the crowd's excitement. Packed to the rafters, my entry to the fixture had trebled the normal crowd. For the first twenty minutes I bounced about like a ping-pong ball, as their kick and run tactics had me running from one end of the field to the other. Up till then I'd only used my whistle for arguments and blatant rugby style tackles. Then, just before half time, I made a fatal mistake. More intent on watching the ball than the players, I gave a goal only to find myself surrounded by angry defenders.

"Off side, Sir."

Already Ajit and his friend's had taken up their places ready for the kick-off. With no linesman to consult and no knowledge of the rules, I had to stand by my decision. The crowd was stunned but, by half time, had turned ugly and, by the second half, was in near riot. Catcalls and whistles were now following my every decision. Then, with only minutes to go in the match, an incident on the half-way line saved me. I blew up for a penalty. Both sides were speechless. Penalty taken, I blew for time. The score line read 1 - 1. Justice was done, and after the match, when asked about my strange decisions, I fell back on my birth right. "We British invented the game, who else in the world could know the rules better ?"

That afternoon cemented my friendship with Ajit and led to an invitation to visit his family in Southern Bangladesh.

"What my family can offer is very little. They will want to give you meat, but they have no money. Your water will have to be boiled, they not know this. They have no furniture. Then there is the problem with toilets and, most important, you cannot speak our language."

I'd experienced all these problems before. I was now used to their well water, thrived on their diet, and even their sometimes exposed toilet arrangements held no embarrassment. Soon sanitized by the sun, ablutions on the road were as varied and as open as the countryside. In some villages, whole fields were set aside as toilets and, in others, maggot infested holes, enclosed for privacy were dug for collection. Between fields I was often forced behind bushes and under bridges, but always I had to step carefully. Caught out without toilet paper I was used to using my fingers and hands for cleaning, so the only thing in Ajit's worries that bothered me was language. Ajit's excuses were now leading to second thoughts and, by the look on his face, regrets, then, before he could withdraw his invitation, I came up with an idea.

"Give me an introduction Ajit. Write it in Bengali. Don't worry about food either. I can pay for it."

"No, they will be insulted. It is our custom. You are a guest. It is unthinkable."

I thought of a compromise. "Let me take them some food. I will say it is from you."

This sealed it, and soon he had me making out a shopping list, sketching a map, translating useful words, and then, with a great deal of enthusiasm, he completed a letter of formal introduction to his father, writing and rewriting it with the delicacy of a diplomat.

Leaving Dacca before sunrise I made good time to Aricha and then, following his directions, crossed the Ganges River by car ferry to Goalundu Ghat. So far so good. Then I came across another ferry crossing. This time his map made no reference to it but there was plenty of traffic around so I wasn't unduly worried and, on reaching Faridipur, I found myself back on course. From Faridipur I turned due south off the Trans- Asian Highway to Madaripur and from this point his map was only sketchy at best. On more than one occasion I caused accidents, simply by being there, and stopping to ask directions created instant throngs of curiosity. Again one footpath crossed into another, one river into the next. Clearings appeared like roundabouts with confusing exits. I lost count of the bridges so important to Ajit's map directions, and one time I rejoined the road in the wrong direction, cycling for over an hour before realizing my mistake. Finally, having covered nearly twice the distance, I arrived at Mostafapur Bridge, and started the next part of my *Cooks Guided Tour of Inland Waterways*, as per Ajit's instructions.

Moored under the bridge just as Ajit described, I saw four small boat taxis, and following his instructions, I took my letter of introduction to the tobacco kiosk owner by the road. "The kiosk owner my uncle. He get boatman to take you to my father's house." I remembered Ajit saying. I approached the uncle as suggested but, by the look on his face, any loyalty to family unity had evaporated at the sight of my white face and I knew that a King's ransom would be due payment for taxi services.

Soon the whole areas was surrounded by a seething mass of bodies trying to get a better look at this strange new arrival. Obviously this was not to be the low profile visit I had hoped for. Nothing was left to chance. Ajit's uncle hand-picked my boatman, fixed the price and ordered his close friends to supervise loading. I was offered tea, my shopping list was closely checked and then cunningly made to patronize his friends' market stalls. The crowd

2.   Labrador/N.F.L.D:
L'anse au Claire's Youth
Hostel

3.   Alberta, Canada:
"THE GREAT ONE" has gone
South. Who's he?

1.   Nova Scotia, Canada:
What this information kiosk lacked in
high tech, it more than made up for in
rustic warmth and abundant Maritime
hospitality.

4.   Nova Sco-
tia, Canada:
The Cabot Trail
on Cape Bretton.

5.   Taihape, New Zealand:
My friend Sonny, sheep shearing.
Working on a farm was a welcome
relief from cycling.

6.   Kilaue Crater, Hawaii:
The road cut straight through the
lava flows. My bike is in the background.

7.   South Island, New Zealand:
The famouse "Round Rock Beach" at Moeraki.

8. South Island, New Zealand:
Cycling between Lumsden and Queenstown. N.Z. had everything, volcanoes, snow-capped mountains, Fjords, plains, deserts and.... "GUDDAY MATE".

9. Northern Territory, Australia:
Burned out cars marked every bend. The land of Oz, birth place of the "STUBBIE", "DOWN UNDER" and "CROCODILE DUNDEE".

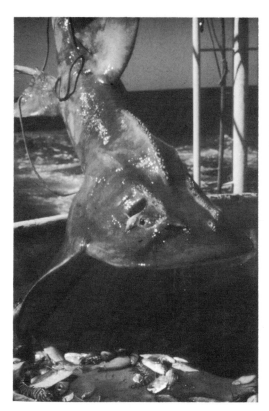

10. *Gulf of Carpentaria, Australia:*
This rare (toothless) "Razor Back Shark" got caught in our nets. We returned it back alive to the sea. Pressganged into work on a prawn boat, due to money transfer problems in Darwin, I spent two months at sea fighting both the captain and the elements.

11.   *Naviti Island, Fiji:*
I only meant to spend one day on the island, but it stretched into six weeks.

12. (above) Uttar Pradesh, India:
Crossing the Ghagara River en rout to Bela.

13. (below) In the Indian Subcontinent, where every
home owns a bicycle, the sight of mine, could shut down
shops, fill streets and empty villages within minutes.

14. Lahore, Pakistan:
Monsoon rains could turn
streets into slow moving
rivers within minutes.

15. *(left) Calcutta, India: Children en route to school by tonga. The natural curiosity of school children would transend any barrier my white skin erected and passing schools, I would empty them like sinking ships.*

16. *(below) Steam trains in India went at a joggers pace due to overloading.*

17. *Lahore, Pakistan: Trucks immaculately decorated from top to bottom in polished chrome and hand-painted throughout were in a league of their own.*

18.   Southern Bangladesh:
Lack of bridges were no problem for bicycles. Here I am going by 'boat
taxi' on my visit to Ajit's father.

19.   Gujurat, India:
Nomadic tribes carried everything
with them.

20.   Punjab, India:
Cottage industry still flourishes, as
this village potter shows.

*Indian Subcontinent bazaar's se-
duced me with their living history
and often I wandered like a fish
ready to be hooked. Shop bargaining often turned to friendships; cups
of tea to supper and offers of free
lodging would come thick and fast.*

*21.   (right) Mysore, India:
Umbrella mender-cum-lock smith,
also makes a mean cup of tea.*

*22.   (left) Jaipur, India:
Cooking stove repairman.*

*23.   Pushkar, India:
Shoe maker and repairer.*

24. *Pushkar, India:*
Took this photo-graph for the cheeky smile.

25. *(right) Delhi, India:*
Family 'brass' business.

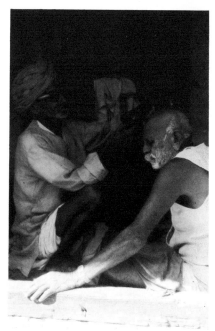

26. *Bombay, India:*
"Anyone for a shaved head?"

27. Bihar, India: Having no language skills, I found playing sports the key to village life.

28. (middle) Nepal: This 'Merry-go Round' was copied from a picture in a newspaper.

29. (bottom left) Nepal: Wooden 'Ferris Wheel'.

30. (bottom right) Bangladesh: The problem Banyan Tree

31. (above) Zanskar, India: Just liked the picture of this Tibetan woman's face. Lines of Wisdom.

32. (above) One of Nepal's many wood-rope bridges. Trekking in the Himalaya's meant, sore feet, an aching back and spectacular views.

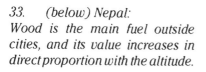

33. (below) Nepal: Wood is the main fuel outside cities, and its value increases in direct proportion with the altitude.

34. India is full of unusual sights and none more so than this Yogi.

35.   Zanskar, India:
The 'Beacon Road' from Srinigar to Leh had many high points. Fortula
Pass at 13,479 Ft. was its highest. It took six hours of blood, sweat and
tears to get up.

36.   N.W.T., Pakistan:
The new K.K.H. highway
follows the old 'Silk Road'
to China. Typical view of
the Indus River near
Patton.

37.   Zanskar, India:
Spring avalanches cut
through the Beacon Road
on the Zozila Pass.

39. (left) Ladakh, India: Roadside chalkham in Saspol.

38. (below) Zanskar, India: Walking in the mountains isn't for the faint hearted. This section near Hanumala Pass dropped away like a waterfall to the edge of a one thousand foot gorge.......Oops!

40. (left) Zanskar, India: These prayer stones directed me off the Beacon Road to Lamayaru Gompa.

41. *Darcha, India:*
You always met a better class of people in the out of the way places. Even if you lose your piece of 'plastic', you could always exchange your boots for B+B.

42. *Land's End,*
Scotland:
A pit-stop is a pit-stop no matter what country you're in. I crashed-out on top of this haystack.

43. *Epulu, Zaire:*
Not known for its world class hotels, but a roof is a roof and who cares after a hard day in the saddle.

45. *(below)*
Uganda's unique
creative toys.
Children are the
same the whole
world over. This
wire toy was
made by a young
boy.

44. *(above) Beni, Zaire:*
The Trans African Highway
during the rainy season.

46. *(below) Nakuru, Kenya:*
Wall paintings where no wall
paper exits

47. *(below) The beautiful*
beaded hairstyles of Africa.

49.   Boiled banana 'Matoke' was my favourite food and staple diet in Africa.

48.   I never went looking for wild-life. If it was there, okay; if not, that was also okay.

50.   Lamu Island, Kenya:
No trip is complete without friendships and mine is no different; Ully & Erica visit my palm leaf house.

was euphoric, and the reflected glory quite naturally went to his head. Everyone knew Ajit, many from school. His name and that of his father was revered in the community and, obviously the uncle's influence would rise and fall, depending on Ajit's future career. Ajit was the son of a poor family made good and in their eyes, I was a gift from God, to repay family and community sacrifice.

Not being a person to overlook golden opportunities, his uncle now turned to the crowd, introducing me with great pomp and ceremony, scoring vital points in the community's popularity stakes, and playing the politician's game of 'use the celebrity' in this instant electoral meeting.

Victim of my own notoriety, I led a small armada of inquisitive boats, and, to prove that taxis drivers on land or water were the same the whole world over, my boatman took every opportunity to give me a guided tour of the canal's network of waterways. First we stopped at his father's home, then made a short side trip to meet his brother and, during the morning we had stopped four times, had six cups of tea and two meals. "How far ?" A stupid question. I was in the Subcontinent. Patience was all. "How far ?" This time my tone needed no translation, but his smile on my boatman's face said it all. BE PATIENT. YOU'RE IN THE SUBCONTINENT.

I arrived under darkening shadows, and the realization registered shock waves of earthquake proportions. Mr Baiya, Ajit's father, was numbed into silence, and his family sent into absolute chaos as children, in their curiosity, to come and parents in their efforts, to go, tripped over each other in total confusion.

Once my arrival had sunk in and my credentials had been read, Mr Baidya set about bringing his troops to order. Tea was brought, chapatis made, and my food gifts distributed. I was now on the verge of collapse. Six hours of heat and glare had given me a mild sun stroke. Instinctively Mr Baidya read my fatigue, and more orders were given. A bedroom was allocated and my mosquito net erected. Then, with only the slightest of hints from my host, I took my leave and collapsed immediately into sleep.

Surrounded by flooded paddy fields, my first morning was seen through a cold dawn mist. Smaller than I remembered, our man-made island comprised five houses, all economically made from reed bounded by bamboo shoots and, together with a cattle pen and small coconut plantation, was no bigger than a junior sized football pitch. Judging by everyone's activities that morning they'd been up for sometime and while they worked, I sat motionless in the shadows of my bed, enjoying a treasured moment of private viewing. Smoke swallowed up the scene in a small out-house where Mrs Baidya and daughters were preparing breakfast. Children dressed in the blue shirted uniforms were leaving by boat. Mohammed, their youngest, was chasing chickens round the yard and Mr Baidya, his brother and son squatted silently, mending their fishing nets. Everything fitted. Shape colour, smell, all parts of this island world had grouped together and, in doing so, had shaped the instincts of the people who made and lived in it. Life centered around paddy, and its limited economy ,on climatic conditions. As in all Asian societies I visited, social systems were based on family commitments, as progressive generations looked after their own and authority linked by age and strength went unquestioned. The forces that forged Mr Baidya's world were far removed from those of his son's, but now I'd seen both. Distanced by different cultures, I could see clearly that invisible link that tied them together. Blood ties run deep in Asia. The term brother may stand for a multitude of sins in some parts of the world, but here it stood for continuity.

Looking back on my first morning those were my only private moments, as one official visit collided with the next in a never ending itinerary of family, school and government functions. Forewarned of my school visit, hundreds of waving children lined the banks to greet me. A trip to the market found me emotionally blackmailed, intervening in community disputes. The regional Commissioner paid me a visit and during the day, prospective marriage partners were introduced for my approval.

One day I was invited to visit the local Catholic Church. As Bangladesh is predominantly Muslim, to find myself in a Christian enclave was strange, and while I answered the priest's questions relating to Western moral issues on permissive sex, he answered mine on conversion quotas, resulting in religious competition. His answers were surprisingly candid. "After the Indo/Pak war, missionaries from Europe saturated this area. Before the war people here were mostly Hindu, but after the war it was dangerous not to be Muslim. Missionaries offered us gifts of aid in exchange for conversion and changes of allegiances to the various Christian faiths in those days depended largely on the yearly gifts of aid, as in Ajit's case, a Catholic scholarship."

There was still one group of men I'd not seen. The army of fishermen who lit up the flooded waterways at night with their lanterns, and on my last evening I looked forward to meeting them. My respect for these people held no bounds. Trapped in a feudal system with little hope of improvement, they were unashamedly proud of their level in society. Lacking that surface smoothness and fakery afforded their official counterparts, they were sometimes brash, and even rowdy, but had an abundance of that special pride and natural warmth characteristic of the person whose life depends on his own achievements.

At first a delegation came to me to formally ask my permission for their visit which, when given, became a prelude to a flotilla of boats. Soon fishermen were slipping in and out of the night to see me. Asked what I would like as a parting gift I mentioned music and, to indulge my request, local musicians were sent for. Soon compelling rhythms filled the air and, by early evening, all the deep-rooted tensions of my stay were released. Clouds of burning incense now mixed with that of burning paraffin and as it lapped around the room, its unique blend courted me like a soothing drug. Some time in the night, I awoke. By now outlines were like mirage images and as the fog of fatigue closed in, again I was eased back into sleep by the muffled sounds of a base tablar.

In the morning I took what had become the ritual family portraits and left, retracing my steps to Jessore before crossing the Ganges River once again. Cycling on to the ferry I supported my bike against a steel barrier then went for a better view. At first nothing was unusual. The same crowds surrounded me and the same questions were answered. It wasn't until the occupant of a white Ambassador Car got out that the trouble started.

"You." He was pointing an angry finger in my direction. "Yes you, put your trousers on immediately."

Not one to avoid confrontations with authority, my bare legs were bound to precipitate one sooner or later. Muslim distaste for bare flesh, especially white flesh, was well known and I'd been warned about it many times. In my island home I'd worn a 'lungi' out of respect; in Dacca, jeans out of choice, and always shorts when cycling, out of need. In Dacca the word, "Disco" followed me everywhere and Ajit explained its meaning. "They call all western clothing, disco. It comes from a popular Indian film. They try to make fun of you, nothing more." Now the word disco would come to my rescue.

"Do as you are told." He wasn't going to take no for an answer. Asked politely, I would have done it, but this wasn't a request. It was a command, and he looked the type of rich Bengali who had seen it all before. Anyway, he'd spoiled the warm atmosphere in the crowd, and if that wasn't enough, he looked obscenely well fed.

"Why?" It wasn't a question to let go of easily. I sat down and waited for the predictable explosion.

"You bloody foreigner. I have you arrested."

I let him continue a little longer. I had the perfect answer, but waited like a professional comedian for an opening.

"Disco, Disco, Disco." I timed it perfectly. Jumping to my feet I pointed to Porky's trousers. "Disco, Disco, Disco."

Suddenly the crowd echoed my chant and, by sheer weight of numbers Porky was pushed back towards his chauffeur-driven car. Then with more than a little help from the crowd, he was forced into the back seat, not to reappear for the rest of the journey.

Bangladesh was not known for its tourist exploitation and in Dacca large posters declare, 'COME TO BANGLADESH BEFORE THE TOURISTS DO.' What they didn't tell the adventurous tourist was that, once away from the city hotels, there was no official accommodation, not even for locals. This became a major problem, since village hospitality didn't lend itself to privacy, and by now weary of being public property, I craved the protection of my own room. It was this weariness that forced me to search out alternatives.

A large painted sign announced Shzadpur Government Rest House. Rest House sounded like some hotel to me. I'd not heard the term before, and certainty I wasn't prepared for what followed. In my naivete I had uncovered a form of shelter that in the future I would link with privacy and together with 'Dak Bungalow', 'Canal Rest House', 'P.W.D. (Public Building and Works) Guest House', and the opulent 'Circuit House' (used by visiting magistrates) would become a familiar oasis of shelter on my crisscross journey through the Subcontinent. Not averse to tourists, but primarily intended for government use, there was never any problem getting a room in them. Built by the British to link the Provinces with the central government in Delhi they were eclectic to say the least, and I could be rubbing shoulders with politicians and judges one night and sharing dormitory accommodation with convicts the next. Reminders of a long forgotten age, my quarters ranged from mosquito-infested rooms, to ones adorned with prize Bengali Tigers. Common to all these rest houses and without whose presence they could not function was the 'Chaki Dow'; this Jeeves of servants, with his stiff upper lip, who could chastise the mightiest one minute, and be the personification of graciousness the next was a constant force to contend with, but one thing about him never altered. He was never around when wanted.

From Shzadpur I continued to Bogra and came across yet another type of safe house.

Where, I ask, haven't the Sixties Children of the Kennedy Dream been to ? These orphans of peace and love, can often by their very presence, spread their own brand of America's Dream, and, by themselves, have done more for the sales of such items as Coca Cola, Ketchup and Big Macs, than the combined millions spent on overseas advertising and Aid Program trade-offs. Where, you may ask, on my global visits hadn't I seen them ? Pioneers in their own right, they innocently propagate all that's nice and apple pieish in this mixed up world. Who, dare I ask, are these people ? None other than the volunteer Peace Corps worker. Thank God for small mercies, thank the Bengali sign writer for spelling Peace Corps correctly and last but not least, thank the volunteers for just being there. Not since Calcutta had I spoken to white faces. Even in Dacca I had drawn a blank. White faces there were like ships passing in the night. That obligatory wave of greeting, no exchange of conversation or pleasantries, all lost in private worlds of travel experience. Now it was time to enjoy myself. For these lads, it was a pleasure to see another white face, an excuse to break routines, and for me, just a pleasure. That night I treated myself to a hot shower with Camay Soap, enjoyed the privacy of western style toilets with soft paper and, best of all, sampled home made Meat Loaf with french fries, before capping the evening off with a Budweiser.

The following morning I set off on a cloud of good fortune and didn't have to travel far to share it. I cycled into a circus. Compared to the mighty Bertram Mills Circuses of this world, what stood before me could only be classed as its poor relative. Canvassed topped in the best circus tradition, its patchwork patterns bore all the signs of continual use and evidence of its worldwide appeal. Although lacking the sophisticated gadgetry of Big Brother, I was soon to find the familiar smells of animals and grease paint more than a match and it reflected in the air of excitement which gripped the crowd.

Curious to get a closer look, I was spotted by the stage manager and immediately adopted by the performers. Given a ringside seat in exchange for the use of my bike, I sat back to relive childhood memories. Clowns and jugglers were the first acts and soon whipped up the atmosphere with stage managed accidents. Hindu gypsy girls, playing in the intervals, simulated all manner of delights, milking both applause and showers of money, while feeding the fantasies of a predominantly 'Muslim' male audience. Soon it was the turn of the animals. Brightly painted elephants danced in sequence, Arabian horses, in formation, and acrobatic bears and monkeys performed in costume. Two tigers, the pride of their country, roared on command, then gave way to a spectacular high wire act. I was introduced to the crowd, and being a distinguished guest, invited into the arena. Meanwhile, one of the jugglers had stripped off my cycle bags and came cycling in amidst a wildly screaming audience and, while the band played on cue, he jerked my bike up on one wheel, before shaking his hands to the audience in an ecstasy of invention."'That was most enjoyable, yes" It was the stage manager, but I was too anxiously watching my bike to answer him. By now the beat created a solid backing to the juggler's performance and, to complete the act, he made three complete circles of the arena backwards before leaping off the bike to thunderous cheers. Finished, my bike was returned and I left more than a little relieved that it was still in one piece.

Compromises are a fact of life, whether private or public, but on the Subcontinent they run through every aspect of it, and no example could be so startling in its effect on modern technology than that which met my eye on the road north from Saidpur. In the

Subcontinent roads were not built for the God of Power, but to the Power of God. Here they didn't live off the land, but on it. Far from trying to tame the land as in the west, successive generations of Indians had learned to live in harmony with it. Revered for its mystical powers and shelter to the holy pilgrim, the BANYAN TREE was central to this unique example of Subcontinent compromise. There in front of me, growing right smack out of the middle of the road, like some great natural barrier of weeping branches, and just as the original road engineers must have seen it, was the problem Banyan tree. On paper it must have looked a minor obstacle, but then the engineers hadn't counted on Hindu logic. Not being students of Hindu mythology either, the unknowing engineers could have been excused for overlooking its powerful significance, and one can only imagine the comedy of errors and misjudgments that followed. It must be hard to imagine the wheels of bureaucracy called the British Empire grinding to a halt over this one hiccup, but maybe this one tree altered the whole course of modern industry. Imagine such a minor problem causing such a major headache. One could well believe its repercussions, maybe they were felt thousands of miles away, even reaching the very seat of Imperial power. Questions in Parliament, the Foreign Secretary's resignation is called for, maybe it even caused the Government's downfall. Did it even reach the ears of Queen Victoria? Did it spawn the Royal Tree Preservation Society? Who knows, who even cares? It's for certain the Senior Engineer involved never forgot it. Maybe he was knighted for services above and beyond the call of duty, Ambassadorship even, or maybe cashiered from the army. Maybe he became an authority on Hindu philosophy or maybe he just fathered the crazy Sadhu who I saw under the tree. Maybe...maybe...

Then just to emphasize the tree's obstructive value, a truck spun off the road in a cloud of dust missing it by inches, only to reappear on the other side where the road started again, as if nothing had happened.

By noon the heat was so brittle it snapped the leaves of branches. The road by now had melted into a dirt track and my only guide through a maze of parallel tracks was the border railway line, which I followed with a great deal of difficulty.

After three weeks in Bangladesh I was looking forward to

leaving. Outside Adjit's friendship I was now tired of the Bengali stereotype. Humble, humble and more humble. The term poor had lost its value by now and bandied around like some kind of verbal currency it was beginning to wear very thin. Every conversation was a continual reminder. "We are very poor in this country." Somehow I found it very difficult to sustain any sympathy. They talked about sleeping outside, but they didn't have to contend with the penetrating damp of Europe, and their continual complaints left me cold and unmoved. I would tell them about my own parents in England. They owned nothing. We complained amongst ourselves but were too proud to complain to others. All I could offer was the ballot box or revolution. "The best fighters are the hungry ones," I told the students in Rangpur. I'd been cornered in a tea shop after their demonstration had broken up. A baton charge by army soldiers had sent them running in all directions and I found myself surrounded by them. I could read it in their eyes. Their revolution lay in rhetoric. They weren't suffering like the poor. They were on the outside looking in. Where would they be when the fighting got hot ?

That evening in Domar I met another band of revolutionaries, but these were front line fighters, putting their lives on the line against a government set on change at all cost, without much thought of their future.

"There is no room in the rest house, can I stay here ?"

Entering Domar I had gone straight to the Government Rest House, only to be turned away, and now I was trying my luck at the police station.

"No problem." The police inspector was more than glad to see me. "I'll find you room in the Rest House. I make arrangements. No problem."

Having just been turned away I was a little confused.

"Please go to my house. You eat there."

I followed him home and was immediately introduced to his wife and children, who quickly disappeared to prepare food. It was during our evening meal that I learned of the guest who now was vacating his room for me.

"He freedom fighter from Assam. Little wound. They fight Indian Army. We are very sympathetic. He has many relatives in this region."

I listened in amazement to the inspector and as his story sank in I tried my best to dissuade him.

"Please don't go to this trouble for me."

"His friends will understand," he replied. "You are guest in this country. It is our duty to shelter you."

I was worried about the friends. What would they think when they returned to find their friend outside, wounded? I know what I would feel. I tried again.

"I can sleep outside in the compound. It is bad to move a man who is wounded?"

Again I was answered as before. "No problem, wound not bad."

After supper we returned to the Rest House, where outside under the verandah, on a rope strung bed, my room's original guest lay fast asleep.

"I am obliged to leave you. Do not worry about this man." He now turned to the Chaki Dow; whose face registered marked disapproval of his new charge, exchanged words and left. Once inside, my room's displaced guest played on my mind and it was sometime before I plucked up the courage to get into bed. Then dampening the lantern light, I drifted off to sleep.

Sometime in the night I was woken. Voices from outside argued, then dropped into silence. Minutes later there was a knock on the door. Silence, then another. At first I didn't want to answer it then, just as I turned up the lantern, the door burst open. Instantly my room filled with armed men . In the confusion my lantern was knocked over, flooding the room with light and, seeing my white face, they froze.

"Most sorry, our comrade sleep outside."

"It is my fault." Their entry had been so quick, I hadn't had time to be afraid. "The police inspector insisted I take his bed, but I should have stopped him."

"You are British?"

The tension broken, they gathered round my bed and soon we were deep in conversation. With no uniform for identity, only their youth and single breached rifles they looked no different from the millions of Indians you saw on the streets.

"My name is Nali, I am their leader." He didn't even look old enough to shave. Educated in Delhi, he had learned the politics of war at university. Products of a Government Relocation Program, many of the group had relatives living in Assam and the government's uncompromising policy of eviction fused this band of young men together in a common cause. Forced to leave their traditional areas in the forest, survival for many had changed from one of subsistence farming to humiliating government hand-outs, as new communities now clung to highways for their very existence by government decree. Many harrowing stories were told that night. Some told of women reduced to prostitution for family survival, others of young men seduced by stories of city life, who drifted down highways never to be seen again, and then, of the new diseases brought in by city traffic that were claiming the rest.

We talked for hours. Nali asking and translating for his friends, who by now mostly exhausted, lay sleeping on the floor. I was about to ask them to leave, when there was a loud knock on the door. Instantly Nali's group united against the wall. Half a dozen men led by a red bearded giant strutted into the room. A heated exchange followed. A rifle was cocked and immediately the room filled with violence.

"What's going on ?" I silenced everyone.

All eyes turned on me. Apparently, tonight was scheduled as a Hind/Muslim political fix-it campaign in the run up to a local election, which judging by Nali's expression, excited nothing but total disgust. My position in no-man's land between the groups forced them to put aside their religious and ideological differences. That night a truce was called and, by morning, both groups had gone their separate ways.

From Domat the road split into numerous village tracks and Chili Hati was reached more by good luck than good judgement. This one way frontier town was dedicated to travellers but not my type. Restaurants overlapped hotels, and, what shops there were, almost exclusively catered, with their stocks of electrical goods to the Bengali gift trade. Within minutes the town came and went and still there was no border crossing. Seeing people milling about with baggage, I stopped to ask directions and, reassured, continued only to end up at a collapsed bridge. I again asked, "Where Customs ?" To emphasize my question, I showed my passport. A finger pointed northwards, this time in the direction of a dirt trail and with a rush of enthusiasm, I cycled on despite it narrowing into a chequered network of footpaths. Optimistically, I continued. Thirty minutes passed. By now the footpath was so bad I had to walk. Initial enthusiasm turned to concern. Where was everyone? Not since arriving in the Subcontinent had I felt so lonely. Had that 'living deity' deserted me? Bangladesh was the most populated country in the world, you couldn't even go for a piss on your own without enlisting spectators. Soon paddy was replaced by scrub.

"Halt."

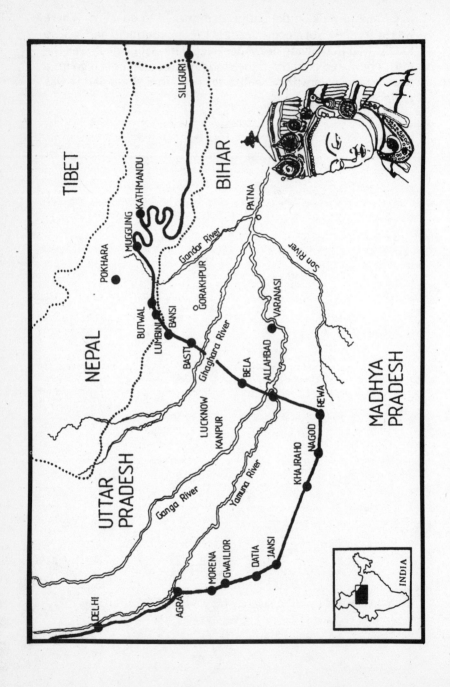

Chapter 14:
Rendezvous with Kama

A SIKH TURBAN STOOD BEFORE ME.
"Passport please "
My passport was studied from all angles, my visas with particular interest and my bike was just too much for them. No one seemed interested in the fact that I had no exit stamp from Bangladesh, and when it was pointed out, they only laughed.

"No one go by road," they said. "By bicycle impossible."

I was their honoured, if not captive, guest and by allowing the sergeant to ride my bike could do no wrong.

"You take Indian tea ?"

Having amused the border patrol, I was directed fifteen miles to Jalpaiguri where I officially entered India. Here, a bewildered railway Station Master doubling as the Customs Officer bore out earlier stories of this little used route and, before leaving, I left him a picture of myself to pin with his other rare guests, in a rogues gallery of travellers on his office wall.

The following morning's crisp, dawn chill opened a vast panorama of rounded foothills and, rising out of the far distance, I caught my first glimpse of the mighty Himalayas. For me the Subcontinent had always been synonymous with Nepal, Kathmandu and Everest and now I had arrived. All day I was in another world. Mother Earth never looked so warm. Irritating distractions slipped by without notice and the night hugged me tighter than at any time on my journey.

From Siliguri I crossed into Nepal and for the next few days I enjoyed views of breathtaking beauty, as sunrise slipped into sunset, setting ablaze a back stage of snow capped peaks. Now with the Subcontinent's suffocating population behind, I could breath and again find time to unwind from its pressures with frequent stops and cups of tea.

Sitting in a roadside tea shop, I watched an old Nepalese man amuse himself with my bike. Squatting in that peculiar Asian way, his hand moved over cables, tracing them from lever to cog. It was a picture of every day life I was accustomed to. People had gathered around whenever I stopped and it was quite usual for

one person, whether from youthful courage or old age, to exam-
ine my bike in detail, sometimes even altering my gears. Because
of this I got into the habit of checking everything before cycling
away, but this man was different. Keeping a respectful distance
his hand gestures moved more in curiosity then out of any need
to tamper. First my bell was rung, then front and back brakes
engaged, but when he moved my gear lever his granite features
danced with delight. Being now a veteran of these encounters I
had lost the hard edge of temper and, not wanting to interrupt the
old man's enjoyment, I waited some time before venturing outside.

"How many speed ?"

"Ten speed ?" I replied, putting my fingers up. Satisfied, the
old man prized himself up, came over to join me, and insisted I
have another cup of tea with him, before changing the conversation to more serious matters.

"What religion do you follow ?" It was a question asked of me
many times and I always enjoyed being swallowed up by its many
answers.

"I do not follow any religion."

"But you must believe in a God ?"

"I do not believe in anything I cannot touch. "I'd bitten on his
question and it reflected on his face. The Hindu Logic was always
trapped by non believers and, after weighing up my answer, he
counted.

"A man without a belief is like a bird without a sky to fly in."

I couldn't help but laugh at his reply. The Subcontinent was
alive with street philosophers, and this old man was no different.

"A man without bike is like a rider with no road to ride on." It
was my turn, and like a pair of old combatants, we sat down to
share both a meal and conversation together.

Two hours later I was being given a guided tour of his village.
Being a grandfather his priority was with children and his prized
gift to them was a merry-go-round. Made entirely out of wood and
wire, he described how it came to be built. While on a business
trip to Bombay, he saw a picture of a city fair in the local
newspaper. The merry-go-round captured his imagination and,
not wanting to rely on his memory, he kept the whole page. On his
return, he sold the idea of building it to the village. Trees were
felled, an old axle cleaned, and wire needed for struts, stripped

from an old army encampment. Local carpenters carved the donkey, eagle and elephant from the picture and, when the wood ran out, two small beds were used in lieu of the lion and the whale. He insisted I have a go and, while he pushed it around, I filled the playground with cheering spectators. That evening a small makeshift platform was erected and, while I ate a meal on it, the whole village assembled below and around me. When I finished, the old man took center stage and for one hour conducted an open meeting, with me being the guest speaker, as streams of questions from my nationality, to the reasons for my bachelorhood flowed from the children. By my sixth tea, I was exhausted and that night found me in the old man's house, sleeping in their only wood-roped bed.

The following morning found me refreshed. I was now eager to experience the physical challenge of mountain cycling and from Hetauda, I gained increased momentum as the road started its ascent into the foothills.

A chance meeting with a travelling Sadhu found me following a little used gravel road from Bhaisedobhan to Bhenphidi "Short route to Kathmandu," he told me. Why was I so gullible ? At Bhenphidi the road predictably ended. Stretching from the Hindustani Plains to Kathmandu, it did circumvent both the Domar and Spyyang Passes, and he was also correct about the distance; it could be walked in a day, but what he failed to realize was that it was impossible to negotiate by bike, at least not mine anyway. Used daily by herds of buffalo, it was the main route and source of Kathmandu's meat, not its traffic and it took me two days to half-carry my bike over its rough trail.

If offered three travel wishes from the sixties, Kathmandu would top my list. Overpowering in its variety of wood carved and stone buildings, nearly every other a temple and, with a never ending street festival, Kathmandu was what dreams are made of. Looking at it for the first time, wrapped in its winter coat, only increased my thirst, and I quickly pushed on from Thankot down the valley.

As in any great city, underground sub-cultures had their own meeting grounds, and central to that in Kathmandu was Freak Street. My arrival coincided with their impending departure, and its transient population had an air of expectancy written in their eyes. Could it be the cold weather that glazed their pupils , an early morning joint of hashish , or could it be read in the way they stole glances at the storm clouds ? Like all migrating birds they huddled together in small flocks. One group all ready for take off milled around a sign penned in numerous foreign languages.

GOA FOR XMAS
ALL WELCOME
200 DOLLARS CASH ONLY
AIR COND. ALL MOD. CONS.
BRING YOUR GUITARS ALONG
LEAVE DURBAR SQUARE 12 DECEMBER

By now my priority was food and as I was on being Freak Street, I couldn't resist the temptation to sample their famous pies. First I tasted a Jumbo Banana Crumble. After that I had a huge slice of Coconut Crisp, and eventually topped up with a Chocolate Cream Flan.

"Are you English ?" A short man with Mongolian features and shaggy beard caught my arm as I left the restaurant.

"Yes I am ?"

"In the big war, I am in Gurkha Army. I fight by side of British."

"My father told me of your army's courage." I meant it.

"I like British very much."

"Thank you."

"You want to change money?" It came so quickly I didn't realize what he said at first. "You want to buy hashish ? You want Coke ? Smack ?" He was now saying them so quickly I didn't even have time to respond. "You like young boy ?" My face must have disclosed something. "Girl ?" His voice now sounded irritated. Then: "FUCK OFF! Stop wasting my time." I instinctively apologized, and he burst out laughing as if what he said had no meaning, then turned and left.

I had given friends two postal addresses in Kathmandu to cover myself against losses. First, the old faithful 'Poste Restaunte' and secondly, the more reliable 'American Express'. I went to the post office first. I had started using the poste restaunte service way back in Australia. Housed in every main city's Central Post Office their counters were invariably hidden from view, but here, in Kathmandu, due to the number of its travellers, occupied a quarter of its counter space. Queues were never hurried and always the air was full of excitement. Letters from home would often lead to tears, enclosed travellers cheques - to cheers and short messages from friend's missed en route - to sad faces, but for me todays events would take a much more unlikely turn. On reaching the counter I handed over my passport and after a quick search of H's was handed two letters. Outside I suddenly felt a shock. My passport was gone. Reaching for my wallet I found it empty I ran back inside.

"Have you found a passport ?"

A shake of heads across the counter answered everything. I turned to the Europeans in the queue. No one had seen it. I went outside again. It wasn't there either. I dashed back inside to try again.

"Maybe it fell into the tray. Can you look under 'H' again ?"

The teller calmly looked through the tray of letters again.

"Maybe it fell into another."

Counter transactions now came to a full stop while every tray was looked through. Had I dropped it ? Maybe it was stolen ? What should I do next, notify the Embassy ? The more I tried to calm myself down, the more I panicked.

Thirty minutes later I was blurting out my story at the British Embassy.

"You are Mr Howgate, Mr Bernard Peter Howgate ?" The official asked.

"Yes."

"Have you any other identification ?"

I handed him my American Express Card. He disappeared, only to return moments later with a sealed envelope.

"This was handed in only moments ago by a Nepalese gentleman. It was marked for your attention."

I couldn't believe my luck. A British passport was worth a small fortune on the Black Market.

"Could you please check all the contents? Then sign for it here,"

The money I had exchanged that morning was gone but that could be replaced easily but, more importantly, my passport was there and inside was a short note, "Enjoy Your Stay." I signed and left a little short of money, but with a new respect for the Nepalese people.

Next stop was the American Express Office. Then, in reverse order of importance, I read through the bundle of letters, leaving a letter from Alison till last.

Delhi/ Nov. 81
Dear Bernard,
    You will be glad to hear I will be at this address in Delhi at least
until February. I am living with a family in Delhi working and
looking after children. Look forward to seeing you.

    I replied at once.

Kathmandu/ Dec. 81
Dear Alison,
    Great to hear you're still in India, looks like we shall see each
other again. Hope you enjoy Christmas with your friends. See you
in the New Year.

    My plan was to cycle south to Goa, spending Christmas on the
beach relaxing under the sun, before cycling up to Delhi for the
New Year. But it wasn't to work out that way.
    I should have checked things on my bike more closely, but
Alison was still on my mind. I was speeding, not paying attention.
Sharp bends went unnoticed. A horn blasted out, I braked and a
truck passed like in a dream. Suddenly there was a blinding flash,
then-silence.
    Smells of oil and burning rubber were replaced by drifting
sensations.
    An unreal calm swept through me.
    People were staring at me from above.
    Nervous giggles.
    Then the pain.
    Two men helped me to my feet. More carried my bike.
    "No, Leave it."
    They were taking off my bags. The man supporting me was
talking but I could hear nothing. I resisted but his grip tightened.
His face turned. There was a look of genuine concern and I
allowed myself to be led away by it. Rice sacks were moved and
I was eased back into them. Water was brought, soap, towel,
cigarettes, and tea.
    My bicycle was a twisted wreck. Lodged between frame and
front wheel a shredded mosquito net told clearly what had

happened. I'd strapped it across the front bags before leaving but it must have loosened, and then trailed into the wheel spokes, jamming it into the frame. The front wheel's frame was bent 90 degrees from its original position, and the back wheel's frame must have snapped under the impact.

A young man bathed my face, locating the source of pain. A two inch long gash to the bone released flesh which flapped hideously over my left eye. Feeling sick and unable to touch it, I sat half blinded. I felt helpless, adrift, unable to cope with the slightest decision so, when someone helped me to my feet, I offered no resistance. My bike was moved again. We climbed the hillside to a small house. My bike was put into a store room. A key held in a loop of string passed before my face. The young guide pointed to the store room door then put it around his neck. Did I understand? Yes, he was reassuring me. I nodded my head, he smiled and we returned to the road.

All this time the young guide had not left my side. He gave instructions and shortly after, a damp cloth was put in my hand and directed to my eye. A truck stopped, more instructions. The driver came over to see me.

More looks of concern followed.

"I take you to Muggling. From there you can get the bus to Kathmandu."

Again my young guide pulled out the key.

"He ask you return when better." the driver translated, "Bicycle safe we go."

I thanked the driver, said goodbye to my guide and got into the truck.

Muggling was twenty miles away and while I waited in the truck our driver found me a bus.

"It leave when full."

"When bus full?" I didn't understand.

"There is no timetable." The driver shook his head, praised Allah, and left.

Thirty minutes passed and still the bus was half full. Loss of blood made my head swim and constant enquiries drained me. After sixty minutes I felt a sudden attack of nausea. Only wanting fresh air, the next thing I remembered was sitting in a small Medical Hut. I'd been found wandering in the road.

"Please still." A young Nepalese nurse was using cotton wool and tweezers to clean grit from my wound. Knees, elbows, and back grazes were splashed with iodine in a fire of antiseptic. Then a loud exchange of voices and once again I was outside.

"Bus waiting in road, go Kathmandu." She gave me a bundle of cotton wool and took me down to where a bus was waiting for me. The bus was packed to overflowing, but still people stood in polite obedience and I was spoiled for choice. I sat behind a small band of white faces. No words were exchanged. Why didn't they speak to me? Their pink skins and new clothes had the scented look of don't touch about them, and I sat in speechless anger, confused by their non-involvement. Reaching Kathmandu, I was teetering on the edge of violence. Nepalese, controlling their eagerness to get off, helped me to get to my feet. The whites ignored me; looked uncomfortable when I stared at them and got down right angry when I asked them for help. I was spoiling their holiday. Tourists embarrassed by my blood stained clothes passed me by without question. I asked a policeman directions to the hospital and not recognizing any of the landmarks, I was soon lost in the crowded streets. Suddenly a hand gripped me. Dressed in rural clothes, his kindly face made instant contact and I followed him like a blind man. At the hospital he took command, passing me through hospital formalities like a royal patient.

My accident had happened before 10:00 am and in the reception the clock said 5:30 pm. I was still in a state of shock and, up til then, I hadn't been bothered about the mayhem in the hospital or, for that matter, its unclean look. All I wanted to see was a familiar face.

At 6:30 pm I went into surgery and within minutes was surrounded by friendly shadows. Children wanting a better look had climbed the wall, and were now framed behind its barred window. An old couple peered from behind a closed curtain and an attendant nurse held my hand. Children now looked on inquisitively, women; caringly and men; with an eye to detail. Everyone seemed to be reaching out with encouragement. Here the link between doctor and patient was not isolated by the mask of technology.

The first series of injections was very painful, and I refused a second, deciding stitching pain would be the lesser of the two evils. After ten minutes it was done. To my relief I wasn't blinded, but I was told I might never be able to close my eye. The skin was so tight the least movement sent shock waves of pain through my forehead.

"You need tetanus injection." They had no more drugs or bandages left, I was expected to buy my own. By now my spectators were as much a part of my treatment as was my doctor, and no sooner had the doctor's request sunk in, when a young man was sent for.

"You give him money. He buy tetanus, foil, and bandages for you."

I handed my doctor my wallet. Money was counted and instructions given and thirty minutes later I was leaving in a bicycle rickshaw put at my disposal by my new found friends.

"Mr. Bernard! What happened?"

I'd left my hotel that morning. Shocked at my appearance, the receptionist rearranged guests and soon a room was found.

Kathmandu's illusion was shattered after this accident. Mornings were cast in freezing mist as winter's penetrating damp rolled off the mountains. Confined to bed for the next two days I sent out for food and rice wine. During the evenings I gained some relief from the smells of urine, as waves of hashish floated up from the rooms below where Europeans fired up for their nightly entertainment. Disembodied music rolled over roof tops, and chemically induced voices talked to the moon. Emotions during this period fluctuated wildly. The least problems exploded out of all proportion and , by the third day, I was glad for the excuse to fetch my bike.

Left to my own devices I spent all morning trying to locate the remote area of my accident. Luckily, a wildly cheering group of workmen recognized me riding in a truck. I was the bearer of gifts, but they wouldn't hear of taking them. Submitting myself to their enthusiastic welcome I spent the next few hours in their company, drinking tea and smoking hashish leaves, and then, cushioned on a cloud of carefree humour, I returned with my twisted wreck to Kathmandu.

Two days later my bicycle was miraculously mended. The back wheel frame had been cut and welded back together, the front wheel was painstakingly beaten straight again. Although not true, I felt the new angles and tilts would soon be absorbed and a trial spin only confirmed this thought. The following day I had my stitches taken out. My eye was still badly swollen but I could partially close it, even if it was painful. I took one last trip to the post office to send a telegram,

Kathmandu/ Dec 81
................Change of plans. Slight accident. Bike much worse than me. See you in Delhi for Christmas. Take care Alison.

Chapter 15:
Cross Roads

C YCLING FROM SUNRISE TO SUNSET, THE DAILY ANOINTing of sun rays had speeded up all surface healing processes but long days in the saddle were draining my insides out. Inevitably something was going to snap and, by my arrogant behaviour to people I met, sooner rather than later.

From Lumbini I crossed into India and straight into the waste land called Bihar State. Neglected by successive governments and sentenced to years of poverty and decay, here, frustrations had become pure aggression and, for the first time on my trip, I tasted fear.

Confused by directions in Bansi I enraged a crowd of onlookers with my temper and, to escape, I took to a maze of smoke filled streets. Screaming children pressed in from all directions. I turned; they stopped. I pretended to throw a stone; they scattered, only for their noise to attract older ones. Violence was now more than just a possibility. I looked back for escape routes. There were none. A young man ran forward defiantly. My invisible threshold snapped. I committed the worst kind of sin. Hemmed in on all sides, I panicked. I picked up a stone and threw it at him. Instantly the street echoed with screams. People, trampled underfoot, fought each other to get away and, within minutes, they had poured back on to the streets again. A stone bounced in the dust in front of me. I cycled towards them. Another stone hit the road, this time from behind. Another, then, another. Suddenly I came under a hail of stones. Some of the crowd broke cover and ran down the pavement towards me. Panic turned to despair.

"TOURIST...TOURIST...TOURIST..."

Waving my hands hysterically at the crowd I screamed out the first words that came into my head. They stopped. A momentary chord of silence tied them to the spot. I continued as if my life depended on it.

"TOURIST...TOURIST...TOURIST..."

My head started to pound. The noise got louder, but now it was with me. They had picked up my chant. The whole street echoed to tourist. Screams turned to laughter and moments later

I was being swept along by an excited crowd. The whole incident had exhausted me. My face was stinging with tears and my hands shook uncontrollably. Sitting down I tried to reconstruct the strands of events leading up to the first stone, but it was impossible. Violence which threatened to tear apart the street only moments before had melted away into a carnival atmosphere. Prominent members of the community came forward and I was escorted to a Christian Mission. "White Lady look after you." They spoke of an old Scottish Missionary and ten minutes later I was pouring out my story to her.

At the mission it was agreed that I should leave to diffuse the situation further. "It's not your safety that is in question, but that of the people who live in the Mission," she told me. "When the Dacoit's (band of thieves) hear that you are in town they will use it as an excuse for mischief, and mischief in Bihar means death. Better for everyone if you leave. My servant will act as guide. We have a mission in Basti. You will be welcome to spend the night there." She looked very serious and, to stress the point, she stood. "Never and I mean never throw stones at Indians. No matter how frustrated you feel, no matter what the situation, or their behaviour to you. Never forget it's their country not yours. You are passing through. They are not. They look at whites in a special way. White means privilege. It means many of the things you take for granted and that they will never get in this life. Today you were lucky, tomorrow you may not be." Then she added cheerily; "You must think I'm an old battle axe. I have been in India for over thirty years and I know these people better than most. You cannot meet a better race of people anywhere in the world. The way you reacted in that mob saved your life, so you must have done something right today."

At Allahabad I missed the direct route to Delhi. Thinking I was on the Grand Trunk Road I cycled to Rewa before realizing my mistake. I'd now added three days to my journey and this thought nibbled away at my confidence. Still I pressed on. The days were getting shorter. The winter's chill bit into my wounds and I cursed the day I'd sent my heavy 'goose down' sleeping bag home. At Gwailior, the fever returned and, entering Morena, I hit another hole. The handle bars twisted out of my hands. I was just too weak and I crashed to the road. The bike was O.K., but I was finished. A farmer stopped in his tractor and thirty minutes later, still pale and shaking. I was dropped outside Morena Police Station. My body now spoke for itself. A doctor was called and a room found.

In the morning I woke to find my bicycle propped up against the bed. The accident in Nepal and seeing its twisted wreck had brought home to me its importance. I couldn't see travel by any other means. It took me from A to B, untapped adrenalin and got me both into and out of trouble but, above all, kept me in the peak of physical health. So it was ironic that, setting off by bus to Delhi that morning, I was in the worst physical and mental state since starting.

My bike was on the roof and the sight of it entering New Delhi Bus Station sparked off near riot scenes, as dozens of porters attached themselves like leaches to my window. Prices were quoted and porters both verbally and physically competed for my business. To them it was work. For me, in my weakened state, an irritation. My white skin had opened up a glorious opportunity to earn a fortune in baksheesh and I played out its game to the hilt. I gave way to the cheapest, only to double payment when his comrades left. My action didn't leave me with good feelings and I cycled away confused with my new found power.

The Paharganj in Old Delhi offered multiple choice of hotels but booking, into its first, I immediately surrendered to sleep. The next day I lost no time calling the number Alison had given me.

"Hello, my name's is Bernard Howgate. Alison gave me this number. I'm an old friend just arrived in Delhi. Is she there ?"

"Yes she mentioned you were coming. She's not living here but I will tell her you've arrived. Where are you staying ?"

"I'm in the Paharganj at the moment, but I'm moving out tomorrow. Do you know Ringo's ?"

"I've heard of it, yes, just off Connaught Place."

I tried to get her address from him but was side tracked each time.   "Don't worry, she'll ring you."

The mystery puzzled me and, after two days' silence, I rang the number again. Within the hour my call was returned.

"Bernard, is that you ?"

Old memories came flooding back. Eighteen months had separated us. We had set off on our different trips within weeks of each other. Alison east and I west. Memories of our time together had distorted like a worn mirror. Bad experiences had long ago been dispatched and there was something unreal about

my life now. On the road I had no firm base from which to push off
from. Life was like one continuous dream of events and the
thought of meeting Alison again both excited and frightened me.

"Can you meet me at Ringo's, Alison ?"

"Yes, in one hour."

"I'll wait in the hotel. Great to hear from you again, lass."

The cancerous excitement spread rapidly. Soon my stomach
was knotted. I showered, shaved, and showered again. I needed
to hang onto something badly. She sounded so strong on the
phone. I was only faking mine. I wanted to make a good impression
and my bike was the only thing I could think of. I took it with me
outside and waited.

"Alison, over here."

She'd not changed a bit, looked even healthier than I remembered, but her forced smile distanced us in a way our separation
had never achieved. We were polite in that strangely British way
and conversation never strayed beyond the borders of small talk.
We went for a walk. I put my arms around her.

"No, Bernard. Indians don't like it."

We walked over to Connaught Place and sat down, then I gave
her a gift of sketches I'd compiled while travelling.

"Your Christmas present, don't open it now."

We'd been alone for twenty minutes and I was waiting for a
green light that never came. Suddenly she stood up.

"We must go. I have a friend I want to introduce you to. I look
after his children in Delhi."

While walking she gave me a leaflet to read.

"This is what I do here."

It was entitled 'Building a Better World', and had all the
hallmarks of militant sincerity. I thought it was obviously some
kind of volunteer work and the wording was full of poverty and
sharing wealth.

I was introduced to her friend Keith in a coffee bar and within
minutes found myself having to justify my trip to him. I talked of
travel. He talked of equality and, everytime I directed the conversation towards Alison, he deflected it. Keith had lived many years
in India and, with a stable family base behind him, spoke from a
depth of experience I couldn't match and the more we talked the
more uneasy I felt. In ten minutes he had systematically under-
mined my trip and I was glad when our meeting finished. We made

arrangements to meet again on Christmas day. Keith left with Alison and I was left holding a big question mark over my trip.

Christmas turned into a pantomime of music and kiddies games. Guitars were played, and soccer sides organized. I found myself joining in whole-heartedly. Yesterday's conversations were put on hold. Now there was something uplifting in their presence. Today I would have to justify nothing. Gone was the anaemic look I associated with travellers. Alison's friends all had healthy dispositions and it was refreshing to talk about ordinary things. I again felt relaxed and in command of my emotions. I was invited to dinner and later went dancing with her friends, not returning until the early hours of the morning to Ringo's. Her friends had immediately made me feel at home and even hints were made that I should stay, help them with their work. For the first time in eighteen months I felt totally at ease with strangers but, mainly, it was Alison.

The following morning she called.

"I'm going to Kerela in southern India with Keith, Shelia (his wife) and their kids tomorrow."

I was shocked. We had spent most of Christmas together and she'd not mentioned it.

"Why so sudden ?"

The question was never answered and before I could enquire further she suggested we meet that night. She quickly described our meeting place then the phone went dead.

That evening's wait was emotionally charged yet strangely false. Why all these formalities and short phone messages ? Why had I been kept waiting like a schoolboy before our Christmas meeting ? What was she hiding ? Each silent question threw up another answer and I was soon lost in a web of intrigue. We met as arranged and went into a coffee bar.

"I kept many things from you Bernard, in my letters."

She started to talk of her time in Israel, filling in many of the blanks left by infrequent letters and, slowly, a picture of loneliness unfolded. She spoke of a desperate effort to rise above it all, her heartless pursuits and of disillusionment, finally ending with her illness and the pain of isolation in Sri Lanka.

"What now, Alison ? You can't just look after other people's children. What of your future ?"

"I have a new family now. In Delhi I've found peace and

happiness. Here we don't believe in possessions. There is no his and hers. Here we all love each other."

Her sentence touched a nerve but, before it could hurt, she continued.

"Did you know that Jesus loves you, Bernard ?"

"Jesus ! What are you talking about ?"

"He loves all sinners. All you have to do is ask him into your heart and you will be saved. From the day we are born we want to do things our way. If things go right, we say it's because we did it, and if things go wrong we blame everyone except ourselves."

For no reason, except it was Alison who was talking, I felt terribly exposed. On the road I had come into contact with various religious groups but their forceful need to convert always left me unmoved. Like all salesmen there was something in the small print they couldn't answer. Religion had no place in my life and Alison must have read it on my face.

"Religion is not the answer Bernard. I don't believe in churches. I only believe in the love of Jesus Christ. Jesus is the passport to heaven. Jesus is the only love. To believe him is to confess him. Ask him into your heart. He's changed my life in so many ways. Ask him. If you love me, you must love him. I love him. All you have to do is ask him into your heart and you will be saved."

"Saved. Saved from what ?"

"I love you Bernard. If you love me ask him into your heart."

The word love held the key to my emotions. Suddenly the flood gates opened. Eighteen months of lone experience exploded to the surface.

"*Jesus loves you.*" I jumped through the sound of her voice. I was gone.

Chapter 16:
Picking Up the Pieces

A SHAFT OF LIGHT ILLUMINATED MY BEDSIDE TABLE. A letter lay open, addressed to Alison.

Kathmandu/April 82

.........April.....four months. What had happened ?

Dearest Alison,
   It's sad you couldn't make the effort to come over before I left, but then, you were my bait. The longer they kept you away, the harder I struggled with my conscience and the weaker I became. You are escaping from the world with a modern Guru, with no basis in reality. They feed you equal doses of love and discipline, then say, if you're not with us, you're against us. Nothing is black and white Alison, nothing is that simple. Please Alison take time away from the 'Children of God', judge it for yourself. Do it now before it is too difficult for you even to do that. I didn't dislike any of the people I met in Delhi. I'm sure they are sincere in what they believe, and they did shelter me, but what a price. It's their fanatical belief that worries me. Anything they do or say, and I mean anything, is justified in the name of Jesus. It's one thing to believe in the Bible and another to believe one hundred percent in what your leader Moses David says. You're isolating yourself from the outside world. Soon you won't have a mind of your own, because to question Moses David is to question God I'm told. Keith talks of systems, hypocrisy and unchanging views, but he is more fixed and fossilized in his own than any person I've met. Come fly with us he says. Fly where ? Can't you see you need earthing just as much as you need to fly ? Much of what I read by Moses David is just plain common sense. The rest sounds like the ramblings of an old man with a chip on his shoulder. Get them when they're young and disillusioned, he says. I've heard it all before, it leads to dogma and narrow mindedness. I was blinded to it for a long time, and it was only your presence, wanting to

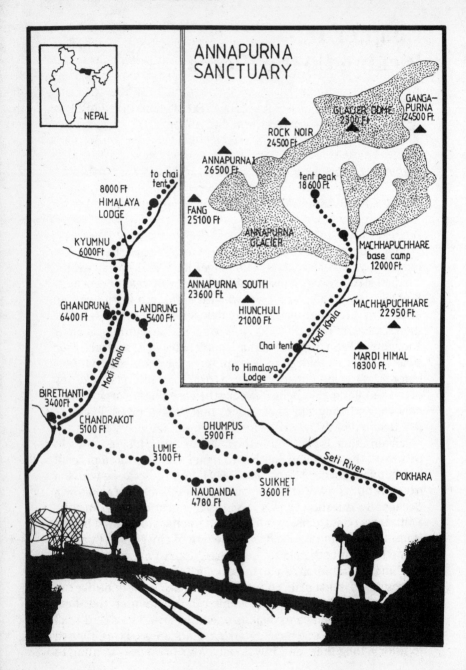

understand how you changed that kept me. The battles I had, coming to terms with unseen enemies. Every day bombarded with M.O. letters. Sex, Power, Money. I was beginning to see demons in every corner. I couldn't leave the house without praying, and at times I was even too paranoid to answer the door. Then there was you. I was put in a different house, and they would never let me see you on my own. The age old tactic of divide and conquer. It worked, didn't it ? Remember they even spirited you away just after Christmas. Some days I didn't know whether I was coming or going. I'd lost complete control, it was getting to the point where I questioned everything I did, and needed reassurance for even the smallest problem. I'm not saying it was all bad, no one forced me to stay and as they said the door was always open for me to leave, but then I'd given them all my money, I couldn't get very far......

I read and reread each word. Did it really happen ? You write truth as you see it, but it's never quite that easy. Was it sour grapes ? After all, it was her life, not mine. What right had I to complicate it ? We all reach cross-roads in life and, when it happens, hold on to that which directs us. I had offered Alison nothing and, the more I critized her new life by pen, the more I felt like a whimp.

It would take me years to come to terms with the decision I had made in Delhi but, as for the present, it was just a relief to continue. It would have sounded guilty had it not been. I posted the letter and that evening a group of tourists gave me the incentive I needed to pick up the pieces.

"Go to Pokhara. The Annapurna Sanctuary Trek will only take you ten days." I needed to set new goals to pull me out of my present state of mind and this sounded right. The mountain air would clear my head, adrenalin, my body and the natural high of going forward, the rest. In Kathmandu I got my trekking permit; in Pokhara, my boots, rucksack and sleeping bag. I was ready.

Starting out from Pokhara I spent all day walking in the basement of a glaciated valley before leaving its Seti River at Suikhet. The following morning I climbed the steep narrow steps to Naudanda. The day's program was set. I would now be following the contours of a high ridge. Collages of green topped by jagged peaks bordered my vision all day and, before it changed channels two thousand feet below in Birethanti, I got the first sighting of my goal, the razor edged Machhapuchhare Mountain. Already the fresh air was clearing my mind and, my constantly changing, happy-go-lucky walking companions were lifting my mood.

Day three was characterized by the Modi Khola River. Tracing its course up stream, first to Ghandruna, them Kyumnu, my tapered vision was edged in by a deep V shaped valley. By now the altitude was effecting me and after an eight hour walking day, sleep came quickly. For the last four days I had met up with the same group of holiday trekkers and in the evenings we found ourselves constantly praising our own achievements in efforts to forget sore feet. Since Birethanti the trail had got steeper and rougher and, stepping off the defined paths for a rest, meant being plagued by the spring's thirsty army of leaches. I had taken the precaution of putting plastic bags over my socks, but my friends were less fortunate and, taking their boots off that evening released pools of blood and, with it, their confidence. The next day saw the final straw for two of my travelling companions. In front the swollen Modi Khola River had to be crossed and the prospect of fording it over a rickety wood-rope bridge was just too much for them. As I pushed on up the trail, they turned back to Himalaya Lodge and a warm fire. There were only two of us left now and, to share our load, we repacked our rucksacks. I would carry the wood while he would carry both of our provisions. We had been told that to reach 'Tent Peak' in the Annapurna Sanctuary and return in one day was impossible. That meant a night out under the stars. Our hopes were now pinned on a little used climbing expedition base camp at the foot of Machhapuchhare but the information on this was sketchy to say the least. No one we asked knew for sure how much protection it would afford or, for that matter, if it had made it through the winter. To make matters worse, we were told that a recent avalanche, that only weeks before had plugged up the valley, had now melted creating a dangerous ice bridge.

Sticking close together we followed a narrow trail through damp clouds and clinging overhead forests and, by mid morning, the steep valley had closed into a deep gorge. Once into its jaws there was no turning back. The day was already half over but, with the trail now following natural glaciated cuts, we were making good time. One minute, the trail would cut deep into rock faces and the next, jut out precariously with nothing but a hundred feet of fresh air separating us from certain death. A loud crack echoed, then opened onto the sight of a huge wall of ice and rock. Time didn't allow for fear and within minutes we were climbing onto the avalanche's naturally formed ice bridge. For twenty minutes we picked our way slowly across it. Large cracks in the ice released terrifying roars from the river underfoot and dislodged stones, brought down by the avalanche and frozen into ice, afforded us our only secure footing. Spring thaws were in the air and, once over the snow bridge, the valley opened into areas of patchy brush. We were making good time but, by late afternoon, gliding snow flakes had turned into a dark blizzard. Again luck was with us. The base camp was marked with a red flag and once inside the makeshift shelter, our flagging morale was immediately boosted by its David and Goliath comedy team. The giant took on the form of a Swiss climber and, by the look of his rucksack, he obviously needed all his strength to carry it. We had unwittingly walked straight into his check list and, while my friend drooled over his vast array of pitons, ice picks and two way radio, I went over to speak to his friend. Dressed in only jeans, yak wool sweater and light weight runners, he looked the typical French Freak I had become accustomed to; underclothed, undernourished, but good fun. We hit it off at once and, while the others planned the following days route to Tent Peak, we set about pooling our resources and soon had the night's meal cooking over a roaring fire. That evening silence gathered only to be shattered by the sound of an express train. An Avalanche exploded in cracks of thunder followed by a frightening roar as clouds of snow raced down the mountain slopes. Darkness came like a light switch and, with it the frost, and we ended up pulling straws for the privileged sleeping positions closest to the fire.

The night moon was still clear and looked strangely out of place that morning as the mountain tops blazed in the red glow of sunrise, illuminating Tent Peak's high plateau in a blanket of orange. Everything looked and felt larger than life. We were over twelve thousand feet up and the Sanctuary entrance was covered in deep snow. After two hours walking we entered a magnificent natural amphitheater. Peaks rose and fell in a 360 degree sweep with Machhapuchhare's base camp far below. By now it was 10:00

am. The sun had just popped over the mountain and it was impossible to continue without sunglasses. Already my nose and cheeks were burned as the sun's rays reflected in the clear air like a mirror off snow.

Noon, and still we hadn't reached our goal. We had left the French Freak behind at base camp and our Swiss companion was now only a speck in the far distance. The snow was melting rapidly. Its frozen crust started to crack and, not wanting to court disaster, we decided to retrace our steps to Himalaya Lodge, and a warm bed.

Shattering news. Gathered around a portable radio that night, we listened in shock to reports of the Falklands. All eyes turned on the Brits and we were bombarded with questions.

"I can believe the French going to war, even the Italians, but never the British. You are supposed to be the most stable country in Europe." An American traveller questioned me. "Is this a legacy of the British Empire?" I was as much in the dark as he was. It was the first I'd heard of the Islands. Since New Zealand, world news had been none exsistant and I found this revelation confusing. I thought Colonial Empires were a thing of the past. Had I been away that long? I couldn't even find a sense of national pride.

The Falklands crisis followed me all the way back to Pokhara. Every night I was glued to the radio. A ship was sunk. Hostilities on the land. I had visions of a global war but, still, I couldn't believe the reasons given on the radio for invasion. Then, "Argentinian forces surrender".

"You bloody British. You're using people as an excuse, it's just their land you want. I bet there's oil under the island." This time I was being questioned by a Dutch traveller. "What other reason could there be, even to the untutored? The strategic value is useless, it has no airfield."

I had no stomach for arguments like these and once, in Pokhara, stayed clear of further questions.

By the time I returned to Kathmandu the crisis was over. The trek had been the tonic needed to get myself fit and the Falklands crisis put my own problems in perspective. I now looked forward to India, Delhi and my bicycle again.

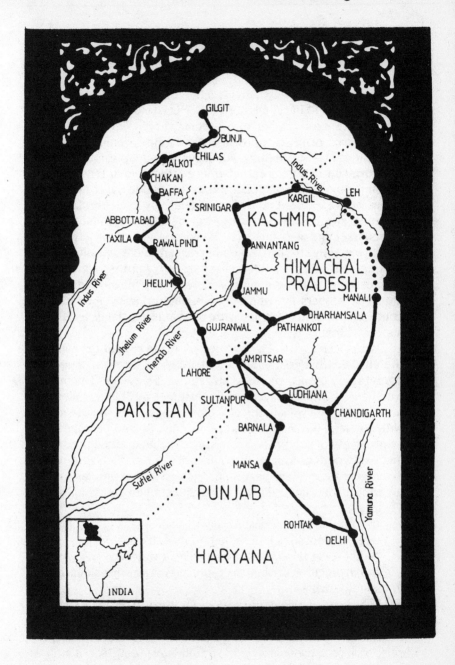

Chapter 17:
On the Road Again

A LOUD REPORT OF GUNFIRE SPLIT THE EARLY MORNING silence. I'd cycled into a sectarian war. Trapped within a maze of intricate passageways I found myself hemmed in on all sides by a seething crowd. Only thirty minutes before I had been drinking in the calm atmosphere of the Golden Temple. Now screams of violence rushed towards me. Suddenly, armed Sikhs appeared. One, bleeding from the head, his eyes burning with violence, stopped. We exchanged glances then a whistle broke our contact and, seconds later, khaki dressed militia appeared. Seeing me, they stopped. An embarrassed salute was offered, as if in apology, then they too disappeared. Another whistle announced the police and, batons drawn, they hit out indiscriminately at passers-by, while people, sheltering in open shops, continued to watch events with the same partiality as if at a soccer match.

With the ferocity of a bush fire, violence spread throughout the city. Death's contagious spirit inflamed its message to all corners and by nightfall, the streets were deserted to curfew. Numbed by violence, yet not threatened by it, the following morning I took a walk in the city. The main streets were teaming with soldiers, bazaar shops were boarded up and passageways were empty of shoppers. Yesterday's garbage soiled the street and packs of dogs fought over the spoils of riot. Small groups of Sikhs were stopped and searched. Allowed to pass unquestioned, my white skin of neutrality stayed unquestioned until the Golden Temple.

"Sorry, you cannot pass."

Over fifty soldiers had sealed off its entrance.

"What was the reason for yesterday's violence?"

A Sikh officer described in graphic detail a sacrilegious insult to his holy shrine.

"The head of a slaughtered cow was thrown onto the steps of the Temple. It was this incident that sparked off the violence." He then described how Temples guards rushed out, seeking reprisals. "For your own safety you should leave. Amritsar is a time bomb. No one knows when it will explode." It was sound advice and, on returning to my lodgings, I made immediate arrangements to leave the following morning.

Since Nepal my travel had gained renewed impetus and walks in the mountains had only whetted my appetite for more. It was now the end of May and, having returned to Delhi by train, I was soon suffocated by the heat. Excuses were not needed to head north, the heat could be felt everywhere. Pavements melted into oppressive hazes and mosquitoes, attracted to body odour, attacked mercilessly. With no breezes, the nights were breathless and during the day early monsoon clouds only added humidity to an already heavy atmosphere. Thoughts of Laddack and Kashmir suited present moods and the day Sikh violence spilled onto the streets around Connaught Place, I decided to leave. I picked up my bike at Ringo's, and headed north up the Grand Trunk Road.

From Amritsar the road started its course upwards to the Banihal Pass where, cutting thousands of feet off the summit, it passed through a tunnel. This tunnel marked the border between Hindu Logic and Muslim Discipline. Married in blood through historic struggle, these two opposing forces are separated by the Himalayas, a geological barrier the British found impregnable. On the northern side the Vale of Kashmir was a blanket of lush greens and, dropping down into the valley, a rarified atmosphere was replaced by the vibrant feel of business and prosperity. Even, at first glance, this mountainous Empire was for India what Switzerland was for Europe, a playground for the rich and, on entering Srinigar, I was accosted by dozens of enterprising young boys. Business revolved around exchange and literally any western good had a price. Even my bike drew offers and, to one group, sixteen hundred rupees wasn't too much, considering the exchange rate, twice its worth. It took me one hour to negotiate a house boat and another to have my bike rowed out to it. Once on board I wasn't in a hurry to leave, spending the next few days planning my trip to Leh.

Leh, situated in Ladakh, was the only remaining part of Tibet one could visit easily, and a quick visit to the Kashmir Tourist Information Office in Delhi had produced one sketchy map of dubious quality, and only a few paragraphs of information.

"Ladakh lies in the North East corner of the Himalayas and is

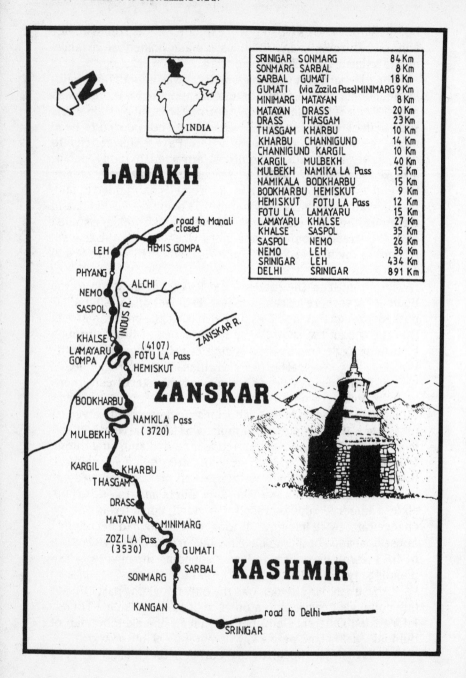

SRINIGAR	SONMARG	84 Km
SONMARG	SARBAL	8 Km
SARBAL	GUMATI	18 Km
GUMATI	(via Zozila Pass) MINIMARG	9 Km
MINIMARG	MATAYAN	8 Km
MATAYAN	DRASS	20 Km
DRASS	THASGAM	23 Km
THASGAM	KHARBU	10 Km
KHARBU	CHANNIGUND	14 Km
CHANNIGUND	KARGIL	10 Km
KARGIL	MULBEKH	40 Km
MULBEKH	NAMIKA LA Pass	15 Km
NAMIKALA	BODKHARBU	15 Km
BODKHARBU	HEMISKUT	9 Km
HEMISKUT	FOTU LA Pass	12 Km
FOTU LA	LAMAYARU	15 Km
LAMAYARU	KHALSE	27 Km
KHALSE	SASPOL	35 Km
SASPOL	NEMO	26 Km
NEMO	LEH	36 Km
SRINIGAR	LEH	434 Km
DELHI	SRINIGAR	891 Km

incredibly dry, as little rainfall can penetrate this formidable barrier. The road climbs over three major passes, and is paved all the way, the only exception being the portion which goes over the Zozila Pass. Due to constant avalanches in spring it is always in need of repair."

The information leaflet wasn't exactly an encyclopaedia of travel and the map's scaled mileages left much to the imagination. In fact, the only information which would remain constant was of the lack of food and water along route and, with that in mind, I bought extra water containers and stocked up with mixed bags of oats, dried fruit and nuts before leaving.

Refreshed from my stay on the house boat I set off on my first stage to Leh. At first Dal Lake's early morning mist blocked my vision and it wasn't until climbing into the foothills that the bone chilling dampness left. Already small villages, I passed through, showed little evidence of tourist exploitation and it was a relief to shake off Sringar's passion for high pressure salesmanship. During my short stay the whole valley had taken on the form of a huge outdoor supermarket. To be a Tourist was to have dollars and everything seemed geared up for maximum profit from them. Now each passing mile decreased my worth in dollars and its balance was replaced by the currency of curiosity. When stopped at tea shops locals insisted on paying for me and restaurants were just as free with their food. All day I followed steep inclines and from Ganderbal the close proximity of trees gave way to the patchy vegetation of mountain flora. In Sarbal ground frost carpeted my first morning and, as it would be sometime before the sun rose above my mountain corridor, I responded by taking an extended breakfast. Having spent the last year cycling in tropical climates, my body was now stung by this cold dry atmosphere and it was not until mid-day, when I reached the foot of the Zozila Pass, that I warmed up to cycling. By now the luxury of a tarmac road had deteriorated into broken gravel. Above, six miles away by road, but only four thousand feet by flight, bathed in sunlight and, in places, twenty foot deep, was the source of the road's deterioration. Cut through by the road, precarious ice-walled corridors were constantly melting and their deep rutted road streams made it impossible to continue except by foot. For two hours I pushed my bike. Excitement mounted as the summit came into view, but relief at reaching it soon went. Mountain curtains shadowed the valley ahead. Steep faces of rock closed down my view and my breath echoed in the silence. Exposed, wet and tired, I chilled to the full force of a biting wind. I had no protective anorak, no overtrousers and I was regretting my lack of preparation. The descent was full of switchbacks and as I sped down, the countryside changed noticeably. Skies were birdless, ground-barren. The valley was a ghostly shell, and it took all my reserves that afternoon to reach Drass.

The following day, I dropped down to Drass River and followed its course up stream all morning to Kargil. The road now started to show constant wear and tear from yearly thaws. Large holes pitted the road and where the valley opened out, evidence of landslides scared slopes like deep red wounds.

Once an important trading post, Kargil was now reduced to an overnight stop for truck convoys en route to Leh. Although the area was still heavily Muslim, I saw, for the first time, Tibetan influences. A group of red robed Buddhist Monks were shopping in its small bazaar. Women from Zanskar, colourfully dressed in traditional clothes, traded goods of Yak wool to local businessmen and children, dirty faced and impish, played street games freely in total contrast to their more disciplined Muslim brothers. Cycling into the center of the town — a ramshackle assortment of new and old buildings with a population counted in hundreds — I stopped at the Yak Trail Hotel. On advice in Srinigar I was keen to try the local brew, 'Chang'. Made from rice paddy, its potency was legendary amongst travellers in this region and at first taste was bloody awful but, after a couple of glasses, it left you with a thirst for more. Soon I was on my third and, on leaving, I staggered two miles out of town before collapsing fast asleep in a small field by the roadside.

By now the scenery reflected a dry arid climate. Skies were empty of colour. A lunar landscape of scorched red boulders dominated my world and although the road had deteriorated badly I made good progress. Army truck convoys broke into my peace once a day but, apart from this intrusion, I was left alone. It had been four days since leaving Srinigar but it all seemed light years away. Loneliness was now my universe and my imagination - my friend. Cycling in the mountains had forged a new me. No pass was too steep. Once again I relished the pain of physical challenge and Namkila-La Pass was conquered easily.

Leaving Kargil had meant leaving Muslim influences. Gone were the austere domed mosques which had seemed to dominate the center of every village passed through. In their place, sometimes perched on the edge of cliffs and sometimes dominating valleys like medieval fortresses, were Buddhist monasteries and that evening in Bodkharbu the disjointed sounds of monks chanting interspersed with horns and bells, rocked me to sleep.

The morning started badly. Half way up the imposing Fortu-La Pass I was caught in a freak snow storm and without shelter I was forced to continue, if only to keep warm. Nearing the top, noises of an army convoy snaked up the pass ten miles behind, and thousands of feet below. Because the switch backs were so shallow I could ride them with no problem and it was a slow motion thirty minutes before the convoy caught me. Passing in smoke screens of dust and exhaust they forced me to stop. At one point, a Sikh army driver stopped for a chat. More joined us. Food and drink appeared. Again I fell into the trap of eating too much and after the convoy left, I found myself pushing my bike, my stomach having grown to unusual proportions. By noon I'd reached the top. At this altitude the air was extremely pure and I drank in its cool crispness like a wine connoisseur. I now took time out to take in the view. My bike was rested; bags emptied. I took out two chapatis, filled them with honey, then sat back into my thoughts.

"TOURISK...TOURISK...TOURISK..."

From nowhere appeared a group of Tibetan children, seemingly more interested in my bicycle than me. I decided to give them an impromptu performance of trick cycling. Nothing impressed them. Soon they became restless. My audience started to drift away. Then I changed gears. Miracles ! They broke out in spontaneous cheers. Time and time again I was made to change them, each time sparking off excited shouts. With a child's appetite for new things they soon wanted more and when I couldn't deliver they quickly showed their boredom. Too soon it was time to leave. Now it was my turn to be a child. Soon I was enjoying the exhilarating feeling of freewheeling down sharp switch-backs, taking corners at blinding speed. Sheer drops of thousands of feet held no danger then, missing a corner, I careered down a goat track. Miraculously nothing was damaged but the shock broke my momentum and snapped me out of my dangerous lack of discipline. Half way down, the imposing view of Lamayaru Gompa dominated the view. Drawn by its oasis I left the main road and soon became the center of attention in a sea of red coats. At the Gompa I was met by a saffron robed monk. By now the whole courtyard was swarming with children. A rope was produced. An old man pointed to my bike, then to the roof and before I had time to object, he had hauled it out of the reaches of inquisitive hands under the roof. "No touch, no harm," the monk said. For the next few days I rested up behind closed doors, reading, writing and sketching from memory the passes I'd just climbed.

From Lamayaru I continued down the pass to Khalse and to my first view of the sacred Indus River. The valley road to Saspol was getting steeper by the mile, but what that day lacked in interesting features, brought on by riverside monotony, was more than compensated for by increasingly surprising views down tributary valleys and of the occasional Tibetan, totally oblivious to my presence, walking in the middle of the road.

My rest in Lamayaru had been counter-productive. Cycle rhythms were broken, dull aches became burning pains. Cramps racked my body and, feeling sick. I stopped at Nemo. It hadn't been my intention to stay, but the doctor had different ideas and, while he proudly showed me around his small clinic, his wife prepared us a meal of rice and dhal. He insisted I stay and that night I slept on a surgical couch, to be awakened with tea and chapatis in the morning.

By now my body was accustomed to high altitudes and Leh was made before noon. I had now completed my first 'planned' trip in nearly two years. I was beginning to feel like a tourist and celebrating the completion of my trip from Srinigar at the 'Dreamland Restaurant' on good old egg and chips, I was already planning another trip.

Chapter 18:
Roof Top of the World

THE DECISION NOT TO RETRACE MY STEPS TO SRINIGAR was made, as many before, on the spur of the moment. A short conversation with an Indian Major lit the fuse of my imagination. He told me of seven mountain passes over twelve thousand feet and two over seventeen thousand feet. It was a chance in a lifetime, and I wasn't about to let go of it easily. I immediately researched a trail from Lamayaru to Darcha and calling in Leh's small Tourist Information Office I was told it was feasible. Passes should be clear now. If not totally thawed out, they would at least be safe from major avalanches. The only foreseeable danger would come from ice bridges, but in all probability, I could by-pass them. With the help of their office staff I constructed a map of village names, distances, rivers to be crossed and most important, the route to take over the two snowbound passes. Having put together what I thought was a reasonable map I set about buying a rucksack and hiking boots, before booking the bike on an army plane to Chandigar, to be picked up later.

Outside, the night was warm and peaceful. Unseasonable winds from the south had punctured mountain corridors and I took this to be a good omen. In Leh I found no one to join me. Either through time or fear, most found the idea of walking for three weeks in the mountains without a guide and with only a home-made map for directions foolhardy, but no-one had been able to deter me either. Buying a rucksack wasn't hard, since many tourists on hearing of my trip were more than willing to help me, but boots were a problem. Big sizes were hard to come by and filling a size ten took over a week. For food I bought six pounds of powdered milk, a jar of honey, two dozen chocolate bars, a dozen packets of powdered soup, a packet each of coffee and tea and a bagful of dried peaches. Now as ready as ever I would be, I lay down in my new sleeping bag exhausted with excitement and slowly emptied my mind of future plans. If I wanted to think of passes, I would have to do it in the clearer light of day, and do as they say, take one day at a time.

Om Mani Padme Hum

The following day I joined a truck convoy going to Srinigar and getting off at Lamayaru, I spent the night in the Gompa Rest House before setting off the following day.

There's always barriers to be broken before you're able to touch the people, and to overcome this you have to do things their way first. Walking in the Himalayas is a great leveller so, five days into the trek, my burned face, tired gait and sweaty brow were all the passport I required. I'd overcome first day jitters in Wanla and, having already put four eight-hour days walking over fourteen thousand feet behind me, any physical doubts about fitness for altitude had gone. Feelings of isolation through not meeting any other travellers only invigorated me and my sense of exploration had been heightened at every pass. Zanskar's hard bitten physical beauty excited me, and its friendly people dispelled any fears I'd felt about the unknown. I'd found no problem staying in villages and what little food I had, was always shared in payment.

I'd left behind the peach orchards of Wanla, the shallow irrigated valley at Fanjila and sheer walls of stone, resembling church organs and ice bridges at Hanupata. Sirsirla's pass of sixteen-thousand-plus feet had baptised me in rarified atmospheres and, on its summit, I found new thresholds of endurance. At Photoksar I waded thigh deep in swollen ice waters and at Bumitsela, losing direction, I tested footing to the limit over a river of sharp glaciated boulders. At the bottom of Singela I was introduced to the natural quilt of alpine flower arrangements and, climbing its slopes, I saw my first snow-bound pass. Every day Chalkams beaconed my way and I was already five of them along going by my surprisingly accurate home made map.

Although past noon the sky was still royal blue and had not diluted in colour since early morning. I'd been walking for four hours since leaving Yulchung and in that time I'd followed a roller coaster of small intermediate passes, each traced with a draftsman's precision in zig-zag patterns up almost vertical passes, and each holding the promise of new and exciting vistas ahead. Underfoot the path had gradually softened from the morning's uneven surface of stone, to that of powered dust and Yak droppings. I was clearly nearing a major settlement.

Suddenly Linshet's green oasis came into view. Splashed in colour thousands of feet below, its inviting smudge opened like the leaves of a book on either side of the valley and, descending into it, my senses were soon bathed in the sweet smells of lavender growing in small pools of shadow around boulder outcrops. The scene that followed couldn't have changed in hundreds of years. Five day's walk from the Leh/Srinigar road and still a further three from the Muslim outpost of Padum the Buddhist stronghold was still secure and, going by the uncomplicated stone houses, one that would last much longer than its present inhabitants. It was here to stay and, like its surroundings, had bent and blended to suit natural conditions.

As I entered the village small boys, their faces caked with dirt and snot, ran towards me. An old man spinning his prayer wheel with trance-like serenity only looked up long enough to give his hand a rest then, having satisfied his curiosity, gave it another twirl. Young girls, heads topped by large floppy hats giggled nervously and my scent set off a chorus of barking dogs. Immediately I was swallowed up by an intricate network of connecting tunnels. Forced undercover by harsh winters the village's dimly lit nervous system soon had me mistaking cells of human occupation for courtyards. I accidently walked straight into someone's kitchen and far from being suspicious or angry at my trespass, I was met with a delightful old world hospitality, and, leaving my rucksack behind their closed doors with an undertaking to return later for an evening meal, I set a program to spend the rest of the day sight seeing around my first Tibetan Gompa.

Likened to many of the great European Monasteries for its majesty and mystique, the Gompa's treasures were soon opened for me to view. Under the wing of a friendly Lama I was taken into its magnificent inner hall, where totally unrestrained children played freely while aged monks, cross legged and bent over enormous books, were in studious debate. Buttered tea (made from Yak milk) was offered, but its taste defied explanation, and I left it for further hall investigation. Inside, niches and alcoves were adorned with silk hangings and private cells for meditation were lit by fragrant ghee lamps. Murals of vivid reds and greens gave life to outer walls and from within, gold Buddhas, future and past, warlike and calm, each with a different expression and posture, looked on, down and sideways from elevated positions. A large spinning wheel secured to the floor dominated one small cubicle, and its adherent, an old bearded man, rotated it, notching up merit to Buddha at every turn. Chantings and incantations drifted down darkened corridors and the air was filled with heavy scents of herbs and dust. I stayed for hours. People came and went, but I was given little notice. The currency of curiosity held no meaning inside the Gompa's walls, but once out, the throng of children soon surrounded me.

That night I slept on the family's roof and as the fires of sunset began to illuminate the mountains, the disjointed noise of horns, bells and pipes announced the day's end and, almost before its echoes were a just memory, stars sparkled in the sky. At this altitude it was hard to estimate time. During the day the sun seemed to hang directly above for hours and in the evening, once it was behind the mountains, it dropped rapidly. That evening the constellations looked so vivid I felt I could touch them and satellites arcing across my roof top horizon, flickered in and out at regular intervals.

From my rooftop bedroom the trail over Hanumala Pass was clearly defined, but no sooner had I put Linshet behind me than I was lost in a confusion of splintered trails. Three times I had returned to this major intersection. With the base of Hanumala hidden by a barrier of smaller hills, it was impossible to gauge which trail to take and my first three choices either petered out into Yak trails or, once over, bore off at right angles from the direction I was heading in. I had spent the best part of the morning, looking for that with which a compass and proper map would have posed no difficulty to find, and when I eventually found the right trail, I pushed on without resting to make up for lost time. That night I knew I would have to sleep outside. Nertse was deserted and Hanumil was eight hours walk for a Tibetan, let alone a beginner like me and the last thing I wanted was to be caught out under the stars at sixteen thousand feet. Resting up at the top of passes was cold enough and, after thirty minutes, I invariably wanted down. Thin air stung my throat and climbing Singela I had suffered a nose bleed. Now, en route up Hanumala, ice cold springs refreshed me, and mixed with powdered milk and spoonfuls of honey, these watering holes were providing much needed pit stops for gaining energy. The pass turned out to be less formidable than I'd first thought and after two hours it shaved off into a gentle rise. Linshet was now only a speck in the valley below and still clear with its light covering of snow, I could retrace my steps from the previous two days, all the way back to Singela. For the rest of the day my course sloped down. Gradual declines dropped into a deep gorge then tumbled onto broken steps of mountainous boulders. Ice bridges again had to be negotiated and at one point they paralleled a waterfall whose mist left every foothold covered in slime. Half way down, the trail lipped over into an adjacent valley and at one point came terrifyingly close to the edge of a sheer thousand foot drop. That day wasn't for the faint hearted and by sunset at the base of Parfila, I was exhausted.

After Parfila Pass the trail dropped into the deep Zanskar valley and for the next two days any lack of interesting features brought about by the blinkered view of the valley ahead was more than compensated by its numerous friendly villages.

Arriving in Padum my first priority was food. Reachable by truck from Kargil for three months of the year, the small settlement was already a hive of activity when I got there. Make-shift hotels, only just opened, overflowed with the season's first tourists and shops, not yet fully stocked for the summer visitor offered little in the way of food. What they had was expensive. A packet of biscuits worth one rupee in Delhi and two in Leh, now rocketed to five. A newly-built Mosque took central position and boomed daily messages down the valley to adheres and non adheres alike and, in doing so, underscored Kashmir's entrepenurial intrusion. Soon there would be no more careless summers in Zanskar. Already the road from Kargil was being upgraded and plans were afoot to push its arteries deep into the surrounding valleys. The new road would drain Zanskar of its unique unspoiled innocence and if change came too quickly, it would be shattered. I thought I'd never passed through a more peaceful picture but it had become a sadder one when I contemplated its future. Soon the natural silence so abundant in the valley would be replaced by man made noises. I stayed three day resting, then, following a truck convoy of food from Kargil, I set off once more.

Unlike the maze of splintered trails which dogged my progress from Lamayaru, the trail I was now following from Padum was well defined and hugging the Tsarap River's gradual slope, I made Tangse by mid afternoon on the second day. All thoughts were now preoccupied with Shingula Pass. Over seventeen thousand

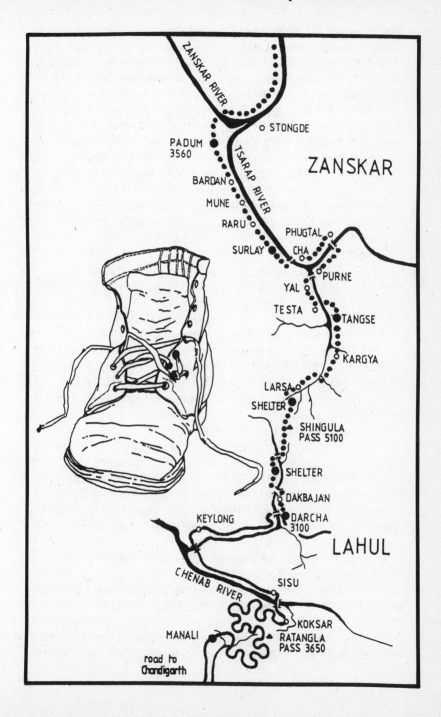

feet, it would be my last and highest climb to negotiate. Snow-bound all year round, it would have only just opened and trails over the snow, I was told, may not have packed down sufficiently enough for walking. I left Padum without any clear knowledge of conditions and left it in the hands of weather conditions and luck.

Camping at the edge of Tangse I encountered a guided tour of American tourists. At first I was intoxicated by their names, Sue Ann, Mary Lou, J.J., Dick, Carl, and my eyes warmed to their vast supply of decorated baggage. A Sony Walkman was offered for my amusement, the Herald Tribune for my starved mind and to feed my aching stomach their Nepalese cook was informed of an extra place at dinner. While one of their guides took their horses down to the river, a plate full of tinned ham and a bottle of Indian beer materialized in my hand.

"Hello. I'm Teddy."

Their Indian group leader introduced himself and soon conversation turned to Shingula. He hadn't come from that direction but, but he added a timely piece of advice.

"Shingula should be O.K., but I wouldn't attempt it on your own. Go back to Padum and hire yourself a guide."

His advice fell on deaf ears. Once bitten I found it impossible to let Shingula go. I'd been thirteen days on my own, crossed six passes, broken old barriers and found new strengths and the thought of being defeated with only one pass to go was too painful to contemplate.

"Is there any danger from avalanches ?"

"No, not at this time of the year. Your only problem is finding the trail. You have to set off early before the snow melts but, in the morning, the pass could be hidden in mist so if you don't know the route, it's easy to get lost." He must have read the determination on my face, so continued. "Have another beer, if you're stupid enough to do it on your own, you might as well make your last one a good one."

Teddy's bold stroke humour and broad veined hospitality was a typical throw back to the days of the British Raj. Sikh in dress, but western in outlook, we spoke in equal terms and that night set the seal on a friendship that lasts to this day.

It was June 13th. I didn't think I was superstitious, but the number hung in ominous cloud formations all day. Ahead

Shingula's snow capped barrier stretched across my path and on reaching Larsa's nomadic settlement, I forked south into a valley of rock avalanches. One hour into its corridor clouds of mist closed in but, by late afternoon, they'd evaporated and I could clearly see the pass as a narrow slit in the distant peaks. I had been walking without rest for eight hours since Tangse and, on seeing the rock shelter Teddy described at the foot of the pass, I cursed my laziness for not crossing Tsarap's tributary when I'd had the chance at Larsa. Numerous fast flowing streams blocked me from my goal and, to make matters worse, a thin layer of slippery moss made every step a balancing act. No sooner had I started to cross than I found myself thrashing about like an upturned turtle in eighteen inches of glacial water. I was soaked and my spirits, so high at reaching this point, were instantly extinguished. At the shelter I took stock of the damage. Boots, socks, jeans all were saturated, but, thankfully, I'd anticipated the worst, and had thrown my sleeping bag over the water first. At fifteen thousand feet I was in no-mans land. In front of me the valley tapered off to a dead end wall of solid rock and behind me was four hours of nothing. I needed heat badly and for the next hour. I scavenged on the valley floor for burning material. Dried moss, Yak dung and my priceless Herald Tribune lit a fire in the shelter, but within minutes they'd gone out.

Luck, that major ingredient in all my unplanned trips, once again came to my rescue. A caravan train of horse-back Tibetans materialized at the bottom of the pass and, seeing my smoke, it changed direction.

It hadn't been unusual for me to spend all day walking in isolation so, meeting this band of people, at this time of day, and in this secluded valley, was nothing short of miraculous. Within seconds they had weighed up the situation. A long length of dried cloth appeared. My wet clothes were folded, wrapped in its length and beaten against the shelter's stone wall. While I stood half naked and shivering, another man, flask of paraffin in hand, went inside to relight my fire then, before leaving, mouthfuls of fiery chang were offered. That night, warmed by a smouldering yak dung fire, beneath a sod roof shelter, I fell asleep.

A moving mass of morning mist blotted out all but the lower reaches of my initial climb. I'd spent thirty minutes on a breakfast of honey, peanut butter and tibetan bread. Even if my clothes weren't dry, I wasn't going to turn back through lack of energy. At first, the trail was easy to follow. Below the mist, vision was good and when the trail rose above the snow line, it was clearly stained in Yak and donkey droppings. Then it happened. Local mist rolled, fell and burst right on top of me. Suddenly the trail splintered. The cheerful countenance I'd had only moments before vanished. To survive in these circumstances you have to control all fear but, at that instant, I wasn't doing a very good job at it. I could still see the trail I'd just come on. I hesitated, then within seconds it was lost to mist. All this had happened on a small open plateau. There were no steep gradients to fence in my path. Lost, I wandered. The stained surface of snow seemed to have no borders. For what felt like hours I slowly climbed. Directions held no meaning. The route I'd chosen got steeper and steeper. Footholds were getting softer and virgin snow sometimes left me struggling, thigh deep, trying to extricate my feet. Two right angle bends were negotiated and an overhang traversed. Suddenly, I was flattened by a burst of air. Ahead a window of mist opened and before me loomed a vertical wall of emerald green ice. Hemmed in on three sides I climbed from one snowy shelf to the next then a vista I'd never even dreamt of exploded around me. In front I had 180 degree unobstructed view of mountain ridges and countless hidden valleys. I was still some way off the summit but, to the east, high peaks forced through hollows of cloud pointed out where I had made my mistake.

Sitting down I tried to work out were I was. Nothing looked familiar. Below and to the south the snow was whiter than white, and the valley I had started in was obscured by mist and jagged peaks. I must have been over eighteen thousand. I thought of all the things that hadn't gone wrong on my trip, but nothing compensated for the present. Slowly I was being engulfed by a feeling of detachment. It had started in my extremities. My toes had deadened in the soft snow and my fingers had been lost to the overhang. By now tingling sensations had reached my knees and shoulder cramps pinched. Frost bite was taking hold. I had to make tracks.

I stood up, bowed to an imaginary audience, and in less than a dozen leaps, half skied and half bounced down the steep slope onto a plateau hundreds of feet below. It all happened so quickly they nearly disappeared from view before I'd picked myself up.

There, less than a hundred yards in front of me and half obscured below the plateau's lip, a saffron robed Lama sat astride a Yak with a dozen attendant monks in tow. I'd stumbled onto the pass's summit in no uncertain terms. Time was now as blue as the sky. I went over to the passes chalkam and placed a stone, I'd been carrying, with the rest of the lucky charms and prayer flags, then sat down to enjoy a well deserved smoke. I remembered little of the downward side of Shingula and when I did eventually surface in the present, it was in Darcha.

The euphoric feeling of achievement didn't last long. One cursory look at my clothes told its own story. My boots were now held together more by luck than thread and sealant. My shirt was shredded, socks holed, jeans split and what remained of my rucksack's tubular frame didn't even bear mentioning. As for my body, once my boots were off, the soles of my feet ballooned and toes webbed. Two nails had started to go black through cold and both small toes looked a ghastly shade of yellowy brown. I stayed two days, healing, feeding and sleeping on the floor in one of Darcha's three postage stamp size hotel-cum-restaurants, eating them out of house and home and all three heaved great sighs of relief when I eventually left on Manali's bi-daily bus service.

Twentyfour hours later I was patronizing Manali's hot springs. Indulgent as ever I had paid over the odds for a private cubicle and, closing the door on the aches and pains of travel, I relaxed into its waves of wondrous heat and friendly humidity.

Before leaving, I visited Manali's European style weekend flea market, but it was not what I expected and its picture would haunt me for years to come. I was shocked by what I saw. Casualties of the once youthful, high flying peace and love movement of the sixties, Manali's floating population of aging hippies had deteriorated into skeletons of human decay. Grouped together, but divided by their countries of origin, they sat in idol worship of the God Shiva and, as they lit up one chillum after another, plumes of sweet smelling hashish rose into the air. Eyes stared out from darkened holes and their owners' occasional movements reminded me more of the patients in a geriatric ward than travellers on the experience of a life time. A young European girl, aged before her years, was trying vainly to nourish her baby from withered breasts while, by her side, her man, bent over a small pile of minute sausage-shaped measurements of hashish, tried with equal results to do business in Manali's potent trance industry.

A small hand stopped me in my tracks.

"BACKSHEESH...BACKSHEESH..."

The white child had already learned to mimic his less fortunate Indian brothers and this memory chased me all the way back to my hotel room. That night images of Biafra overlapped those of hippies and the following day I decided to leave before these scenes burned any deeper.

Chapter 19:
Silk Road to China

A QUICK VISIT TO AIR INDIA OFFICES IN CHANDIGHAR completed an overdue reunion. As in previous years, worries about my bicycle's durability to take air travel proved unfounded and, after a meticulous check of mechanical parts, I left to find Teddy's house.

It had been my habit not to renew acquaintances when on the road, and when Teddy insisted I visit his family in Chandigar I was at first reluctant. Generally I refused such invites, if not outright, then with a delicate politeness, always maybe, but no sooner was I announced when I was adopted like a long lost son and slipped into family life with the ease of an oldtimer. For once I wasn't treated like a V.I.P. and could come and go as I pleased. Food and drink were readily available and I never felt that I was the object of curiosity.

"Nothing is permanent in this life without sacrifice." Teddy had said and, on reflection, I could see it clearly. Although free spirited on the surface, Teddy, like most Indians I met, was entwined in the spider's web of family influences and commitments. I had relinquished these for my trip. Responsibility was like a millstone around my neck and now I found myself envying Teddy's life. Chandighar would always be his home and, if need be, he would fight for its survival. His travels would take place in an aura of family warmth in his living room, swapping stories and experiences with the orphans of travel like myself.

It didn't take long for the ground to set hard around Teddy's hospitality, but when the monsoon rains broke one morning I knew it was time to leave. The question was; to where ?

One evening Teddy's father came visiting and our conversation followed the historical pattern of India's Independence. Spawned from India's Spare Rib as he humorously called it, he talked of the beauty of their northern-most outposts.

"Take the K.K.H.." Teddy's father said. (abbreviation for the Karakoram Highway) "It follows the Indus River towards it source near the Chinese and Indian borders." (Officially opened in 1978 to connect with its partner's road in China, it follows the centuries

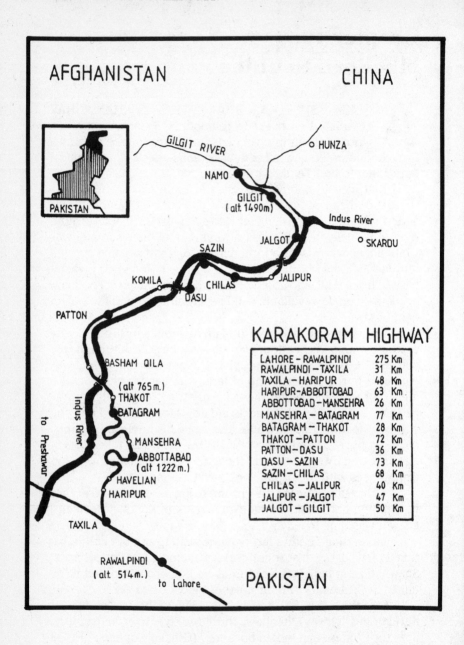

old caravan trails used by silk traders and was hurriedly completed after the Indo/Pak War to secure the northern borders, marrying its friendship pact with China) "Before the highway was built, camel caravans braved the mountain passes to China. There is still a bustling trade over the old trails, but it has now degenerated into black market."

He continued to paint a romantic picture of intrigue and as the evening misted over under large quantities of liquor, his description of Pakistan's untamed North West Frontier lingered just long enough for me to map out the next stage of my journey.

Three days later I arrived in Lahore and, as a direct result of earlier warnings, searched out the Salvation Army Hostel. Three months earlier in my swing through Delhi from Nepal I'd called into the Canadian Embassy. (not wanting to carry excess money and surplus passport around, I'd left them there for safe keeping to be collected later) Here an eye catching notice in bold red letters spelled out a warning to budget travellers; pinned under the heading BEWARE OF LAHORE'S BUDGET ACCOMMODATION, newspaper cuttings, personal letters and an official Embassy Memo gave graphic detail of drug plants, assaults, and hit and run robberies, all with the same sanction if not downright collaboration of local police. There seemed no reason to pick out Lahore for such special treatment. Every major city I'd passed through suffered from this disease and, for some travellers I'd met, it only added to the excitement and reality of their travel, so why Lahore? The Embassy Official enlightened me.

"Since Afghanistan closed its borders to overland travel, foreign currency is as rare as gold. Entrapment is a very real danger. Unscrupulous hotel owners will go to any lengths to get dollars. We have evidence the local police in some cases are in collusion with them, especially with drug plants. It is no good giving you names of safe hotels. The ones listed in the article," he pointed to a cutting from the Delhi Times, "do not exist anymore and that is from only a few months ago. No sooner does the government close down suspect hotels, than they open up under new names, sometimes under the same roof. Your best bet is to stay clear of Lahore if possible, or spend extra money and go up market." Then as an after thought he added. "There is always the Salvation Army Hostel. It should be safe, but I am not sure whether they are still taking in travellers."

Not wanting his warning to become a grim reality I had taken his advice, and settling back to a night of rules and regulations at the Salvation Army Hostel, I slept secure in the knowledge that the grounds outside were being patrolled, if not to catch robbers, at least to deter them.

Alone in the only dormitory I became a prisoner of continued rains. Downtown Lahore was in a constant state of flood and I took this opportunity to catch up on writing to family and friends. Not since leaving Alison and the Children of God in Delhi had my mind been clear enough to write and now I threw myself into an orgy of communication.

Lahore July/82

Dear Mum and Dad,

.............just to fill you in on a few gaps. I left Delhi and religion behind in April and took off to Nepal to get my money and go trekking. Would you believe the bank in Kathmandu had my money all the time. When I first passed through Kathmandu in December they said they had no record of my bank transfer. Yet my lawyer in Canada advised me the transfer was made in November. I eventually had to get the British Embassy in Delhi involved when I ran out of money. They kept me solvent for two weeks when I was broke. One letter from them to the Bank of Nepal in Kathmandu did the trick. Nothing like an official letter to cut through red tape. Heading north now to get away from the rains.

The rain continued unabated for five days. Confined for long periods to the dormitory I was beginning to get claustrophobia and when, one morning, the skies cleared, I was away.

I was very tired when I decided to call it quits in Gujrat. That day I had realized in no uncertain terms that differences between Pakistan and India were not only religious. Everywhere buses, trucks and cars reflected an economy open to imports. Japanese pick-up trucks and compact cars contrasted starkly with their more bland neighbour to the east, and buses immaculately decorated from top to bottom in polished patterned chrome rivalled even the Australian 'Road Trains' in macho brilliance. If that wasn't enough, Indo/Pak stereo music blasted out at maximum decibels, putting the rainbow shaped buses into a division of their own. Even the trucks, hand painted from back to front in miniature pictures, defied description but, above all, the most important difference to me that day was calculated in speed. Since I'd arrived in the Subcontinent it had been my habit to ride in the center of the road, not out of any death wish, but for safety. Here, it was customary to give way to the biggest, and bicycles on the road were easy prey. Right from the beginning I chose to break this code. My rule was based on high visibility and it depended completely on the speed of oncoming traffic for its success. It wasn't my intention to have showdowns with vehicle, but, had I left the road every time I heard a horn, (like all other cyclist) by now my bike would have been a wreck. The continual pounding due to dropping and mounting the road's paved curb would most certainly have led to breakdowns and slow progress. Riding in the center allowed oncoming traffic time to see me clearly as a tourist and, invariably, they would stop honking and slow down, even if only out of curiosity. This allowed me time to cycle to the road's edge and although they would pass within inches I soon got use to it. Almost without exception they offered me lifts and, at the very least, a wave of recognition, but sometimes, and thank goodness only rarely, a driver seeing my white skin would see red and purposely try to spread me across the road. My game plan in the past had depended entirely on this golden rule of visibility, but Pakistan's passion for speed now made it too dangerous to follow. Speed was a natural passion in Pakistan and it wasn't unusual for me to be brushed off, even into ditches, as trucks and buses alike raced through clouds of dust two abreast down the road.

From Jessore the countryside slowly changed. Richly irrigated and cloaked in green, the Punjab plains slowly dried out into barren savanna and oppressive heat forced me to continually stop for refreshment. Just before the K.K.H. turn-off I stopped at a small roadside bazaar. Sitting outside its restaurant a small group of men centered by a huge ginger beard were arguing, and as I passed their table, my hand was suddenly held in a vice like grip.

"Join us brother." It was ginger beard.

His grip tightened into a command.

"My name is Abdul Mohammed. Take tea, brother."

The word NO, was not in his vocabulary. Instructions were rattled out with the rapidity of a gattling gun and immediately the chairs were rearranged.

"Please, sit by me."

A forceful pat on the shoulder directed me to the seat and soon the table was full of spiced teas.

"You are hungry, yes?"

Before I had time to conjure up resistance, a large plate of curried meat appeared then, within the space of thirty minutes, Abdul had pried out my life history and, to use his words, we were brothers. Now related by the common bond of friendship he spent the rest of the afternoon trying his best to convert me to the advantages of being Muslim.

"Mohammed very great man."

Attacking from all sides, his approach and persistence would have been the envy of any second hand car salesman, and his enthusiasm for religious debate was equally matched by his overwhelming hospitality. Although eventually accepting defeat on my conversion, he refused to abdicate center stage to his friends and turned his attention towards marriage.

"Why no wife? I have two."

"I was married once."

"Get another." He was full of the occasion and his friends responded by falling about with laughter. That afternoon welded a personal friendship which overlapped in to his family and, before continuing to Taxila, I had been introduced to all his child daughters with a view to marriage.

In Gujranwal I'd been guest of village hospitality. In Jhelum, an opulently furnished 'Canal Rest House' played host for the night, and now in Taxila I experienced, for the first time, a Subcontinent 'Youth Hostel' and, with it, all its cumbersome officialdom. All forms had to be completed in triplicate, and the British passion for job titles was much in evidence. Tiers of officialdom begged acknowledgment and I passed from manager to submanager and warden to subwarden, before I was finally admitted by a young room sweeper.

At sunrise I set off from Taxila determined to make Abbottabad before sunset. After Haripur I could see the mountains of Kaghan in the distance and crossing the Dar River at Havelian the road started its relentless course upwards. By now it was mid-day and there was no escaping the heat. At this point I was beginning to regret my earlier decision to continue. Just at that moment a truck stopped in front of me.

"It is too hot brother. I take you to top."

The driver was insisting. I didn't want or need a lift in his truck, but after a long discussion on sun stroke we came to a compromise. A rope was tied to the rearside of the truck and we agreed that I would be towed to the top. With one hand tightly gripped on the handle bars and the other on the rope I soon found my new road skiing technique exhilarating and, with the help of his horn to warn me of approaching traffic, I slipped in and out of the protective shield behind his truck. After only a few minutes a small convoy of vehicles, seemingly more intent on watching my movements than passing, were following us. Then nearing the top one car pulled parallel to warn oncoming traffic of my presence and nearly precipitated a head-on collision. This in turn awakened me to the dangers of my tow and I let go. At the top my lift was waiting. We exchanged greetings, shook hands, then, before leaving, he handed me his business card.

'Name: Patel; Private Carrier; Licence from Furniture to Livestock.' Where else in the world could this happen, I asked myself?

From Abbottabad to Batagram the road wound through gentle hills thickly planted with pine and fruit trees, and then crossed a ridge from which a sturdy wall of mountains imposed themselves like a huge barrier on the distant horizon. Suddenly the road banked. Ahead my panorama froze. Blue skies arced, mountains traversed, then the ground hit me. Immersed in Pakistan's rugged frontier scenery, I'd cycled straight off the road.

Once up, I checked the bike from spokes to frame. At first I saw nothing, then a large swelling confirmed all my fears. Ending up in a ditch, my front wheel had cushioned the impact and in the process split my warn tyre's rubber tread. An inch long tear had opened, laying bare a bulbous mass of inner tube, begging puncture. With my spare tyre recently lost to careless packing, I knew I would have to return south. Spares of any kind, especially of the western variety, were impossible outside cities and the nearest was Rawalpindi. I waited twenty minutes by the roadside for a truck-lift, and when none came pushed my bike just as far as the nearest tree.

In the Subcontinent, where every rural household owned a bike, mine had been a catalyst of many a conversation. Daily, people had gathered round whenever I stopped. It could shut down shops, fill streets, and empty villages within minutes. Instantly people could relate. Tyre pressures, brakes, cables, everything that could be was checked, compared with and argued over. On the road, city street philosophy was exchanged for rural street mechanics, and there were none better to pass the time of day with than the Subcontinents' countless roadsides 'bicycle repair men'. Often housed under trees and sometimes under umbrellas they were in a class of their own. On the plains of India they would often flag me down, sometimes even stepping out in front of me from sheer excitement. They constantly demanded my attention, and their childlike enthusiasm could at times be an irritation, but now I needed their expertise badly, so when I walked straight into one, it was like a Godsend.

In front a whole tree had been converted into a bicycle repair shop, and resting in its shadows, surrounded by the tools of his trade was its owner. At one side of him, a neat row of bottles filled with oil, and tins filled with glue, bordered a large bowl of water. Sacks spread on the ground held spanners and files of all sizes and, hanging from home made nail hooks like shelves from the tree's trunk, a vast assortment of tyres, coggs, rags and chains, blotted out its base. Above his head branches acted as natural stores, as old and new inner tubes used for both patches and replacements hung down like decorative streamers. An ancient foot pump propped up by the roadside advertised his services and a stove of steaming tea, evidence of his hospitality.

It wasn't long before my presence had attracted dozens of inquisitive hands. First my bike bell was rung, then brakes applied, but when my gear lever was engaged, its grating noise shot through the crowd like an electric shock.

By now the bicycle repair man was full of himself. Cog teeth were counted, ratios calculated and, within minutes, he had made himself an authority on ten speeds. In the excitement I'd almost forgotten the reason for our meeting, then the sight of my swollen tyre galvanised him into action. Within minutes my bike was the center of an amazing scene of improvisation. One hour before I'd given up hope of continuing, now I was sitting back with a cup of tea watching my repair man set about his task.

First he brooded over tyre sizes. Heads were scratched, second opinions called for and then, after due inspection, he set about his work. Having lost my spare tyre in Lahore I was open to anything and, like a person suffering a terminal disease, gladly allowed him his chance for a miracle cure. First he measured the split, then cutting a strip off an old tyre, he proceeded to sew the patch on. Once that was finished, a strip of rubber inner tube was glued like a bandage on its inner side and when blown up, bulbed out like a cancerous growth. The whole episode lasted less than thirty minutes. Payment was refused and with a feeling of a patient on borrowed time, I continued north.

Just below Thankot the road dropped sharply into a rocky chasm before exiting hundreds of feet below into a landscape of bleached rock. Although small at first sight, it still took me over an hour to locate its only Rest House owner. Finding him in restaurant, he greeted me with great ceremony, thanking God, my bicycle, my luck and the British Empire for getting me there. After a correct time had elapsed on these formalities I was shown my room. It was obvious even at first glance I was being given his family room.

"No cyclist stay in Rest House before, it great honour." And before I could protest, he ordered his servants to remove their personal belongings.

"No, please don't trouble yourself."

"No trouble, my room, best room. You are my guest."

I had experienced Muslim hospitality before but, this man, albeit for reasons of business, brought to life its very tradition and while furniture was exchanged and the room made ready, his wife prepared a meal. Helped by her daughters, we were waited on hand and foot. Half hidden in the wings, looking like delicate ornaments poised for movement, they watched intently for gestures, always there when needed, but rarely seen. Throughout the meal we were surrounded by their graceful patterns of silence and as one plate emptied another was filled. Everything had its place, everyone a task. The whole family knit neatly together in a tight web of confined space and organization. Obviously this required much submission and, from what I saw, mostly by the women, but was this submission, or just another view in space ? I'd learned before the pitfalls of questioning other cultures too deeply too soon and for that evening immersed myself into the part of privileged guest and, with little prompting before bed, answered a stream of questions from my host's wife and children.

Leaving Thankot the road made its first of many crossings of the Indus River. From here it paralleled its course northwards and while the river gathered turquoise waters of melting snow, the road became a catchment area of rock slides and pot holes. Cut through deep gorges, rock overhangs echoed to the sounds of continual breakoffs and deep ruts in the road surface suggested continual erosion. Sheer faces of rock stretching hundreds of feet above the road and sharp turns in the river, cut distances down to less than a thousand yards and one minute I would be cycling in an atmosphere of thunderous roars, only yards from a turbulent Indus and the next I'd be clinging dizzily to the road, hundreds of feet above the river. By now the road traffic was almost non-existent and what vehicles did pass me announced themselves in the screech of low gear changes, as their noises echoed down the gorge long before I saw them. By noon the Indus valley was a furnace of dry heat and, with little shade, the sun was a continual source of discomfort. Dehydrated, the disciplined mixture of speed and rest needed continual rebalance. Surface river breezes and feet dangled in ice cool waters acted better than any aspirin against sun migraines and, taking advantage of these periods, I brewed up constant supplies of tea. Halfway to Komila the scene changed dramatically. The road rose, switched back and skipped over the valley, only to expose the Indus's course millennias ago. Streaked in silver-grey, pink and violent hues were enormous deposits of gravel and sand. High and dry, and looking totally out of place, this proved to be the only oasis of colour that day and, with only the thought of hidden valleys ahead to encourage me, I was relieved to make Dasu. Since Taxila I'd not seen a hint of cloud in the sky, and with the prospect of another hot dusty day in front of me, I decided to spend more than usual on accommodation. Going up market, I booked straight in Dasu's P.B.W.D. Guest House.

That evening I was invited to join a diplomat and his family for a meal on the verandah. Himself attached to the Pakistan Diplomatic Corp, his wife was a working journalist and this in itself made them a unique combination. Since entering Pakistan, Muslim's patriarchy had distanced the gap between the sexes to impossible proportions and it was common to see women like frightened sheep on rural sections of the road, either scampering over walls, round corners or just turning their backs on me. It was making my days very one sided and without the shapely female form for company, a depressing one, and that night I didn't need a second invitation to join them.

In the opulent surroundings of chinking china, stainless steel cutlery and a clean table cloth, I took advantage of the menu's relaxed formality, and ordering a bit of this and tasting a bit of that, I indulged my taste buds to the limit. Then, just as the meal's sweet course was served, there was a power failure. Plunged into darkness, my friends continued without breaking step and while I fumbled around trying to find plates of food, they continued as if totally unaware of the new circumstances. I couldn't even detect a tone of irritation in their voices. Although accustomed as they must have been to the material benefits of the west, obviously modern technology was only a luxury to them, to be played with and not govern their lives. Too embarrassed to leave the table and too embarrassed to stop eating, I carried on, dropping food and spilling water until a servant brought a lantern light. I had thought my years of travel had stripped away these complex dependencies, but this one small episode with electricity had proved otherwise.

In '78 I lived through the news of New York's two day power failure and with it, all its incumbent mayhem. Air conditioners, so much part of the North American way of life failed, and the resultant temperature rose in direct proportion to people's tempers. Shops were looted and Federal Guards roamed the streets with unlimited powers. Riots were the order of the day and people's suppressed hatred erupted in an orgy of street violence. People died from panic, claustrophobia, inter-family disputes and, with no television to feed their fantasies, loneliness. The only positive thing to emerge from that summer of discontent was the statistical peak in Manhattans birth rate.

From Jalgot irrigated paddy fields sprouted out from nowhere. Buildings, glued at precarious angles to steep glaciated river walls, piled on top of each other, as life once again followed a zig-zag pattern up the Indus River. At the foot of Mount Haramosh the road came to a junction and, leaving the Skardu road to the east, I followed the Gilgit River and once more the valley shallowed and, like Zanskar before, filled itself with mile upon mile of peach trees. It had been nine eventful days since leaving Lahore and nearly a month since Teddy's. In all that time I'd encountered only one tourist. Foreign experience and sunsets, as beautiful as they were, were still no substitute for human contact and now thoughts of arriving in Gilgit seemed like reaching the end of a rainbow, a rainbow I somehow had to return on.

She smiled at me and instantly I was happy. As luck would have it. The first person I met on arrival in Gilgit was an Australian traveller. Immediately we coupled and, for the next week relaxed in each others company before separate plans parted us.

Not wanting to retrace my steps down the K.K.H. I looked for alternatives. First I tried the Shandur Pass to Chitral, but after two days' riding on pebble filled roads, I surrendered. Next I visited Gilgit's airport where I found that subsidized flights left twice a week, but seat priorities went to the army. I booked in advance, then for the next two flights, I stood back powerless as one businessman after another played the game of baksheesh, leapfrogging over my reservation. Giving up, I tried the market truck stop. Packed to overflowing with everything from livestock to sacks of grain, the sight brought back bumpy memories of Burmese travel and I passed onto the bus station. Looking poor relatives to their chromeplated brothers of the plains, I decided on the lesser of the two evils and resigned myself to an eighteen hour bus journey back to Rawalpindi.

Chapter 20:
As One Door Closes,
Another Door Opens

B Y NOW THE DRY SEASON WAS IN FULL SWING AND September's fire ball lost no time burning away morning hazes. Fields coated in a mire of red muddy soil only two months before had long since hardened and aged like human skin. Cool mountain air had given way to burning heat and movement at this elevation was infinitely preferable to sweating on the spot. My diary of day's events since leaving Rawalpindi added up like penances and temperatures on the Punjab plains now settled at the upper limits of endurance. Everywhere the country slept. Bullock carts were not seen till early evening and rickshaw drivers dismounted at the least gradient. The schedule of daily mileage, inescapable heat and fitful sleeps began to affect me. Beneath that glow of health, my concentration wandered. Objects ahead shook like jelly and everywhere there was dust. It got in my eyes, my nose and lodged in my throat. Thoughts of Delhi were now all that drove me. Cool showers, fan ventilation and clean sheets, but above all news.

The clerk at the Delhi Post Restante quickly checked my passport then handed over my mail.

No matter how close we think we are to people can anyone preguess their response. My letter to Alison had been received, but her reply read like a challenge. "If you want to see me again, you have to see my new family". All the accumulated points since leaving Delhi now evaporated. My time in the mountains now meant nothing. Even my body, that well tuned machine, offered no confidence. Could nothing be gained without corresponding debt ? Had I really sacrificed my relationship with Alison for selfish goals ? I always felt alive on the road and thought this strength reflected in my letter to her, but it sounded like it had backfired. I only had wanted to see her again before leaving India, to give her my point of view face to face. The last thing I wanted was to meet her on her own ground. Surrounded by her 'family' as she put it, I would stand little chance of influencing her. I knew

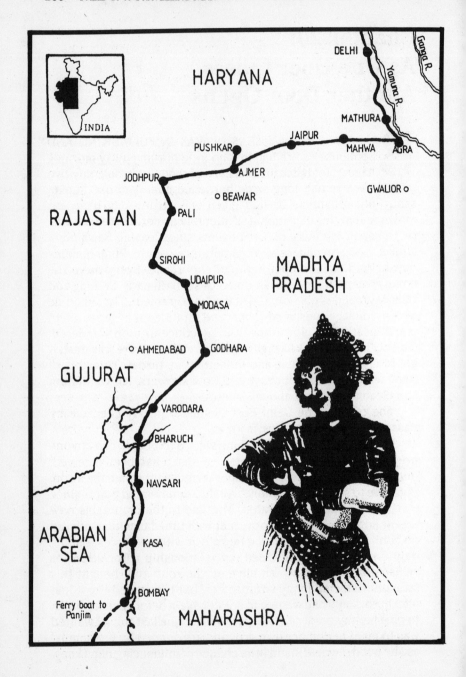

from my past experience of living with them that my presence as a 'backslider' would intimidate them. But I went anyway; I didn't have a choice.

Due to my status as an ex, they kept me waiting fifteen minutes outside while, within, they went through their ritual hype, setting the stage for an emotional entrance.

"I love Jesus, Bernard."

The world love had lost all currency, and my expression allowed no space for apology. I wasn't within her orbit of friends any more and, invited inside, this showed within minutes. Every question I posed had a predictable answer. Every answer I gave was predictably questioned. As one family member wilted another took up the mantle. I lost my temper and they shut me out. Bernard the backslider had to go and that night my divorce papers came symbolically wrapped in a brown paper parcel. Personal gifts to Alison, all evidence that a partnership had once existed were waiting for me on my return to Ringo's. The door had been slammed shut. There was only one thing to do: open up another one.

If childhood was a foreign experience then by now its mystery was too overpowering. Years of analysis had been taken past the point of contradiction and it had been reached in the critical phase of travel. In Australia the opportunity to return to engineering had been too great a pull to discount easily but, now two years on, there was no certainty I could pick up those pieces. Memories were grey in comparison with new frontiers and contact with friends had dwindled to the obligatory postcard. Only my parents kept in regular contact. By now one and a half feet were in travel and a 'round the world bicycle trip' looked like a reality, if not a necessity. In front I saw a whole new way of life and to return at this stage would be like leaving a job half finished.

I'd learned much in the last year from people where technological advancements were not an everyday part of their lives. In the past my life had been dominated by speed of action and high tech, and dependency on it had surfaced on more than a few occasions. In rural Asia, I had experienced people whose lives were governed more by external forces of climate than man made influences. Their slower pace of life and economy of need, no matter what the reason, had planted a seed that wouldn't go away easily, but was it any better than what I had just left? Ignorance of past mistakes had led to renewed famine, but still there was something strangely attractive in their carefree attitude to life's disasters.

Leaving the Iranian Embassy in Delhi I felt relieved and the reason was one obtuse piece of paper stapled inside my British Passport. The sight of my Canadian Landed Immigrancy form was enough to remind the custom officials of past indiscretions and my application for a 'Transit Visa' had been refused. In those days the American Hostages were still on everyone's lips and Canada's involvement, spiriting away nearly a dozen of their officials under the guise of Canadian Nationals, was all the ammunition the Iranian Embassy needed to refuse entry. My escape route for a quick return to Europe cut off, I now became a welcome prisoner of the Indian Subcontinent.

Where the previous week was a serious game, today blossomed with good humour. Captains of industry stepped out onto Connaught Place with naked Fakirs and rickshaw whallahs saluted my exit from Delhi with a chorus of early morning bells. There was still allot of petrol left in the old tank and having made plans to spend Christmas in Goa, I hit the road to Agra with renewed vigour.

A full moon lit my first view of the Taj Mahal and I wasn't disappointed. Jet set tourists mixed with shoe string travellers and, inside, the whole scene took on a carnival atmosphere. Powerful photo flashes and video lights exploded on the old tomb's surface while, below, a travelling band of permanent residents did business. It was one huge commercial bandwagon. Prices had increased three fold since I'd arrived a few days ago, but who could blame them. Full moon viewings of the Taj were only possible three days a month and Agra's tourist economy was based almost entirely on this astronomical fact. Inside, fortunes were made and lost and, by the sound of it, marriages also. Outside the tomb's perimeter another scene took over. Street sellers competed with each other in an unholy guantlet of profit and, swarming around a fleet of A.C. buses professional beggars picked off the aged, as tour guides tried their best to extricate their charges.

From Agra I entered the heartland of India's Peacock Throne. Khaki paddy fields disappeared into hazes of heat and, dotting the barren landscape peacocks on the 'mate' erected plumage in sudden bursts of blues and vivid greens. Camel caravans competed with buses for road space and, hemmed-in on either side, flocks of goats drifted in perpetual clouds of dust. Cottage industries of rich clay pots spilled out onto the roads while women in make-shift shelters wove reed baskets. Village barriers of maize stretched fully across the road, as buses and bikes alike threshed where no threshing machine existed. A travelling band of musicians en route to an autumn wedding gave me an impromptu roadside performance and everywhere I stopped there were children, hundreds of children. I was beginning to feel like some ageing gunfighter, as each village passed through would offer up its batch of youthful challenges. Appearing from nowhere boys would often race me through streets, only stopping when I had crossed over the invisible lines of territory. By now Delhi's cosmopolitan uniforms seemed light years away as Rajastan's tribal costumes took over. It was a country of little benevolence to the exposed. Dried out river beds reflected unremitting sun and it was no wonder the inhabitants adopted a proud stance against nature. Towards evening the land softened. Bland constructions of bleached white buildings were washed in ripples of evening shadow and plain colours turned to shades of yellow and orange. Sunset came quickly and surface heat disappeared as night chilled into sleep.

Jaipur came and went and took with it some money. Shops displaying infinite varieties of multi-coloured garments attracted me and I indulged in one of my rare spending sprees. Cycling towards Pushkar, my tailor made silk shirts blended into the tribal scene, if not in style, then at least in their splash of colour.

Pushkar was one of those unique spas of healing that shoe-string travellers could depend on. Known to the hardened few its name was bandied around as the place to rest up in and it attracted a rare cross section of long distance travellers. Manali may have its freaks, Varanasi its religious adherents and Delhi the business type, but Pushka attracted them all. Hidden away from the main stream tourist traps, it was home away from home for the nomads. I had first heard of it back in Bangkok. Even in those early days I had learned to match personalities with their favourite places and going by the looks of that traveller I could now bring life to his beads and pendants.

Following advice, I booked into the lakeside 'Pushka Hotel' then decided on an early evening bath. The distance from the dormitory balcony to the lake could be calculated in the faith I had put in that one conversation in Bangkok. Splitting the early evening silence I executed a perfect half somersault complete with belly flop and, after recovering from the initial shock, revelled in the refreshingly cool waters.

"Hey Bernard. What's the water like ?"

"I don't believe it. Roland is that you ?"

My trip usually took me off the beaten track and to meet travellers twice was unusual,and to bump into them five times was nothing short of miraculous. Roland's dislocated movements were his greeting card and stepping out from the dark in long rambling strides, his unmistakable giraffe like features gave him away.

"How's it going, Pommie ?"

Roland was the thinking man's traveller, a calculating machine who hated machines. His encyclopaedic knowledge was backed up with a library of books and, when emptied, his backpack would litter his room for days. This insatiable appetite for knowledge was only matched by his craving for illusionary drugs and I had seen first hand his journey into space. We had first met nine months before in Raxaul crossing the border from Nepal. Five months later it was in Zanskar, again in Leh, then finally six weeks ago in Delhi. Since our first meeting I had followed his progress with increasing alarm. At first I put it down to solitary travel and that instinctive distance we use to insulate ourselves against any hard knocks, but in Leh I had noticed he was never without his supply of hashish and by the time we met in Delhi he had almost permanently withdrawn into a private world. Manali had cured my fascination for the 'translucent trip of life' and now it held no relevance. At first it had a deliberate function. It broke down barriers, stripped away pedigrees and transcended the need to articulate. I indulged whenever it was available. My attitude then was, if it was there, that was O.K., and if it wasn't, that was O.K. too. It wasn't until Manali that I first recognized its serious undertones. Setting themselves apart from the rest, Manali's Shivite followers brought a religious element into their communion and the sense of friendly participation vanished while elitism took over. Mind games where the name of the game and manipulators of this art were a dime a dozen. At this point I stopped taking the drug and soon entry into its groups was refused, but obviously to Roland it was still part of his trip.

As travellers go, Roland was a solitary figure. His swing from albino white when we first met, to chocolate brown, characterized his personality of extremes. He had strange perceptive powers, never more evident than when 'under the influence'. Always the one to contradict dogma, our chance meetings would coincide with new philosophy and, when parting, I was always left questioning it. On one occasion while in the middle of a heated discussion on the existence of God with fellow travellers, he pulled out his dictionary. "Look here, if God is in the Oxford dictionary, that's proof enough for me." He could be a hard act to follow and many a dark night was illuminated in his company.

We spent ten days together. By now he'd taken to smoking from the hallucinary chillum, and its fumes possessed him. Gradually I was loosing the battle to his illusionary world. Insecurities, once easily spotted on his character, now followed a natural course and turned inward. Conversations so invigorating only a few days ago, were now increasingly punctuated by gibberish and his once childish enthusiasm for adventure had deteriorated into a total lack of interest. I argued, bullied, threatened. I tried all I knew to snap him out of his apathy, but nothing worked. His new philosophy now had little space for reality. In his words, he was 'IT'. To be ordinary meant boredom, compromise, and systems. In India he could explore the universe or return to its source, but could he cope with its realities, or for that matter, would he accept them? He was in the grip of a habit whose appetite he could little afford now, let alone when he returned to Australia. Already his return had been postponed twice. I agonized over leaving him. Was it survival of the fittest or indifference that drove me on? No-one held a gun to his head. "Think Goa sounds good," he said when I was leaving, but there wasn't much heart in his reply. "Maybe see you there. I'll drop you a line at the Post Restante." I left feeling relieved, but I never saw him again.

Soon today's experience washed away yesterday's event and freedom of the road detached me once again from relationships. Jodhpur and Udaipur held me for days. Bazaars seduced me with their living history and I wandered narrow streets like a fish ready to be hooked. Again doors of hospitality opened and I accepted one invite after another from shop owners. Bargaining turned to friendship, tea to supper and offers of free lodgings came thick and fast. From Udaipur, clefts of rock and parched brown hills gave way to plains and, following my nose, I escaped off main roads, seeking out dirt tracks leading nowhere.

Driven by thirst, a throne and a prayer mat became a welcome refuge. Sitting in a box-like cubicle with the air of a priest at confession, a roadside temple's resident Sadhu waved me over. Curtains of shade drew back and a supporting cast of garlanded deities greeted me. Before me a prominent statue of Shiva was smothered in rose petals. Peacock feathers surrounded another of Kali and sandalwood incense assaulted my nasal passages. In one corner empty tins of Nescafe took pride of place and in another, a small stove was surrounded by cooking utensils. A crochet picture reading 'Home is where your heart is', spelled out welcome to all visitors, and above its dreadlocked owner, plastic flowers and a calender gave permanence to this strange scene. I'd arrived halfway through his evening pugaree and having trapped my attention, he continued as if meeting Europeans was an everyday occurrence. Miniature cymbals now filled the space of noise between bell ringing, and his ritual chants followed the scale of my humour.

"Greeting friend."

Once his pugaree was over,we exchanged pleasantries while he made tea.

"You speak excellent English."

Born into a Bombay Textile family, I wasn't surprised to hear, he was a product of private education.

"Why did you give up the family business ?"

"Maybe it was middle age. My family are all grown up, either married, or living away from home. I reached that stage in life when all youthful goals have been achieved. I wanted for nothing, houses servants, cars. Life lost its meaning. I had surrounded myself with the trophies of success, yet I was becoming increasingly dissatisfied with its ground rules. Everywhere in my life I experienced excess. I wanted something different, not just to amass enough wealth. Achievements shouldn't always reflect themselves materially, don't you agree ?"

"Yes, but what about your wife, what did she say to all this ?"

"At first she resisted strongly. We broadly shared the same views, but outside pressure to conform affected her more than myself. When finally the decision was made, it was made jointly, but I can see now how selfish I was to leave her isolated at the mercy of family criticism."

"What is she doing now ?"

"She returned to nursing. She's an independent woman now, makes decisions for herself, and I know from her letters she's also found new meaning to her life."

"When did you leave home ?"

"I left Bombay two years ago with only the clothes on my back. Since then many of the preconceptions I had of spiritual advancement have been crushed. First I sought out a teacher. I walked to Almora in Uttar Pradesh. My first weeks were the hardest. Begging doesn't come naturally to a man who spent his life selling labour for profit. Villages can spot fakers a mile away, and if it wasn't for their help during this time I would have returned to Bombay a failure. From Almora I went to Rishikesh. It's so commercial there. Everything is aimed towards you Europeans."

"What do you mean ?"

"Ashrams-places of retreat, that's what I used to believe. I tried to gain entry without success. If you're white, no problem. They may even risk taking you in first, without payment. Maybe they look upon it as an investment, but for Indians, letters of introduction are required. In short, money. This commercial exploitation of Hinduism made me very angry. Hinduism is now treated as a national asset to be traded to the highest bidder. I was told it started with the Beatles, now everyone beats a path there. It's disgusting. Needless to say, I didn't stay long and I didn't miss it when I left."

"Walking ?"

"Yes, I set off along the Ganges to Allahbad. I wanted to attend the Ardha Mela Festival."

(Held every six years, it attracts Yogis and intellectuals alike. They meet during the festival to purge India's more radical Gods and to induct others. The Hindu Hall of Fame as Roland put it)

Unknowingly our paths had crossed during this period. Following my route to Delhi in Dec/81 through Bihar State, wandering holymen had peppered my route south. Near Bansi I had passed one complete with his complement of disciples. Arm erected in penance, I saw it had withered to matchstick proportions; another outside Basti, naked as a new born baby, carried aloft a three forked staff of office to Shiva, but strangest by far was the man I passed just north of Allahbad. Throwing pebbles down the road, he repeatedly retrieved them by crawling on his belly, but here I had found myself in the presence of a Sadhu, who impressed me more with his honest humility than the sum total of his more flamboyant peers.

"What of the present ?" I asked.

"For the last week I have been helping the village committee fill in government forms. They are trying to obtain an irrigation grant."

"That's a long way from the spiritual path isn't it ?" How arrogant. I knew immediately that my words had hurt him.

"Remember I initially told you I searched for a teacher. Well, I found him in Varanasi. He told me to stop fighting my past. He corrected my course, redirected old habits and steered old skills towards different goals. I gave up my pursuit of philosophies. He told me to help the illiterate, advise the ignorant, so now I write letters for those who cannot and help in commerce whenever asked. I have become a travelling consultant," he said with a laugh, "and I am enjoying every minute of it. I ask no payment, but all my wants are met."

"Do you keep in contact with your family ?" It was the most asked question of myself and I was curious to hear his reply.

"When you are in the throes of new experience, you grasp at them, and I am ashamed to say they have all but consumed me. I have little time to write. My wife understands what I am doing and my children have something interesting to tell their friends. They all know I will return when the time is right."

"When will you know that ?"

"I will just know, I cannot explain the future, I just know that when it happens I will be ready to grasp it. My teacher in Varanasi, when asked to explain the fear of returning home to a group of Europeans, illustrated it this way. In Europe you believe the world is round, but in India you find it is flat. Now position India right on the edge of the world. To leave now, you will have to believe the world is round again. If you can't then you will find it impossible to return home, because to leave at this point in your travels will be to fall into the void of ignorance and, to survive, you will have to forget all you have learned in India."

We spoke no more that evening. He made another tea, cleared a space for my mosquito net then, while I slept inside the shrine, he slept outside guarding my bike.

The next few days saw me climbing back into the shell of travel. Roadside attractions took second place to road concentration as, on reaching Varodara, I left the quiet village tracks for the noisy realities of commercial traffic. Entering Bombay, I was again sucked into the teeming chaos of trucks, bullock carts and rickshaws and it wasn't until I saw 'India Gate', with its backdrop of sea blue shading off into the sky that I allowed myself the luxury of relaxation.

Using the Salvation Army Hostel as my base, I spent the next few days making plans to go by boat to Goa, and getting permission from the hostel's warden, I stored my bike in their lockers until after Christmas.

Chapter 21:
Trouble in Paradise

THE ATTRACTIONS OF GOA'S BEAUTIFULLY SCULPTURED bone white sands need no further explanation, or do they? Stories I'd heard in Bombay varied from laid back to mind killing and with my second Christmas in India only weeks away I had arrived in Panjim harbour full of apprehension. Now into my sixth week in Goa I felt like an old timer and able to comment on the residents.

In Goa you could cast off that 'living deity' label rural India gave white flesh. Some came here to get away from there and some just to be ignored. Here, no-one cared if you were a pop star; son of the wealthy; an aristocratic runaway daughter, or a working class lad. We were all here to either unwind, or windup, it made no difference. Your past wasn't relevant, and who gave a damn about your future ? Here Guru's could be found on top of every sand dune and, for most, this was their once in a life time chance to hit the big time, to follow their hero's footsteps. "I was Marareshi's favourite disciple. I carried Jimi Hendrix's guitar." Bhagwan was the flavour of the month in Ahrambol, Syd Babba in Anjuna. My old friends, the Children of God, monopolized the fallen in Calangute, and in Vagator, Timothy Leary, the undisputed King of the Acid Freaks reigned supreme. Here the traveller was forced back on his own resources, expected to succeed with the same grace as he was expected to fail, and Goa had a nasty habit of sorting out the men from the boys, as the failures at Panjim Sanatorium could testify. Indians called it the 'Enlightened Syndrome.' Once Buddha-hood was attained there was nowhere else to go. After all, as they put it, "Who wants to live with a living God ?" If you could get used to this indifference, you could even learn to enjoy yourself, but to the stop over traveller, who never explored under Goa's surface, these words could fall on deaf ears, because to truly experience Goa, you had to get your hands dirty, join the nameless band of followers and go searching. To the winners went the ultimate. A return ticket home, an older and wiser person. To the loser, a one way ticket to Panjim Sanatorium, and a free trip to the telephone exchange. "Hello

Daddy."

Why Goa, you may ask. "It's cheap, it's different, and there's no bloody computers," is the usual answer. For some it meant anti-materialism, yet for many it was trade in consumer goods (computers and cameras) that paid for their extended stays. Many didn't even understand their own cultures. Most, if pressed, would tell you they just didn't care. Then there were the 'Gloom and Doomers', self destructors with their message of the all powerful mushroom, and offering in the process their own 'magic variety' as a form of escape. For the 'permanent residents' it was just plain hard work to exist. Arts and crafts and the ever present drug traffic were seasonal trades, with Goa their biggest market place. (Anjuna Flea Market) To some of the more fortunate, begging was their only alternative, and in this they had to compete with the none too pleased Indians.

For the Germans it was an escape from army call-up; for the British, it was a winter haven for the seasonal worker out for a cheap suntan. For the rich, it was a chance to be down and out; for the fashion conscious Italians it offered an abundance of clothes at bargain basement prices, and to the philosophical French a mountainous supply of their favourite drugs, but the prize must go to Goa's original trail blazers, the loveable American Hippy. Born winners, but secret losers, Goa offered them one last chance for the big one, IMMORTALITY. And last but no least, the mixed up Indian on his cultural trip with white flesh. A chance to shoot film like David Bailey and take photographs, putting reality to those sexed starved fantasies that western tabloids portray.

For the political, left wing revolutionaries from the 'Red Brigade' to obscure hit squads plied the beaches more than willing to offer the disillusioned a multitude of causes to fight for. Whether your pain lay in your head, or your stomach, these bandaids of society stayed poised in the wings, ready to pounce, like vultures, on the fallen, offering beliefs to the spiritually poor rich, and relief to the spiritually rich poor. In short Goa had it all.

"Trouble in Paradise."

Those words were my first offering of reality from a young Indian on arrival at Panjim. In Goa for the Christmas souvenir business, his face looked down cast.

"Bottom's fallen out of the peace and love market. I come here every Christmas, but recession no good." His conversation tapered off as if quoting prices from the New York Stock Exchange, but I wouldn't have to wait long to experience his words' serious side.

In Vagator my rented house soon became free accommodation to the homeless and its swinging doors of entry were always rotating. Faces came and went and naked flesh was always on display. As always I liked exploring possibilities in myself and with the exception of Goa's booming trance industry, I indulged in all flavours and fetishes Goan lifestyles could offer.

Acid, punch and cocaine parties offered ample opportunities to display male or female cosmetic body paints and together with their nightly costume fashion parade, they drew viewers with a round the clock gallery of living pictures. Better than any underground telegraph system, party locations were advertised by Goa's spin-off economy. Instant restaurants surrounded locations and found themselves competing for business with Goa's permanent residents. By now, Christmas party season was in full swing and Goa's nightly countdown menu of punk rock music battered the brain. Hardened party goers danced themselves into tribal groups of trance. Morning announced the body worshippers. Tai Chi experts, defying the laws of movement, danced in slow motion to the Gods of Martial Arts, and Yoga classes attracting the most nimble, sent limbs through every known barrier of elasticity. During the day communes devoted to everything from sex to aesthetics kept both body and mind active and hidden away, known only to old timers, a small library of English books from westerns to romantic novels did business in 'exchange and mart'. For the searchers of eternal youth, Goa offered mud baths and their so-called mystical properties attracted the aged in hope of miraculous reversals. Possessions were old fashioned, but secretly hidden, and only minds and bodies were exchanged. Relationships were transient and anarchy was the invisible badge of acceptability. People worshipped the sun, themselves and sometimes their partners, infact whatever took their fancy. It was perfectly acceptable to swing in private or in public, be lesbian or homosexual, dress up or dress down. In short ordinary was not in the vocabulary and to speak for so called normality was to swim against the tide.

By now the sun's daily diet had rounded my tan and Goa's

surface rhythm of eat, sleep and be merry had regulated my day. I played all her games with wild abandon then, one morning, the surface cracked.

Two dead bodies found in a week and a stolen passport was enough to dent anyone's confidence. The first body surfaced during an early morning swim, a twisted shell draped in silk. Then, a few days later, the bloated second body was washed ashore. Both were colourless. In India, where life and death were courted openly, dead bodies were not an unusual sight, but these were white. I'd already served an apprenticeship in the open air morgues of Calcutta, and whatever mystique remained had turned to ashes on Varanasi's burning ghats, where the vipers of funeral fought over its trade. Death held little significance, but this time I couldn't escape its consequences by riding away. Only days before I had met both people in the normal circumstances of beach life. They had been acquaintances to me, but no-one owned up to them. In death they had lost friends. To come forward now to identify them would lead to embarrassing questions, over extended stays, lack of visas, and of course, funds. To the police they were now stateless, but I knew them to be French. To acquaintances like myself, they were nameless, yet they must have answered to something. Who cared ? Who wanted to know? They must have had friends ?

Between these deaths my passport was stolen and came a distant second to mortality. It didn't devastate me as I thought it would and even the irritation of returning twice to Bombay to the British Embassy didn't bother me either. By now Vagator had lost its appeal and, trapped in Goa by an Embassy 'Travel Document', (awaiting the issue of another passport) I explored alternative beaches to live on.

Just over a mile from Ahrambol, a secluded lagooned, beach was home away from home for the last true survivors of the sixties peace and love dream. Here, back to earth life styles were taken to extremes, for, to own clothes, was to be exclusive. Here the badge of conformity was to be naked. Too far for the average daily visitor, Ahrombol was a paradise of seclusion and its residents could do their thing without coming under the magnifying glass of curiosity. Homes made from palm leaves dotted the cliffs and each was moulded to the character of its owner but, as I was to find out later, ownership was based on the age old principal that 'possession equals nine tenths of the law'. Squatters were common and suppressed anger needed only the right key to unlock it. Even paradise has its darker side and surface love, its sinister hate, and it was one of these property disputes that eventually erupted with deadly consequences.

At first I searched the cliffs for suitable vantage points, but all except the most exposed were taken. The same applied around the lagoon at the back of the beach and finally I chose a spot above high tide on the beach, shaded by palms. It took me three days to build a lean-to out of woven palm leaves and within the week I had dropped into a daily routine of exercise. Soon co-existence with my new neighbours was strained. The proximity of the friendly neighbourhood Shivite meetings increasingly concerned me.Within spitting distance of my front door, nightly guitar music mixed with the sweet smells of hashish. The trance industry was everywhere. I thought two dead bodies had nailed down the lid on re-entry, but the pull to retrace my steps back into its experience was now a powerful one. In Vagator there were many diversions and exclusion from one group was no great problem. Ahrombol was very different as night life was non existent outside the Shivites.

Christmas and New Year were quiet times and I was already planning to leave when a chance meeting with an old girlfriend ended with a night in Mapsa. Having left hospital days before, Hilda had walked twelve hours from Anjuna to Ahrombol then, without realizing it, straight into my hut. Still weak from a recent operation her stitches had burst and already the scar was pussing. She was far to ill to stay on the beach and I lost no time taking her back to the hospital in Mapsa, where before the night was out, I had made arrangements for her return home to Austria.

When I got back to Ahrombol nothing seemed extraordinary. It was too early for the Indian tourists and the fishermen would still be out at sea, but still it was strange not to see any people on the beach. My night in Mapsa had been my first night away from there since I'd arrived three weeks before. Could it have coincided with a beach party ? Was this the reason ? I picked up my pace and, as I came round the point, the mystery was solved. Two police passed carrying a bamboo trestle . The funeral in Calcutta flashed across my eyes. A deep purple gash sliced to the bone. Dried blood clotted and a man's head rocked hideously to the beat of its bearers. Stunned I watched two other lifeless bodies pass me. Tears and cries followed in a group of girls. By now I was running and instincts took over. I met another group. Shock took away all translation. They spoke only French, but anguished looks spoke volumes. A young man cried openly, then I spotted a familiar face.

"What the hell went on ?"

"Your neighbour, the Golden Avenger flipped his lid." I'd not once passed the time of day with him yet he only lived less than one hundred yards from me.

"Where is he ?"

"Vanished into thin air, could be half way to Bombay by now." He shook his head. "He just went berserk. Started about ten in the evening with an argument. First he chopped up this guy he found squatting in his home. The he tried to get his girlfriend. Remember that French guy, the one that was worried about going home this week ? Well his worries are over. He copped it just in front of your place. Then he crossed over the lagoon. Killed one of his buddies with his bare hands."

I blotted out the rest of his story and set off on a macabre pilgrimage of death spots. Already small groups, possessions in hand, were drifting off the beach and those remaining walked around in dazed states. Conflicting stories were rife, but most agreed his violent eruption was sparked off by the guy he found living in his hut, and now all were frightened that he might return to settle old scores.

By late afternoon a dozen armed soldiers turned up and immediately started to comb the cliffs and jungle at the back of the lagoon and, before nightfall, they had already lit fires on the beach. That first night was my worst. The slightest noise set off chain reactions of frightened calls.

"Any sign ?"

"Nothing here."

"All right."

Residents now matched their guards in number, but still most were drawn together into vigilante squads of security. I was invited to join in but declined and that night luck came to my aid. Making continuous brews of tea bought my own private army and for five nights I shared my palm leaf accommodation with the soldiers. Inevitably they gave up the ghost, either through boredom or officialdom, and one night spent without my protectors proved one night too many.

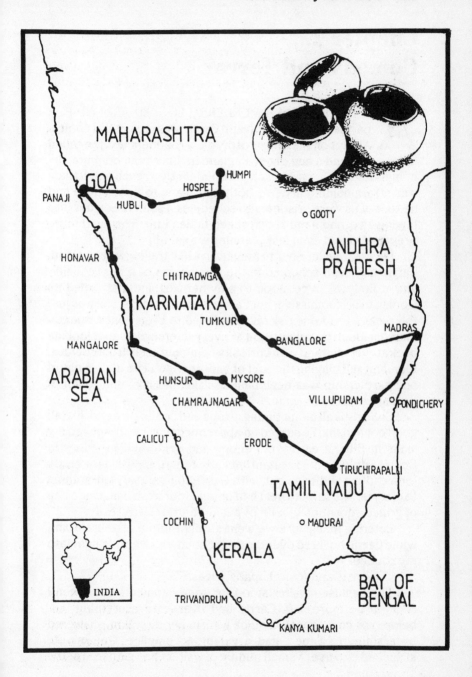

Chapter 22:
Comedy and Terror

AFTER THE BEACH MURDERS, I LOOKED AROUND FOR partners to cycle with and Carrie was the natural choice. Always on the fringes of my daily routine, she often called in for a chat and a cup of tea. England had been our common denominator which, on a beach predominantly French and Italian, was a rare commodity. We both had plans to head south and neither of us were prisoners to schedules. I soon talked her into buying a second hand single speed Indian bike. Then with little preparation and even less planning we set off.

Up til Mangalore her presence was like trailing a heavy load. Carrie had been schooled in the classrooms of sexual equality and at first was in no mood to play her part. India expected its women to be submissive, but Carrie had other ideas. She was just too reckless and one risk taken only led to bigger ones contemplated. I found myself waiting at every intersection and, looking back at every hill and with curiosity hemming her in from all sides, found myself playing the part of 'mother hen'. The early gloss of our partnership was beginning to flake and it took a touch of comedy to unite us again.

Comedy is all about timing, props and confidence and, like all good comedians, I'd served an apprenticeship. I'd sharpened my skills in Bihar's earthy tea shops and smoothed its edges in Delhi's sophisticated restaurants. My repertoire was now ready for a captive audience but, with Carrie to impress, I left nothing to chance. Unknown to her I had bought four fresh bananas, a bag of grated coconut and a tin of peanut butter. I was ready.

Entering Mangalore we went straight into a restaurant and while Carrie hovered over the sweet counter, I went straight into my routine.

"Two teas and four chapatis, please."

The bemused waiter stood for some moments but, when I ordered no more, left. Carrie had overheard everything but, before she could speak, a quick wink in her direction, answered by a smile, told me I had a willing accomplice. One minute stretched into five. A small huddle of waiters had gathered at the counter, then within seconds the owner was at our table.

"Two teas and four chapatis, yes ?"

He repeated my order. I nodded in agreement. He then looked at Carrie. 'Why my restaurant ?' He didn't say it, but I could read it in his expression. He couldn't weigh us up. Either we were freaks, crazy or rich: whatever, he wasn't going to take a chance. He barked out orders to the kitchen staff and soon our teas and chapatis were brought.

Behind the counter, the owner couldn't hide his curiosity and, behind me, as if trying to catch a magician in his trick, our waiter stood rooted to the spot. I had played this game numerous times before and knew what to expect but, still, to extract the most from our dinner time audience, I exaggerated all my movements. I stood up slowly, went out to my bike and returned moments later with the tin of peanut butter. Then with deliberate slowness I spread thick layers of peanut butter over our chapatis. There was an audible gasp. By now everyone had stopped eating and inquisitive eyes were following me everywhere. I went back out to the bicycle, this time for the bananas and no sooner was I back than I peeled and squashed them all over the peanut butter spread chapatis. It was just too much for my waiter friend. His eyes rolled with disbelief and when I eventually rounded off my performance by sprinkling the grated coconut over them, had him exhausted with laughter. By now the restaurant was packed full with onlookers and when I held up my home made sandwich for tasting I soon had the good humoured audience queueing up for free portions.

More chapatis were ordered and more sandwiches made and, in repayment, Carrie was given free reign at the sweet counter. That afternoon we left satisfied that sandwiches would be a long time coming to India, but by the party atmosphere that followed us onto the street, the recipe would stay on their lips long after we had gone.

Since leaving Goa the coastal route to Mangalore had been flat and, with Carrie riding a single speed bicycle, just the right medicine for a beginner. I'd calculated on forty miles per day, but hadn't made allowances for her detours. Our open route on starting had turned into one of universal options. Every temple had to be explored and every beach bathed in. One detour led to the next, and I hadn't the heart to put my foot down. What should have taken us two weeks to cover had taken a month. More importantly our money was running out. We had both made bank transfers to Madras before starting and now it was imperative we get a move on.

Leaving the restaurant we decided to separate. The coastal mountains had to be crossed and leaving Carrie and her bike at Mangalore bus station, with a promise to meet up later, I set off on my own.

Within the day I was already cycling up steep inclines. Coastal suburbia had melted into forest, open fields into gardens of tropical flower and cool sea breezes into penetrating dampness. Pyramid-like elephant droppings bore out earlier warnings and, the following morning, I sighted my first wild herd. I was still riding the crest of new experience when, suddenly, a black object had me riveted to the spot.

Moments before it had looked like a black labrador dog. Now, less than one hundred yards away, its shiny black coat was unmistakable. I'd surprised a black panther. At first the sudden encounter had stripped away all fear. It turned to face me, raised its head to my scent, then with the air of curiosity loped diagonally across the road. It came so close I could see its muscles ripple and, when it bared its teeth, I felt nothing but excitement. We stood watching each other then, with a hiss, it turned and was soon lost to undergrowth. The incident had only lasted second, but took minutes to register. I even got off my bike and went searching then the sound of a branch cracking underfoot slapped me down to earth. Fear now gripped me. I raced back to the bike then, suddenly, I felt the road. I'd fainted.

With curiosity about wild life cured, I now blinkered myself off to everything except the road ahead. In Mysor I again met up with Carrie and, with money the overwhelming priority, we set off immediately for Tamil Nadu and Madras.

Chapter 23:
Excuse Me, My Dreams of
Madness are Waiting

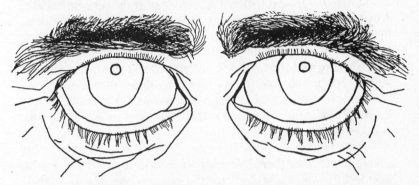

AGAIN MONEY TRANSFERS WENT ASTRAY. RESERVES had already dropped below the critical level at Tritchy but the bank transfer from Canada to Madras before Christmas had cushioned any worries. Now living almost on thin air and with Carrie gone before I realized my mistake I had to make a quick decision. "Should I stay in Madras, prisoner to red tape ?", or "Should I chance my arm on Indian village hospitality ?" The British Council came, if partially, to my rescue. A quick telegram to Canada redirected money to Bombay and a letter of cancellation to the Bank of Delhi, released me.

Since Bangalore, shadows had chased me. Constantly exposed to the sun, I was dehydrated and left exhausted. Lethargy trapped me. I got complacent, going without food and drink for long periods. The pain of fatigue increased awareness of my surroundings. A cow gave birth. Red ants on suicidal missions crossed the road to spilled grain sacks, and buzzards fought over the spoils of a dead roadside bullock. My eyes fixed on a line of trees in full blossom. Reds now blazed patterns in the stainless sky and the sun's light penetrated this regimented wall of colour at hypnotic intervals. Slowly, objects both outdoor and in merged. Tyres working the road's surface picked up its rhythms, and my brain its heartbeat. Cymbals now crashed and drums exploded in my head. The blossoms' blood red colour burst in my pupils, gears meshed in my mind. Euphoria mixed with pain. Interstate consciousness was achieved. It was the natural high of a lifetime, a traveller's nightmare.

"Is there anybody up there ?"

"Beam me up Scotty."

Sunstroke ? Malnutrition ? Delusions of grandeur ? I may have only travelled twenty miles that day, but inside I flew a million. Riding took on the form of flying, and showdowns with buses were like dog fights with no quarter given. Mirrored images melted into haze. Young and old smiled in my presence. I was adopted by a village. Food, bed, everything was provided without question. Flickering lanterns and falling stars passed in and out of my vision. Then someone pulled out the ignition switch and I was plunged into silence.

I lost two days to my condition. Everything seemed to be asking me to stay there. My legs were leaden and my bed was wonderfully quiet. Children were a constant source of amusement, but not of communication. By the third day I began to think the whole episode had been a figment of my imagination, but the struggles I now had to stand indicated otherwise.

I could stand. It was the dawn of my third day. I checked my body. No cuts, no bruises. I found a mirror. I still looked the same. A pail of water was brought with soap and towel and I was left to my own devices. Breakfast with the family announced my recovery, and, leaving to the cheers of this anonymous village, I continued north still embraced in the gratitude in a million 'namastes'.

Hampi became a welcome relief, and provided a foothold back on to the tourist trail. Since Madras I'd not spent one rupee on accommodation and village food had taken care of the rest. Now after three days 'drinking' in Hampi's reservoir of tea shops, my reserves had dwindled from sixty to twelve rupees, but it was money well spent and, before leaving, I was given the address of Panjim Catholic Cathedral for help.

"They are used to helping people with no funds. Goa has a way of stripping its visitors and these priests can spot the genuine article a mile away. I'm certain they will help you."

My previous experiences with the established church had always been linked with hidden catches and the last thing I expected was for them to part with money but my friend was so certain that I changed course and headed west towards Goa and the coast.

Two days later I arrived in Goa. Just to prove that there was no such thing as an ex-Catholic but only lapsed ones, on realizing my baptismal bond with his denomination, the cathedral's resident priest offered money to cover the ferry fare from Panjim to Bombay he also insisted that I accept enough money to cover one night's stay in a hotel.

"Can I have your name ? When I get my money in Bombay I'll send it on to you ?"

"No, that is not necessary."

He was having none of it and even looked hurt at my offer.

"Just do the same for someone else. You never know in this life. Next time the roles may change."

Our meeting had lasted less than ten minutes and, in that time, the load of beggar had slipped off my shoulders. The dreams of madness, so dominant only days ago, had gone.

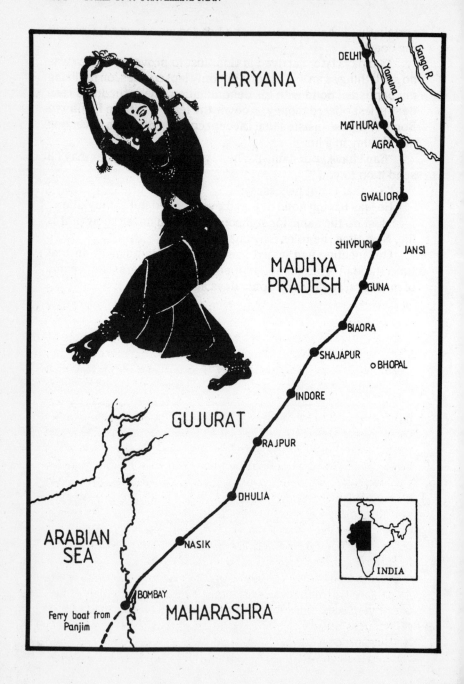

Chapter 24:
A Full Moon Called Dhawali

OFFICIALDOM SMILED ON ME IN BOMBAY. MONEY transactions had come through without a hitch. Now flushed with funds and in the peak of health, I set about the final stage of Sucontinent travel. Attitudes to India had changed since my courtship with madness. I believed nothing more could be gained by prolonging my stay. India had seen my highest highs and my lowest lows. I knew it was time to move on and, after Delhi, I promised myself the heralding of a new chapter. I hadn't any specific country in mind, but it was certain that Africa would be the next continent.

Pushed on by thoughts of imaginary victories, I entered a race of my own making and, leaving Bombay for Delhi in an all out burst of speed, I set goals of one hundred miles a day, if only to prove it was still in me.

Entering Maharashtra's barren savannah, I was astounded by the purity of its centuries old life styles. Unchanged, yet not unchallenged, tribal people riding in camel trains by the roadside were India's link with the past. Carrying everything from home made wood-rope beds to a gleaming assortment of brass water bowls, they contrasted dramatically with their more technologically advanced road neighbours. Their proud manner and unashamed smiles bore evidence of a people whose source of strength centered on unbroken chains of history and whose life was built on solid foundations. At their head, women dressed in black robes were adorned from ankle to neck in solid silver and gold bracelets. Looking like the spoils of war, these historical dowries were evidence, if that was needed, of battles won against technology's seductive powers and their unblinking stares reflected this inner strength.

Thirsty and tired, on arriving in Indore, I holed out in one of its privately owned dairies. Although only small, its owner was overjoyed to see me and, thirty minutes later after a guided tour of stainless steel vessels, antique compressors and a modern bottling process, I was invited to a rice plate meal, and later washed it down with glasses of refreshingly cool 'lassi', a yogurt, ice and milk mix.

From Indore I climbed into the fortified hill cities of Madhya
Pradesh, where nearing Maski, winding nose to tail over the hills
ahead like a slow moving sea snake, I saw a wagon trail of bullock
carts. Each bullock cart displayed its own unique colour combination. Men wore turbans like family crests in a multitude of
primary colours while women, both young and old, sparkled in
multi-coloured waistcoats inlaid with miniature mirrors. It was
market day and a magic cocktail of sound and colour announced
the oncoming "full moon festival", as India prepared for
Dhawali.(Festival of colours)

My days were now split into two phases. I cycled from sunrise
to sunset. Then, after a few hours' cat-nap by the road, I would
continue late into the evening. By day a spring sun filled in the
shadows and by night a moon chilled them. Roadside attractions
reawakened childish ambitions to play clown. During the day
India's bursting population of children acted as my audience
while, at night, noises of bullocks, bells hung loosely round their
necks, mixed with exploding fireworks, as rural India now gripped
in the fever of festive preparations let off excesses of excitement.

The day Dhawali burst onto the countryside, make-shift road
blocks manned by both adults and children extracted light hearted
ransom for more than willing drivers, as both trucks and buses
were splashed good humouredly with colour. On more than one
occasion, bags of coloured powdered dust were thrown in my
direction, and soon my bike and clothes were stained with their
contents. Village festivals spilled out into the streets, and human
blockades often brought traffic to a full stop. Wherever I was seen
I was given tea and often somosas for free. In one village a rice
plate full of spiced sauces, vegetables, and parathas required
eating and, before leaving the village, another restaurant insisted
I sample their pancake-like dosas.

For three days I rose and fell on the tides of festive excitement. One town offered an animal market, and I watched for hours
while men washed, groomed and painted their charges. Camels,
decorated in multi-coloured beads, competed with bullocks for
centre stage, as horns were shaped, sharpened and belled, ready
for sale. Bull races, dangerously marshalled in shallow muddy
ditches, brought out man's betting instinct and, at intervals,
these half ton beasts escaped, scattering both punter and viewer

alike. Fire eaters, snake charmers, and fortune tellers attracted the curious and street musicians the rest. During early evening, open air street cinemas offered continuous programs and, for the first time in India, power failures stopping performances short, precipitated near riots. One evening found me judging a village 'disco' contest, as wires strung between power lines ran free electricity to their antique record player. In another village; a request to show them how people disco dance in the West found me doing the twist on a raised platform to a wildly appreciative audience and, in repayment, village women, having changed into their best sarees, danced for me in a spontaneous gesture of good will, accompanied to the tunes of village instruments. In yet another, my evening was highlighted by a village feast in my honour and, while I ate under the umbrella of lantern light, school children sang songs of welcome in both Hindu and English.

I was experiencing India's icing on the cake. I'd spent over two hundred nights in villages and scores in temples. I'd seen their simplistic life, come to terms with their poverty and borne the living deity mantle like a second skin. Now I found myself letting my hair down. Maybe it stemmed from naivety, or maybe the festive excitement was a drug of equality. I joined in, held hands, touched, sang, danced, was painter and painted. For the first time rural generosity felt natural. All feelings of being different dissolved in a mass of excitement. For three days no one cared what caste you came from or, for that matter, if you were a Muslim, Christian or Hindu. Rural India now linked arms in an unbroken chain round the full moon and it was a sad day when it was broken.

Seemingly hung by an invisible chord, the moon's fluorescent disc was unusually bright the night I made camp outside Biaora and, although days past its fullness, it still illuminated the temple's most sheltered crevices. I'd stopped just after sunset in a roadside Hindu temple and, having erected my mosquito net, now lay naked behind its screen watching a Sadhu go through his ritual bathing. Since arriving we'd not exchanged one word. A nod here, a gesture there. Villagers brought food just before nightfall, even offered a wood-rope bed, but I declined for the cool surface of the temple's polished stone. After eating, the Sadhu stripped, covered his body in ashes, rubbed vigorously, then washed himself down with water from the temple well.

The setting was dramatically beautiful. Erotic carvings in all manner and positions of copulation adorned the pillars. A many handed Kali centered in the open courtyard burst out in exaggerated curves, and within the inner cloisters, burning insence sticks gave fragrance to an atmosphere already heavy with the rising moon. I'd often seen the naked Indian physique, but never in such surroundings. Now cleansed of ash he rubbed oil on his body and

then laying down a reed mat, began his yogic exercises with the controlled discipline of a ballet dancer. Even the slightest muscular movement became magnified under the moon's glare. Only yards from me, he looked long and hard in my direction. Then he stood. Bathed in light; his feline features sent a strange shudder of excitement through me. "Are you shocked? Wouldn't you like to rub up against a new experience?" A silent voice said no, but my body answered in a different language. I'd slept in scores of temples, and it was quite usual for Sadhus to sleep next to me; before. Their motives were always protective, but this time I knew different. Minutes went by. Was I to make the first move? He was so close I could hear him breathing but I dared not look up. Suddenly a warm hand glided over my cheeks, then rested on my thigh. My eyes were closed, my body rigid. Guilt mixed with joy. I couldn't respond. The answer was not in my power. The hand stayed only moments, then slowly followed the arc of my spine, before returning to its owner. I asked the question, left myself open and my Sadhu answered it. There was no embarrassment, no break in mood and, standing up, he returned across the courtyard to his mat. Another mystery stayed intact.

My last day's riding in India took me from Agra to Delhi. It hadn't been my intention to cycle it in one day, but second wind and thoughts of finishing my cycle trip of India on a high note drove me on. Still twenty miles from from Delhi, the traffic became chaotic and heavy and, without road lights after dark, bad vehicle lighting blinded. Then, just as I was going to stop, help came in the form of a Sikh scooter driver and for the last ten miles I glided along on a human tow of mechanical power.

The following day I visited travel agencies in Connaught Place and made tentative enquiries about African flights then, driven northwards by early monsoon rains, I retired my bike in Ringo's and took off into the mountains by bus.

Chapter 25:
Hello - Goodbye

THERE WERE NO GREAT MYSTICAL REASONS FOR choosing Dharhamsala. I had visited this home of the exiled Dalai Lama the year before and chose it again now for its friendly Tibetans and fresh mountain air. Life on the plains of India had been like kicking the ant hill of rush hour traffic and in the mountains, I hoped to escape its teeming chaos if only for a week. Africa, for the moment was put on hold and any thoughts of air tickets were left behind in Delhi.

I had just arrived in Dharhamsala and the 'Rising Moon' restaurant matched my mood. Having come to terms with leaving India I looked forward to spending a week of carefree walking and also felt open to share it with people.

Entering the restaurant my eyes rested on a young girl sitting on her own surrounded by unwritten postcards.

"Hi, can I join you ?"

Her smile was all the invitation I needed and we were soon exchanging names, routes and experiences, as we both slipped into the well worn phrases of acceptable conversation. Mikey was German, not the typical blond, blue-eyed airian, but dark-haired with deep brown eyes and, like myself, within days of leaving India. Our meeting at once had that quality of mystery and sexual attraction that, once raised could not be put down easily and in it surfaced an on going weakness. Since leaving Toronto my bike had dominated my life, but even that had taken second place whenever a relationship had beckoned. Relationships had been few and far between on the road and whenever they did cross my path, I felt powerless to leave. Afterall hadn't I turned Yogyakarta into a race to meet Janet and Singapore had only been a stop-over till Xzera, and, if it hadn't been for Alison, wouldn't I have left India over a year ago ? Now this youthful German had touched the same nerve. Experience had taught me the importance of setting goals. Africa had been my latest. Relationships, I had told myself, were transient, time consuming and their goodbyes-painful. I'd weighed up all the pros and cons before. Logic had always told me to leave well alone, but instincts, so much part of my life, now would always send out different impulses. The last thing I wanted before leaving India was involvement but that night I didn't want to break its spell either. I simply had to ask her out. Within minutes of our meeting, Africa had flown out of the window, but the more I tried to replace it with hints of a personal nature, the more I lost my way. I'd forgotten how to frame the all important question but, that evening, we parted with an unspoken agreement to meet again.

Hidden from view above Dharhamsala, I found Mcloud Gange home away from home for hundreds of Tibetan refugees. Paper thin, its facade of village stone soon gave way to timber-corrugated dwellings, as first, second and third generation refugees squatted together for protection in tiers of patchwork shanties. Held together more through family ties than religious allegiance, prayer flags strung from roof to roof gave the overall scene a feel of permanence.

Arriving early the following morning in Mcloud Gange I followed a prearranged route into the foothills and soon found myself a paying guest in a thriving village 'bed-sit' land of occupation. After setting in, I walked the one mile back to Mcloud Gange and straight into Mikey. It was obvious, on meeting, that neither of us wanted to push our friendship past that of casual, but the next few days found us meeting in an embarrassing web of coincidences, as we both stood one side of a morning lie, only to find ourselves confronting its other side in the afternoon. Mutual attraction had sent us both in opposite directions yet, amazingly, whatever escape route we took, it invariably led us back together. It seemed that friendship-maybe-more was inevitable. Not since Alison had I felt this natural blending of wills and before we both left for Delhi, we were sleeping together. Like children with a new toy, sexual attraction couldn't be put down easily and whether we walked hand in hand or lay together its natural electricity demanded outlets. Up til Mikey, Subcontinent travel had been an asexual experience and now I took every opportunity to make up for lost time. Strengths were supported, ideas spawned and friendship sealed and the gloss of our sexual attraction filled in the rest. I now knew that our time spent together would be enough to bridge any gap her impending return to Europe would enforce.

Five hectic days followed Mikey's departure. Botswana, my

first African choice, proved too expensive. Then Zimbabwe fell through and Tanzania had too many currency problems. Rapidly my options were running out, then a quirk of fate threw up a budget ticket I couldn't refuse. A cancellation and baksheesh secured a flight to Nairobi. Kenya was to be my stepping stone into the African Continent.

It was my last day and for sentimental reasons I took one more walk around Connaught Place. I didn't recognize her at first. Isolated from her friends she looked much older and, when spotted, she offered me only a glazed look of acknowledgement. It was a working day for her and street leaflets took priority. So many travel experiences had overlapped since I last saw her and even the impact of our meeting, or its significance in being my last day in India was lost. Time had evaporated all pain. I could still picture my experience with the 'family' clearly enough, but that specific arrangement of events, that special detail which set the whole incident apart, and my involvement, had gone. She now looked no different from the hundreds of other street converts and a quick conversation read more like a bible class of psalms than what one expected from a close friend.

"Can I pray for you ?"

"That's up to you, Alison."

Four hours later I was in the air en route to Nairobi.

Chapter 26:
What Tribe Are You From?

WITHIN MINUTES OF ARRIVING MY JET LAGGED BODY was injected with African spontaneity. Already the rhythms were in my blood. A woman, a fellow passenger from Delhi, so plain and unnoticeable on embarking, now literally danced down the corridor towards me. Everyone had picked up on Africa's contagious spirit and when the passenger's baggage finally rolled up to be collected, everyone seemed to be falling over each other to give helping hands. Some time later my bike was wheeled out.

"Please can I ride it ?"

Can you picture a porter riding between passengers towards the customs desk ?

"Jambo, welcome. Welcome to Kenya."

The officer shook my hand, his grip leaving me with no doubt as to my welcome.

"What tribe are you from ?" The customs officer was pointing to my passport.

"Tribe ?"

He burst out laughing. Tribe, caste, class, some things never change.

"Enjoy your stay, but beware of the lions."

My head was still at twenty thousand feet and still leaking essential ingredients and, going by my shaky start on the bike, leg muscles also.

Leaving the airport I encountered a herd of zebras grazing lazily against the perimeter fence; they didn't even give me a second glance and further on a lone giraffe stopped only moments before continuing his leafy meal. Suddenly the sound of a passing car exploded a group of gazelles from nowhere and, jumping in high arcs, they crazily zig-zagged down the road, before disappearing into the bush. Further on, roadside houses, built of mud parched red by the sun and blended with straw, contrasted vividly with sky-skrapers in the distance and exemplified better than any words   Africa's headlong leap into the modern world. Tacky shops devoid of variety dotted the roadside

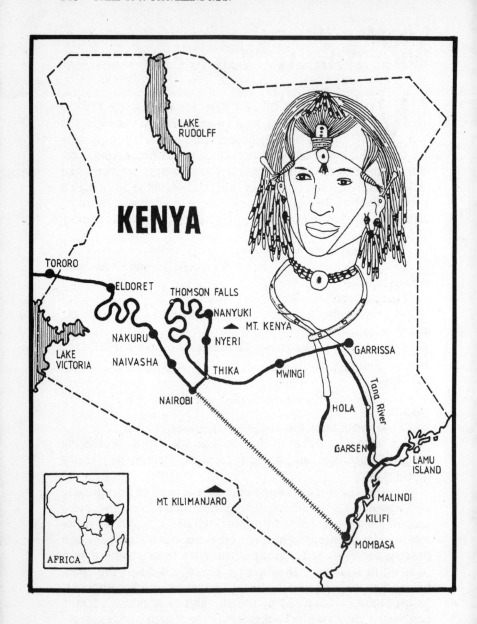

KENYA

like confetti and, on reaching the city centre I felt I had time travelled centuries. Nairobi was not what I expected. The streets were clean and manicured and pedestrians, dressed in pressed trousers, shirt and ties, could have fitted in any western city. Brand new Toyotas and Mercedes cruised with Range Rovers. Traffic lights, working, but more startling, controlling, dominated road movements in a way their Indian counterparts never achieved. A group of half naked Maasai, wrapped in tongas and adorned with neck beads and large drooping ear rings looked totally out of place and judging by the stares they attracted were obviously unwelcome reminders of old roots. Billboards advertising America's mega-hits dominated sidewalks and shops displaying the latest in European fashions competed with a tribal spin-off trade for tourist dollars. It was all too much too quickly and soon I retreated to the outskirts of Nairobi in search of cheap accommodation.

I stayed for one week while adjusting to my new home. Makeshift pavement restaurants were visited, cooked beans sampled and 'mandazi', a local fried bread seasoned with sugar, replaced the plain flour based chapatis as my staple morning diet. I spent hours watching African's playing their own unique brand of bottle top chequers, as games were won and lost with the excitement and speed of Olympic sprinters. My daylight hours were spent exploring Nairobi's dusty red yards and in the evenings I cruised River Road, seeing Africa's seedier side of street gangs, pavement gambling and sidewalk prostitution.

'Shillingy' had displaced the Indian 'paise' as local currency, while hand shakes of biting grips replaced 'namaste' on greeting and soon my hand ached with welcome.

One day I tried Africa's minibus service, the 'matatu'. Conductors dressed like street urchins and hanging out of sliding doors, shouted terminus destinations to all and sundry, waylaying pedestrians at the least sign of recognition. Packed in like sardines their V.W. convertible drivers paralleled, in their excitement, their eight track stereo music and following one hairraising chase through city streets, a tight curve delivered a rather overly curved lady on to my lap, and in doing so, punctured that invisible cage India had erected around both sexes.

It wasn't long before I was on my bike again and soon I was tentatively exploring Nairobi's surburban network of dusty red roads. It was Sunday and already the sounds of voices rose and fell intermittently like smooth curved waves. Everywhere I saw people walking. A man, a woman, sometimes couples, families and even large groups. Umbrellas were used for shade and wellingtons to protect feet against mud. A baby strapped to her mother's back peered inquisitively at me with jet black eyes and young children laughed nervously on seeing. Where were they going ? Did it matter ? Here they weren't caged by wordly problems. There was no rush, no appointments to be kept, no incentives to pursue. God wasn't worshipped at special times and church congregations were in a constant state on coming and going. Distances were not walked but danced and their springy step suggested a life with few long standing burdens. Within the week, I was hooked. Outside the city limits, life followed nature's rhythms. Like the spontaneous roadside dances I'd witnessed, every dance was different, every step based on todays mood. I was now seduced by this flexibility and, like India before with its layers of living history, Africa's element of surprise would end up wrong footing me on more than one occasion in the months to follow.

I was now two days from Nairobi and, to my right, Mount Kenya rose into a mushroom dome of clouds while, opposite, bathed in sunshine and covered to its summit in dense forest, was the Aberdare Range. Cycling in this mountain corridor the blast of cool air intensified, turning into bitterly cold winds, and clouds like flotsam blotted out the sun's rays one minute with stinging rain, only to have its weakness searched-out the next. For three years I'd watched cloud formations come and go and I prided myself on being an expert judge of weather conditions, but the speed of these changes and resultant temperature fluctuations surprised me. It was late afternoon and I was exhausted and, at this elevation, (7000 ft.) being unfit only magnified the conditions and soon I felt sick. I'd no waterproofs and although the sun dried me quickly, I never felt warm.

The next day followed the same pattern and turning west at Nanyuki away from Mount Kenya's umbrella I immediately exchanged smooth paved surfaces for a dirt track. All day I climbed in search of sun with only giraffes and gazelles for company. Progress was painfully slow and the nausea I'd felt the day before returned with a vengeance. Arriving at turn-off, I cycled straight into an invitation and, choosing my host's flat roof, I took advantage of the clear night. The view from the roof was spectacular and the stillness, eerie. Below me unfolding to the north, was a panorama of violet plains shaded off to a royal blue skyline and, opposite, silhouetted against the sky like a huge pyramid was Mount Kenya.

I woke to cold sweats and, as I'd done many times before, chose the medicine of exercise over rest. My original plan, flexible as it was, was to head north into the wilderness areas of Lake Turkana but now, under a blazing sun, I changed course back down the valley towards Nagobit. I was now cycling in all my clothes, even my jeans, but still I felt cold and, like an abscess, my sickness grew.

"You sick, you sick?"

My eyes sought out the voice but the light was too painful.

"You sick?"

Was I ever. My fever had grown hourly and this was my third restaurant stop in five miles. "Yes. You have bed?"

"No, no hotel here. You go Nagobit."

"I can't go any further, too sick."

I slumped over the table to add shape to my words.

"No. You no stay here. Very bad place."

She broke into Swahili and more figures appeared.

"Please, I'm too sick."

I couldn't go. It was impossible. Surely they could see that. I tried to stand.

"No. Wait!"

A bicycle appeared. It was mine.

"Please. We go. You sleep my bed."

She led me like a child through the kitchen into an open yard full of chickens, and the bike followed with its own audience. Three wooden shacks reminiscent of shanty dwelling stood in front of me.

"Here my room." The door almost fell off its hinges.

"Sorry." She apologized in nervous giggles.

For the first time I looked at her. She couldn't have been far into her teens, yet filled every inch of her cotton dress.

"Sorry. It very bad place, no good."

I'd never questioned offers of rooms before or, for that matter, begged for one so desperately. Over the years I'd been spoiled and taken hospitality for granted, even to the point of believing I did people good just by staying, but how I felt for this girl now made that seem insignificant. I under-estimated her resistance and now, looking around her small room, I could understand it. Daylight chequered her roof, puddles of mud, her stained floor and her bamboo bed resembled a battle field. Immediately she set about the room. Clothes were stuffed into a metal chest. Knickers pinned to a line were folded, A straw mattress was brought and an old door placed over the puddles.

"Sorry I put you to so much trouble." It was my turn to apologized but somehow words didn't fit the occasion. She shot me a look that bettered any speech she could have made.

"Take it or leave it."

In ten minutes her room had been transformed into something more resembling a kiddie's playroom, as posters of Michael Jackson were straightened and Stevie Wonder repositioned. Finished, she now gained the naive confidence age dents but, on leaving, her cheeky smile betrayed her other side. "I work night. Come back change clothes."

Fever had drained me of all strength and, within minutes of unpacking I fell straight into sleep.

A voice woke me. It was dark. I heard giggles. A zipper. Flesh was slapped, then rhythmic noises pushed me back into sleep.

"Christ.........."

A foot shredded Michael Jackson. Then a thigh. Panic turned to jitters, and then to detached fascination. The picture lay bare a gaping hole only inches from my face. It was a girl. Familiar legs were open and between them a man thrashed. I felt like an observer at a sex show and the longer I watched the less I felt. Events coupled, cavorted, then vanished. Twice more the quiet was broken. Twice more she entered my room and twice more she changed her knickers. "Sorry, I work nights."

In the morning, explanations were neither asked for, nor given. It was a working night for a working girl and, other than for the fact she used a foreign bed, no different I guessed from any other. We exchanged small talk.

"You feel better?"

"I feel great."

I really did. We shared a breakfast omelette together and a mug of ginger tea but, before we could finish, it was back to work.

I made Thika before noon and my downhill progress found me zipping round bends at high speed as strength poured back into weakened legs. Lake Turkana was now out of the question but a return to Nairobi unthinkable. I still hadn't experience the "bush". I wanted to taste its dust, smell its dew and listen to that special hush, every one had been telling me about. My dreams were of prehistory, of turning corners into the unknown, meeting tribal warriors and of pitting my strength against nature. On the plane over I'd heard of Garrissa. "It's a frontier town.", a man told me. "So most who live there didn't come by choice. It's not that kind of place. Most are transients. There's big foots, small foots, eccentrics, concentrics. It needs the army to keep the lid on. It's not a place for the faint hearted either. Black market is rife. Fortunes are made and lost. It's the blacks who make it and the whites who lose it, so keep your hands in your pockets and your arse against the wall." Then, as an afterthought, he added with a laugh, "Watch out for the Somali men. Their women are beautiful and they know it." I liked him so there was no reason why I shouldn't like his town.

At Thitani the road suddenly haemorrhaged and a paved surface gave way to a red mixture of rubble. Again progress slowed and, on reaching Mwingi it came to a full stop. An army check point blocked the road. I'd now entered convoy territory. An officer, none too pleased with my presence, set about the embarrassing task of relating his county's lawlessness. "There are shifters (bandits) here. We are too few to police this area. To cut down on robberies we send armed escorts to Garrissa. It leaves tomorrow at six. You buy ticket, put your bike on bus. No problem, many hotel. Thank you." I spent ten minutes finding where I could buy a ticket and half the night negotiating one for my bicycle.

In the morning there were no fights to get the best seats. All had been reserved. Soldiers were stationed by the driver, by the door and they also filled the back seats. Guns were readied, cigarettes lit and drinks opened. Passengers helped me lift up my bike and rearrange suitcases and then we were off. For the next hour we all watched helplessly as one item after another blew off the roof.

"Can't stop."

"That was my sleeping bag!" I insisted and when we eventually stopped a loud cheer went up and, while the soldiers were deployed into the bush, passengers hastily collected, repacked and rearranged their roof baggage.

After two hours I could distinguish the first signs of change. Under the dazzle of an intense dusty light the haze of scrub brush became denser and shrub, once sparse, began to cover all sandy clearings. A large metal radio mast marked our destination and a burst of brilliant greens marked the Tanya River basin. Once again the road stepped down and soon cultivated fields of maize prevailed over the surrounding bush. Our high speed convoy had arrived.

Seeing my bike off-loaded, children swarmed around me. Then came the women selling trinkets. As for the men there was no change in their attitude. Had pride taken on a new meaning? Was it calculated, a snub meant to appeal, an act to sell some kind of illusion? Desert warriors, no matter how destitute, do not bow to tourists, whatever the reason. I stayed for four days and I wasn't disappointed. A makeshift cinema ignited nightly to the movement of Kung Fu. Markets lived up to expectations and bartering arts exposed old weaknesses for the bargain. Women were as described - beautiful, and their men - as expected, possessive. The army, ever present when not needed, managed to keep clear of trouble.

As with Garrissa, stories of Lamu filtered down through word of mouth like water through sand. I'd not read about it and it wasn't in any tourist literature I'd seen. Yet, its description, second hand and romantic as it was, painted a picture of golden sands and deserted beaches, and a cultural mix that wasn't hard to remember.

"It's the Kathmandu of Africa.", a traveller in Garrissa said. It was a common phrase used to describe the island and even if it turned out to be half as interesting as I expected, I would be satisfied. I'd been less than one month in Africa and already I'd found little diversity in the cultural landscape. I'd had my moments but, apart from the sunset over Mount Kenya and the occasional wild life, all it offered was a monotony in different shades of green and red. My batteries were now in need of recharge and Lamu sounded the ideal place.

The first stage of my trip to Lamu followed the Tanya River south and, leaving Garrissa at sunrise, I hoped to make Hola before sunset. Again I found myself cycling on a base of pebbled stone and, notwithstanding the occasional rise, the horizon allowed me to see no further than the next bush. Road surfaces were not only difficult, but frustrating. Often I was forced to seek out shallow ruts to escape large stones and the road's corrugation did not help matters either. Since Australia I had made it a rule not to stop during these dry sections, putting the pursuit of distance before caution, but the threat of punctures and broken spokes always left my nerves shattered.

By now the sun was high and, with no yardstick to govern distances, I kept expecting a village around the next corner. Continual dust choked me, heat parched what remained of my throat juices and over-drinking, too soon, had led to stomach cramps. Two thirds of my water had gone already and, to compound problems, the village I had banked on was deserted. Still I wasn't worried. Forewarned of these problems I'd enquired before leaving about public transport. The Malindi bus was due in one hour so I decided to wait for it.

It wasn't the bus but, then, any noise in this desolate place was reassuring and the driver stopped, more out of surprise, then on request. It was a road grader and, as luck would have it, my bike fitted neatly into the blade. Encased in the elevated cab and travelling much faster then I thought, we made excellent time to Hola where I exchanged the isolated but more direct gravel route to Garsen for a parallel track of baked hard mud. Since the lift we'd tapered slowly towards the Tanya River. Tropical bush now lined the road and encroached to its edge like strangling weeds. As always these tracks acted like arteries of village life and clearings filled with mud timber frame houses, for the first time since Garrissa, dotted the roadside at regular intervals. Unlike India, wheel power was a rarity in Africa and, more often than not, foot prints rubbed out all other signs of transport. En route wild pigs were a persistent problem and, on seeing them, my driver would accelerate anticipating dinner.

"Watch out!"

Not wanting to give way, a matatu chanced its luck against us, only to end up, on its side, on the road. Curses were exchanged and immediately emptied the bush of silent spectators.

"Stupid. Those drivers no good. Always too fast. Always too many passengers. Many accident." On and on my driver went and, within the hour, he'd gone the full circle of his memory as accident after accident was recollected in graphic detail. We parted company in a small town market and, wanting to experience village life again, I continued by bike some miles before erecting my mosquito net under a mango tree in the centre of a village clearing.

Curiosity is a child's gift that can bridge any barrier and, like their Indian counterparts before, children, catching the corners of my vision, were my first signs of acknowledgement. At first they were frightened. Then the nerves of laughter crept forward. Eye contact was sought and attracting my attention became a game. Ten, twenty, thirty of them, and I soon was completely circled by a moving mass of bodies. I advanced, they retreated, and soon an improvised game of chase and be chased took over. Women, encouraged by their children, joined in, and before the sun died my audience encompassed the whole village. A radio instantly created movement and within minutes melted all resistance. Men joined in and elders were introduced. A mud hut was put at my disposal and my mosquito net and bicycle taken inside. In the evening singing took over, as songs lying somewhere between Calypso blues and punk rock brought fluctuation in moods and, sung in Swahili, I could only guess their meaning. Always there was emotion, always hope and, always, their voices had that quality of innocence.

There's only one thing worse than being lost and that's finding yourself in an area you shouldn't be in. At Wenje I had two choices. Either to rejoin the Garrissa-Garsen road some four miles west of the Tanya River, or to throw caution to the wind and follow the network of riverside footpaths. Past experience had taught me that wherever you find water, you find villages and although none were shown on my map, I knew they existed. It was the monotony of the more direct route to Garsen that tilted the balance. Now on the footpath and, surrounded by angry baboons, I wished I was bored. Entering a clearing, I'd cycled straight into a pack numbering at least forty and they weren't going to step aside for me. Years before, in the Canadian Rockies, I had surprised a wolverine when I was out for a walk and it was only ignorance of danger that saved me. Life in the wilds had its attractions and being vulnerable to it only added spice to encounters. My saviour in the past lay in not searching, but letting it happen. This time was very different. I knew I was cycling through a game reserve and, thankfully, much needed advice from the warden was remembered.

"Always be calm, don't forget they're just as frightened as you are. Look for escape routes - not yours, but theirs. Don't ever get between a hippo and the water. When you see elephants, look around for any sign of cubs, and don't, whatever you do, come between them and the herd. If you want to rest by the river, choose the high ground or, better still, climb a tree. Crocodiles are scavengers, so keep out of long grass. Bison and rhino are unpredictable so, if you see them, best go in the opposite direction. Never approach lions. If you see one in the open, stand still. If he doesn't approach you, move slowly away but don't turn your back on him and never move quickly. If he does approach you and there's no escape, roll up in a ball on the ground and play dead. Lastly, if all else fails, ring your bell and pray like hell, they've just eaten. The secret is being heard before being seen if you're travelling through."

It worked. Ringing my bell sent them bounding in all directions. I had never thought that baboons were so dangerous before. Seen from the roadside in ones and twos on the bus they looked so playful but, when I was surrounded, like hungry hyenas. With this incident still fresh in my mind safety came first and, that night, I slept in a school building while, outside, crashing through the undergrowth hippos grazed. I reached Garsen the following day and within two more, through swampy jungle, Mokowe. Now only a strip of water separated me from my new home.

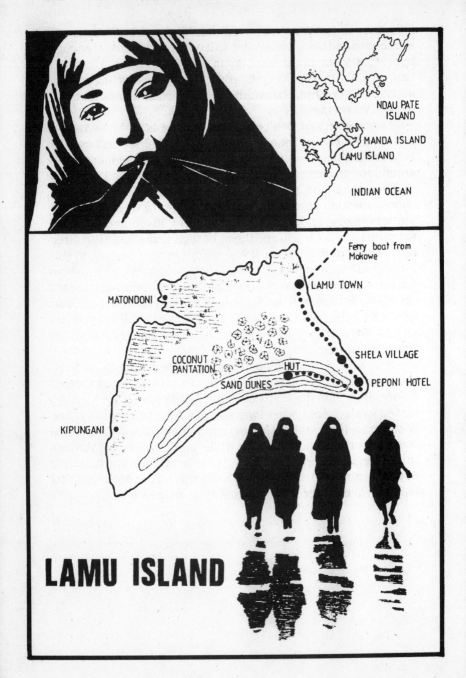

LAMU ISLAND

Chapter 27:
Lamu, an African Cocktail

INSIDE ME THERE'S A SPECIAL FEELING FOR ISLANDS. MAYBE it's because, deep down, I'm British and identify all islands with home. For centuries few influences had spanned the British channel and conquests, in my time, came from within. First we accepted the war refugee. Then, in the 50's over-night sun tans became the vogue. Now, so dependent is Britain on their second generation, they can't do without them and to roll back their influence now, would lead to mass hospital shut downs, bring local transport to a full stop and starve taste buds of their favourite curries.

"You don't have to leave Bradford to travel."

To my mates, all aspects of life walked Bradford's pavements and if I was to believe their words, then Lamu would be a world unto itself and, being much smaller, would accentuate all its aspects. Built on the slave trade and Muslim in influence, Lamu's chequered history was an enticing one and with only the cool sea breezes for company, I looked forward to entering it.

On the boat ride over I reflected on my missing links. Parting from Mikey had been one goodbye too many. I had a strong urge to stop, to mould something permanent from my trip, make some kind of connection and leave an impression longer then my stay. I wanted people to remember me, not just as a one-off, a transient, but as someone they could rely on, a person they could visit when I'd finished. After three years in the vacuum of travel, I needed something more than the "here today, gone tomorrow" relationships.

The boat trip was short and seeing my bike offloaded ignited a chorus of laughter and my now long hair brought on instant nicknames.

"Hey Rasta man!"

"Masungu!"

"Bob Marley."

"No road here, mate."

Jokes gave way to business and soon market forces in the guise of beach boys, pushed down hotel prices.

"Private house. Four hundred shillings a month."
"Single bedroom. Twelve shillings a night."
"Six shillings a night. Best price in Lamu."
Prices fluctuated wildly and description also.
"Many travellers stay my hotel. You come look."
Those were the words I wanted to hear. The priority was to be around my own kind. Bargaining over prices could come later. The decision was made and arguments stopped. Immediately the crowd of beach boys retreated back into the shadows to await the next boat.

Kiswani Hotel overlooked the harbour and, true to his word, its balcony was full of white faces. A cup off tea appeared and a ritualized tour began. I chose dormitory accommodation, then turned my energies to more pressing problems. I stored the bike, changed some travellers cheques, checked the poste restaunte for mail, showered and, slept the clock around.

"Oh Allah Akbad.....Oh Allah Akbad....Oh Allah...Hahhhhhh Akbad."
It was my early morning wake-up call and its echoes seemed to jump out from every corner of the room. Allah was in good voice that morning, and all it took was a whiff of sea air and I was ready to go. Lamu was to be a holiday, and I couldn't wait to explore. Narrow passageways spread out like branches and shade like blankets. Mosques marked every intersection and groups of young men wearing long white robes marked every restaurant. Women, veiled in jet black Bui Bui's searched me with their eyes and children, with their hands. It was 9:00 am and, already, the passageways were filled with people and every tight corner released a new surprise. A market place gave way to Lamu's prison and instantly the instruments of British Policy were exposed. Police Station, Bank, Post Office, all tightly knit together and all tiered in order of importance. A jeep parked where no road exits pointed out, the trappings of officialdom and a sign marked, "Commissioner" revealed its owner. Boats from Mombasa bringing their once weekly food ration, unloaded at bargain prices where, as I found out later, fluctuated around their arrival. Fish, freshly caught, still had their natural colour and demanded purchase and mangoes by the sackful, couldn't be ignored either. Oven fresh mandazies melted in my mouth and

powdered ginger teas, sweetened with spoonfuls of sugar worked better than any coffee to open my eyes. Boats like galleons from a long forgotten age of sail from India, were under refit and, marking the harbour's low tide in staked out rows, thousands of ebony coloured mangrove trunks piled neatly one above another, bore evidence of their continental harvest. Coral used for building material was being unloaded and donkeys, weighed down with their loads,tailed off up into the towns many passageways . Children playing spontaneous football games had a quality that was impossible to referee and beach boys were trying to impress with trials of strength that were impossible to judge. I could have watched Lamu at play for hours, but a deceptive heat forced me back to my bed.

Night brought to life the scents of perfume and shops, emptied by the heat of day, refilled with custom. It was the time for the women and, although inhibited by religious constraint, they now took what little freedom they had to the ultimate. Veiled of bodily curves, their only power lay in eye contact and one wink, one slide up or down, exhibited in their daring glances, a quality of eroticism that dreams are made of.

At first I wished for no more than to eat, sleep and unwind. A week passed before I ventured out of town and yet another passed before I explored the island's miles of golden beaches. One night I visited Tetley's Bar. I'd gone for a drink looking for humour and left, disappointed, so when invited by friends in Kiswani to leave, I grasped at the chance with both hands. One morning was all that I needed to prepare and, by afternoon, I'd exchanged the bustle of Lamu Town for that of Shela's spacious Colonial style living.

From the start Shela welcomed. Barbecues spilled over into parties, conversation into evening meals and sundowners (nightcap drinks) were all the excuse needed to fall into unbroken sleep. Once again I found comfort in armchairs and the time to appreciate a well-manicured garden. Sculptured objects warmed to the touch, well designed spaces warmed to the eye and cool verandah balconies were soothing to the skin. My new home offered both privacy and colour and, within its ten foot perimeter wall, the freedom to be naked with friends. Inside, I wanted for nothing and, although the allure of the beach was strong, I went no further than my home's white washed walls. Mornings were spent skinny dipping in the pool. Afternoons were spent sunbathing and evenings were spent lounging about and reading. Boredom was never a problem and any gaps left over were soon filled by Shela's unique cocktail of permanent white residents. Liberation struggles were relived with ex-mercenaries, big game safaris with retired hunters and European roots with Lamu's hidden tax exiles. Time passed too quickly. In two weeks the owner had returned and, with him, new house guests, but Shela wasn't finished with me yet. Taking up an invitation to Peponi Hotel, I was offered, and accepted, my first bath in nearly two years and so began a rich relationship with its owner. I stayed on for four days as their house guest then, once again a new home beckoned and, returning to a life of confined spaces, I exchanged the opulent surroundings of Peponi's for that of anchored yacht life on "Merlin."

After experiencing life on a prawn boat, if someone would have told me that I was going to spend three months living on a yacht, I would have told them they were crazy. Yet, within ten days of meeting Roy, I was rocking about on water again.

If some people are naturally eccentric then Roy is one of them. Soft spoken and gentlemanly in the extreme, he personified all the traits of his chosen vehicle. Like all travellers he had courage but unlike most, his quality was born from solitary endurance which, in the natural course of events turns all expressions inward. Roy's whole world revolved around his boat, Merlin, as mine did around my bike and in this we had a common base. But that was as far as it went. Roy had lived the hermit's life for two years at sea en route from Europe down through the Suez Canal and, because of this, had developed that sensitivity peculiar to all sailors. At sea, where everyone pulled together, this worked well, but when transferred to land, could lead to disillusionment. He was continually being let down and his hospitality abused. Cocooned and barnacled by sea life, Roy needed friends like I needed solitude and whenever we met our needs surfaced. On land, his thoughts were always at sea and, when at sea, they were always on land. He needed someone he could trust, someone to share the everyday load of boat security.

On board my first lessons were costly ones. "If it moves, nail it down and if it doesn't, tie it down." Sensible advice but within the week I'd lost a bucket, miscellaneous cutlery, two shirts, a pair of shorts and a towel. At first his reaction was one of amusement then, silent pressure made caution advisable, as everything from underwear to buckets was tied down. One week in my temporary home, life's early stutters were over and, being mosquito free, a pleasant one. By day, dozing and reading on deck, a sea breeze cooled me and, by night, shore music drifting over me in natural currents was soothing. Soon we'd slipped into friendly routines and alternate nights ashore found the other rowing over on ferry duty. Occasionally we both went ashore but Roy never strayed far from town and was never more at ease then when he was on his yacht. Some days he opened up and, interspersed between stories of sudden squalls, near capsizes and sea piracy, his other side surfaced. It became clear that Roy's knowledge of countries went no further than their harbourside Colonial bars. One day, in a fit of pique, he commissioned a local shop to make him a British Ensign. Then, observing maritime tradition, he raised and lowered it every day, paralleling that of the Harbour Police's Kenya flag and thus implanted on Lamu, his own uniques brand of one upmanship.

At first the daily menu à la English greasy diet, required adjustment. "A good chip is a thick, crisp one." Eggs and chips for breakfast, dinner and supper were too much for my well travelled stomach. Roy wasn't one for variety, especially when it meant breaking with old patterns. To him a plate full of chips was a journey, a constant reminder of home. Variety was adding Ketchup and he wasn't about to change for any visitor. "You can tell someone's personality from his balance of salt and vinegar." He was the fortune teller of chip-butty-sandwiches, the fry-up's Guru and whenever eating I knew I was in for a story.

We were both Brits but, unlike me, he was still cocooned in its past and, central to this link with home was the "British Overseas Network". Every night it spoke to him. "Two Way Family Favourites " with its 60's music could glass his eyes. Cricket scores would bring on smiles and the nightly Shipping Forecast pricked up his ears. A night of nostalgia was planned and with a promise of Hancock's Half-Hour he had no problem filling his boat with eager listeners.

Eventually my bike was brought over from Kiswani and, when secured above deck, it became yet another landmark of local conversation and with it, a new nick-name, "Ten Speed".

The weeks stretched into months then the inevitable happened. It was too late to abdicate responsibilities now. I had invited myself on to his yacht to get him off. I though, at that time, a change of scenery would do him good. Maybe he could see a bit of the country, take in a few night clubs on the mainland, even get a woman. Now he was going to Mombasa for spares and thoughts of being left responsible for $50,000 dollar's worth of hardware were daunting.

"Don't worry Roy. Go and enjoy yourself. I can look after things here." I was trying my best to sound confident but talking and doing are worlds apart. He had taught me how to anchor, readjust for tide changes and how to use the anchors to manoeuvre the yacht. I could start the engine, recharge the batteries, operate the sump pumps but, seeing him off, I was already planning to share the load if not the experience, with a friend.

"Ully, pull. Harder....Harder!"

Five minutes before we had been locked in a mutual game below deck. I had not noticed the tide changes, A clap like thunder shattered our fun and, in a flash, I was out of bed but, sadly, what caution the shock ignited went up in a puff of smoke and, immediately I entered a comedy script of errors. On deck my worst fears were confirmed. The anchor had dragged and we were drifting across the tide like a slow moving pendulum. Another crash! We'd struck our neighbour's boat on the stern.

"I'll use his anchor-chain. That boat's smaller then ours."

"Don't fight the elements, let them work for you." For a split second Roy's advice entered my head. My first reaction had been to swim over to our neighbour's boat. The current gripped even on the dive and, before my eyes had time to adjust, I was swept downstream.

"Bernard watch out."

Miraculously I had drifted into our starboard anchor buoy. Pitch black, hands tearing on barnacled chain. I fought my way back as a calm Ully watched in amusement.

"Let's get the dinghy over."

On board I should have taken the time to sit down and clear my head but speed consumed me and, returning to the water, I swapped one mistake for another. "I'll row out to the anchor buoy. When I've lifted the anchor off the bottom, pull me back. Then I can row out to the stern and reposition it."

"Pull.....Harder....Harder!" The combined weight of anchor, Ully's pulling and my position in the dinghy capsized it. Again water closed above me. I was exhausted. A night of pleasure had turned into a nightmare. Underwater the dinghy lit up like a fluorescent halo. Plankton now illuminated my struggle to surface. One second I was struggling for air and the next I'd surfaced. I had lost every ounce of fight and Merlin's dinghy too.

"It's alright. We've stopped."

I hadn't the strength to answer her but, looking over my shoulder, I could see we had drifted in the opposite direction and, now, a correct distance separated our anchorage from the neighbouring boat. I'd done nothing right. I'd spent thirty minutes fighting the elements only to give in. My hands were now shredded with deep razor cuts, my knees were bruised and sore, and our wooden dinghy, Roy's pride and joy, lay some fifteen feet below the surface still secured by rope and its outline still illuminated by friendly plankton. I was too tired tonight to retrieve it and the boat damage would have to wait until morning.

Daybreak brought good news. The dinghy, albeit waterlogged, proved little problem and, when aboard, it dried quickly. As for the scene of our nightly adventure, only paintwork scratches were in evidence and a few dabs of paint would restore it to its past glories. For the next week everything went smoothly and when Roy returned I reluctantly handed back responsibility. His return brought news of the impending arrival of another friend which was the signal for my departure to yet another home.

Rising out of the sea like a fireball the sun announced the beginnings of another day. From behind, palms shaded my new home, and surrounding it at receding elevations to the sea, some two hundred feet below, sand dunes rose and fell in recorded shapes to the Indian Ocean's trade winds. At first signs of light my acacia tree would burst into life, as the tree's night shift of bats returned, displacing a multitude of noisy and colourful birds. Snakes would spiral up into my bamboo roof each morning to sleep while crabs on the scavenge would appear from minute caves in the sand in and around my cooking area. Wild bush buck peered at me inquisitively from the surrounding dunes and

wandering goats, more daring, lined up to watch my daily routine at breakfast. A typical day saw me shaking off the cobwebs of sleep with an early morning swim. Driftwood had to be collected and a morning breakfast was cooked on an open fire. While I ate chapatis, lone joggers far below would be registering patterns on the otherwise virgin beach. While sun was boundless, water was a continual problem. I drank tea constantly and every day I was forced back to Shela for refills. My daily diet varied and was dependent on village stocks. I could be eating anything from fresh vegetables to over ripe fruit, while home-made chapatis were made by the dozen.

By mid morning the skies were starched blue and, as the sun moved, the tides of sand moved with it. It was still too early for the sun worshippers and the dune's abstract shape of light and shadow was my only company. After ten, the silence would be broken. Groups of tourists would appear from nowhere. Some would group together for protection. Others, more daring, would search out more secluded spots and, from my high elevation, I could observe them all. Soon predictable patterns of beach life would develop. Families would search out shade, lovers, seclusion, and singles, the golden beach. Territory was staked out with towels and, at intervals, they dotted the four miles of unspoiled beach in splashes of isolated colour.

By noon all colour would be bleached. Shadows disappeared. Dunes, one climbing on top of another, lost all definition and views melted into a heat haze of monotony. Flat seas were lost to the horizon in mirages of fluid light and even the hardiest sunworshipper was forced back from the beach. To walk bare footed only invited pain as sand, baked by the sun, burned flesh easily. It was noon, time to escape the heat and the beach would empty. At this time my palm/bamboo house offered welcome relief and, retreating inside its aerated space, I took advantage of the cool sea breezes.

Some days I filled in this period devouring books, writing or sketching, and others, I had only the strength to fall into a sleep of heat exhaustion. Being one and a half miles from the nearest settlement and hidden high in the sand dunes, my hermit existence offered boundless solitude.

By late afternoon I was combing the beach for building material. House renovation was a full time job and additions, a constant source of experiment. My home had been two weeks on the planning board and then, after leaving the Merlin, it took a further two weeks to make it. Thirty palm leaves needed cutting, carrying and weaving and the framework of bamboo driftwood had to be collected from the beach. A mat washed ashore roofed my verandah and one donated by Peponi's covered my sandy floor. Shells decorated the interior and discarded tins were used for storage. That old inbred work ethic was still with me and I never felt more at home than when in a sweat.

Sunset always drew me back from the beach and, if vegetables were available, a stew was made. It was at this time of the day that visitors would come. Life in the dunes was an exposed one at the best of times, filled with insecurities and loneliness but evening forged a new drawing card and long spells of daily solitude were easily broken. Budget Travellers dropped in for a chat, jet setters for the experience and artists for the view. Inevitably my notoriety spread to the mainland and surprised visitors on guided tours dropped in to see "the freak on the hill". Some days the law paid a visit but, valuing my presence to deter beach thieves, they generally left me alone. Sunset was last orders, drink up time and, for whatever friends were visiting, it was time for them to stay for the night or go, for to be caught out in the dark could lead to an eerie three mile walk back to Lamu town. Once again silence would return to the beach and nature's currents would cleanse it for the following day. As the sun would exit, violet hues would streak the sky. Pale blues turned royal and within minutes darkness soaked up the beach. Some evenings shooting stars traced the night sky and others nights, lit by the full moon, covered the dunes in imaginary snow.

During the night, Peponi's offered my solitude a welcome break, and friends, calling during the day, reciprocated hospitality in the evening. It was the last building before the beach and the first and only building to tempt me off the hill. Peponi's offered me a slice of the good life and, in its owner, a friend whose value could not be gauged until missed. Guests came and went, but always a hard core stayed. Being isolated from the rest of Lamu subtracted all pressures to conform. Here I could touch the untouchable, see the invisible and interview the nameless power brokers of industry. Private chambers were opened and inner cloisters experienced. I became their resident bar mascot and without the owner's sponsorship I would not even have touched first base. In repayment I wound up the bar jokers, deflated the arrogant and philosophized with the philosophers but nothing I said or did could even the balance as gourmet meals offered were hungrily devoured.

After two months in the dunes my humble beginnings had turned into a monster. With no one to share, criticize or stir friction its real estate value had lost all value. Then, in November, a letter demanding action came to my rescue. Mikey was coming in December.

Chapter 28:
Trans African Safari

"C HRIST, YOU'VE BROUGHT EVERYTHING EXCEPT THE kitchen sink." In front of me a bemused Mikey was surrounded by the baggage of our first compromise. Mikey had left nothing to chance. Unlike my paper thin needs, she had answered travel's every question, then doubled its requirements and, so heavy was her baggage that bike and all had to be ferried into Nairobi by bus.

From Nairobi I took her to Lamu then, from within its boundaries we sketched out the plan of our Trans African Safari. Excess baggage was halved, visas checked and routes gone over for weakness. Our plan was to travel coast to coast, ending in the Cameroons by April and, past that, all options were left open. On Lamu Mikey settled into a period of readjustment. New phrases had to be learned, new diets accommodated and temperatures more extreme than Europe acclimatized to. Her body would have to be tanned and toned before travel and while she took long walks on the beach I set about saying my goodbyes. Six months had been a large chunk of travel. Unknowingly I'd taken root. Sunk back into Lamu's sand I now blended in just like any other of its permanent residents and this didn't make my goodbyes any easier. I spent one week visiting old haunts, shaking hands and shedding more than a few tears. Old chords had to be severed and I was relieved when it was all over. Now, into the second week of January, broken clouds spreading to the sea's horizon announced the oncoming rainy season; it was time to make tracks. We took in one final sunset and, by sunrise the following morning, we had gone. Five unhurried days saw us back to Nairobi and after another five spent in last minute preparation, we were ready.

Our first day started smoothly enough, but by noon on the fourth day the sun had distanced us. Mikey had something to prove, if not to me, then to herself. Pain barriers had to be broken, hills conquered and rhythm found. On the road I was the pace setter. Cycle touring wasn't for the faint hearted, not the way I approached it and, in Mikey, I hoped to find a sympathetic partner. The Rift Valley's steady slopes were our first hurdle and broke our muscles in easily but continued exposure to the sun soon led Mikey into heat exhaustion. On our first day Naivasha was reached, but we were never to cover the same mileage again or, for that matter, try to. At Nakuru, on the third day, we turned west and started our climb into the nine thousand foot Mau Escarpment Pass and the first of our many crossings of the equator. Now, rising above the plains we could see its stretch marks as banks overlapped, compressed and rutted into deep gorges. Already the tropical vegetation so thick in the foothills gave way to forests of pine and, once above five thousand feet, the dampness chilled in the shadows. Traffic so thick around Nairobi, had drained to a trickle and, cycling on good paved surfaces, we were making excellent progress.

Outside Nairobi we were at the mercy of African lifestyles. Food would depend on availability and accommodation, on hospitality. Small villages were devoid of stores and long distances, of habitation. We had to eat where possible. Hours could be spent cycling in isolation then, a splash of colour, a burst of activity, and once again we would be surrounded by abundance, overfilling, like camels, in the market restaurants, for the next stop. Not wanting to break the spell of the unknown I was reluctant at first to carry food and based all my decisions on instincts.

I'd now put over twenty thousand unplanned miles behind me and, in doing so, had compiled a wealth of travel experience. I had lived the American Dream; experienced the laid back currents of the Pacific; Kiwi's rugged countryside had hardened my body and Ozzie's crude hard surface had sharpened my wit. I had tasted the spice of South East Asia and even India's crystal ball had not intimidated me. In over three years I had played many parts and in each case lived them to the hilt. In those days I had been the observed and, for sanity's sake, had erected shields of silence. With only myself to answer to I had never been limited by other people's ideas and, before Mikey, had never been put in the position to articulate them either. My partner's arrival had confronted me with a whole new dimension of travel and, in Kampala, it found me having to explain instinct with logic.

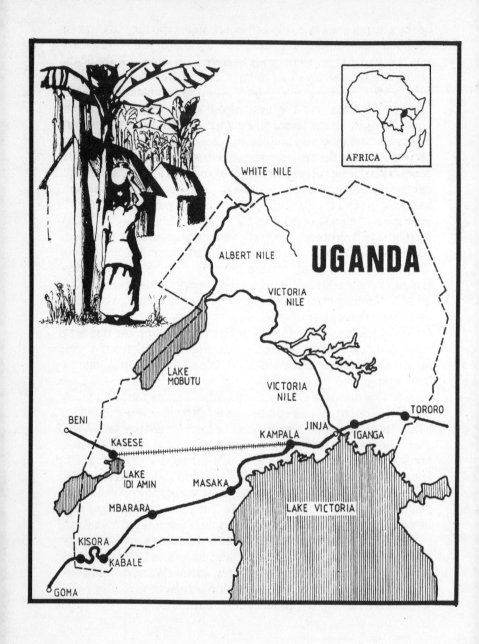

Chapter 29:
A Blood Bath Called Kampala

"**D**ON'T WORRY, THEY WON'T HARM US."
"He says don't worry!" Mikey exploded. "There is a war outside our window and he says don't worry. Maybe you are used to seeing bullets flying around, Bernard, but I'm not. Explain yourself. Try Bernard. Try and give me something to hold on to. There is no common denominator to your decisions. You're not on your own Bernard. I want to feel confident in you. I admit this world of travel is more you than me, but I'm in it with you and if you can't explain it I'm lost. Ever since we entered Uganda, you've said don't worry. Those police and army road blocks you rode through. Don't stop, you said. Some of those soldiers had guns and they were not pleased when we didn't stop. In Nairobi everyone I asked about Uganda said ,don't go there. You said, Don't worry."

Kampala's nightly spasmodic firing had erupted into what sounded like all-out war. Automatic gunfire peppered the night and, bursting through our barred windows, was a wall of panic-filled noise. Screams tore through the darkened shanty village below and now and again dropped to wailing cries. Something told me that we were safe, but that was no consolation to Mikey. Those instincts, so much a part of my life, hadn't even rippled at the noise. "Lock the door behind me. I'll be back in a minute."

Once outside I tried to piece together the week's events. The slippery slope had started with a letter to Mikey from a friend. The tentacles of "Big Brother" had managed to span thousands of miles from Europe through her friend to grip us. In Germany, Uganda was the flavour of the month and the world's press was having a field day. The World Bank was in town. Milton Obote was negotiating with them for an Aid loan but Uganda's Popular N.R.A. guerilla forces had other things in mind. The last thing they wanted was the World Bank propping up a regime they were trying to overthrow. Their objective was to destabilize the government. White businessmen were their target and the result was a blood bath called Kampala. She had translated the letter for me. I could smell fear in every sentence and, from that moment, I had been thrown on the defensive. Something had told me we were safe but, trying to explain it, when everywhere shouted danger had got us nowhere. Her blind trust in my decisions had been punctured. From that moment I'd started to my doubt instincts that only days before, I would have acted on without question. I'd been frivolous in danger before, even thought it was the greatest expression of freedom, but then I had only myself to consider.

The following day we visited the German Embassy.

"You want to cycle through Uganda on bikes? You are both crazy. Didn't you come across road blocks?"

I didn't have to answer the official, my expression gave me away.

"I do not blame you for not stopping. Milton Obote does not believe in paying his soldiers. Road blocks are just government sanctioned robbery. How else can the army survive? It is a case of turning a blind eye. Last week I would have strongly advised you both to stop at them, but that was last week and events have spiralled out of all control since then. A few days ago, a small group of European businessmen were stopped at a police road block en route to Entebbe. The police turned out to be guerillas in disguise. All were killed and robbery was not the motive."

Mikey's face dropped.

"Which way are you going?"

"West to Zaire."

"Well' you have come through the worst. The guerilla forces are not after tourists, not your type anyway. They are after publicity and it's the big fish they want but, be careful."

In the afternoon we visited the Republic of Zaire's Embassy for visas. It was like David meets Goliath but, this time David had left his catapult at home and Goliath was armed to the teeth with red tape. I got nowhere while Mikey, privileged at being a German passport holder, didn't need one. I argued, begged and grovelled and, after what felt like a predetermined time had lapsed, was given one. My embarrassment didn't end there either. I had left Nairobi without checking Kampala's Embassy list. Central Africa Republic had no embassy in Uganda. To get to the Cameroons we would have to pass through it. I needed a visa again and Mikey didn't. Now, I would have to trust my luck at the border and, if that proved impossible, it would put another two thousand miles on to our trip to Kinshasa and back. My lack of advance planning was a fundamental weakness in her eyes and, for once I agreed with her.

Leaving Kampala our slippery slope soon became a veritable ice field of crevices. I passed one too many road blocks without stopping. We'd cycled through an obstacle race of tyres in the road, ignored the hand waving and shouts of soldiers and were nearly half a mile further on when we were stopped. It had to happen sometime but the speed and resourcefulness of the sentries surprised me. Suddenly a matutu spun to a halt in front of us.

"Stop......stop!"

Two soldiers not long out of puberty spilled out onto the road.

"Go back, police want passports."

Seconds stretched into minutes and mistrust into frightening suspicion. Abject fear led to involuntary shakes, and even though they were all brandishing automatic rifles, it was hard to imagine these child soldiers using them.

"Go back."

"Bernard, don't be stupid."

Prudence was the better part of valour and, swallowing my inflated pride, I slunk back up the hill where, on arrival, more guns tilted in our direction. Youth surrounded us, They weren't aggressive but their stance held the promise they would win in the end and their guns were all the equalizers they needed to level off our ages. Immediately Mikey took command. Passports were shown, excuses made and apologies given. She calmed the situation and, before leaving, extracted a promise from me never to cross a road block again without stopping.

Past Mbarara, road blocks disappeared and surface tension evaporated. Once again we could enjoy Uganda's lush green country but within it could also be seen the core of its people's uneasy apathy towards tribal violence. Bread basket of Africa it might have been but, without trade links to unite it, one village's abundance clearly led to its neighbour's famine, as excesses of harvest rotted by the roadside awaiting collection that never came. Colonial style buildings, reflecting a once thriving economy, now stood empty, ghostly shells of their former selves and signs over deserted stores showed a country now devoid of trading expertise. The scars of war were everywhere. Roads were pitted and bore signs of tank convoys and every town we passed through had its own story of scorched and bullet ridden buildings. Looted furniture decorated every roadside restaurant we stopped at and pictures of old and new leaders reflected a country punchdrunk with instability. By now we both wanted to leave Uganda behind and, not wanting to take any side trips, we pressed on into the mountains and the promise of Zaire.

Before us, a road barrier blocked our progress. Caught in a heavy downpour the day before we had reached this point in a hangover of dampened spirits. "Is this it?" A tattered signpost above a deserted concrete building was the only hint of customs. Not the most popular border crossing in Africa, we had chosen Kisora to escape the guerillas, only to find officialdom hiding from us. Zaire's customs was only two hundred yards away across no-man's land, but our exit from Uganda looked light years away. For three weeks we had experienced a country torn apart by conflict and now the last thing we wanted was to be stopped at the final hurdle.

"Good afternoon." From nowhere a pair of pressed trousers and white shirt appeared. "Have you been waiting long?" It was the customs officer and he immediately fell into a well rehearsed pattern of action. Apologies were made. He had been having a late breakfast. Chairs were rearranged, desk drawers were unlocked and paper forms spread out with deliberate ceremony.

Thirty minutes later we left on a cloud of euphoria but, within the hour the worst that could have happened did.

Chapter 30:
The Miracle of Baptise Eglise

IT COULDN'T HAVE BEEN WORSE. I'D NEVER BEEN UP TO THE demands of cycle maintenance and now I regretted never learning the skills.

"My derailleur gear's broken." Putting pressure on the pedals my chain had slipped, knotted itself round the derailleur's arm and fractured it.

"Can it be mended?"

"Not the derailleur but maybe I can fix the chain on one gear."

Of all the places to be tested, it couldn't have happened in a more remote area. Ahead, overhanging bush shaded off our vision into darker areas of green and underwheel, volcanic ash none too even, bore little evidence of motorized vehicles. Since Idi Amin's overthrow trans African traffic crossed further north and our chosen southerly route, now rarely used, was almost lost to jungle undergrowth.

Up to this date, my list of bicycle breakdowns read like a "Scrooge's" balance sheet. Maintenance had been minimal, whether by good luck or good management and the list, considering the road conditions I'd encountered over the years was nothing more than miraculous. With only ten punctures, six broken spokes and a replacement cog and chain, my Raleigh Roadster ten speed bike's only major expense had been the purchase of over twenty tyres.

"I'll freewheel her down the hill. No good stopping here. Let's get to a village." Goma was still two days away and, with it my only chance if not to fix it and that was a chance in a million, then at least of getting a truck lift back to Kampala.

Then: "BAPTISE EGLISE"

Sticking out like a sore thumb from the surrounding bush, a large concrete sign pointed in yet another direction. Winding round an open compound our senses were suddenly assaulted by the geometric proportions of a well-constructed mission. Here in the reservoir of Zaire's knotted jungle, lurking disease and mud huts, we had stumbled on an oasis of American Apple Pie; and, invited to stay, we were soon housed in an Alice in Wonderland

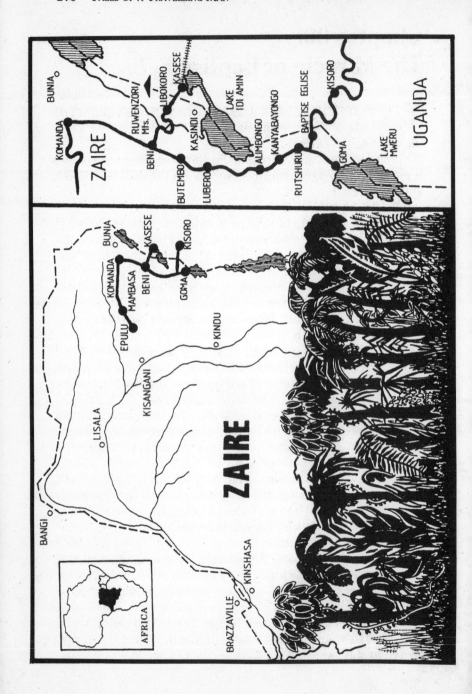

of strawberries and cream, video gadgetry and mosquito-free rooms.

Just like in all closed societies, news of our unannounced arrival at the mission sent shock waves through its members and we instantly affected their lives. Well oiled patterns would have to be broken and rigid routines bent. A community meeting was called and their calendar of events changed to accommodate us. Our arrival had been infectious. The air waves were full of our news and soon, all the more remote missionaries were told via C.B. Favouritism was not to be shown and, sleeping in a common dormitory for visiting guests, we were encouraged to share time equally with its six American families. Daily engagements were pencilled in and, for the next five days, we found ourselves guested out for meals from its oldest to youngest member.

Once again the contrasts of rich and poor touched old nerves. In Indonesia, hospitality had surfaced even within its cess-pool of open sewage. In Thailand it came in the form of bamboo huts and, in India, like mirages. I had shared their homes, entered their hearts and given them dreams to hang on to. Both guest and host had been touched, but these excesses of luxury foreign residents sometimes enjoyed had no easy answer. In India whenever I dressed like them, it confused and whenever I resisted a bed, insulted. To step down as I saw it was difficult for the transient, so was it right to expect the same from its permanent residents? There were no easy answers and each one had to be balanced against its worth.

Born into faith, our Baptist hosts had little in common with their more militant 'born again' neighbours. Arguments of faith did not intimidate and, when questioned as to their motives, felt no need to excuse them and, because of it, felt no need to judge either. Faith long ago had been absorbed into their blood stream and with it came a strange type of submissiveness, as many of our eccentricities went unquestioned. At first, as with a new toy, they were fascinated by our hidden depths but, within days, our notoriety had cooled and once again we blended in like so much furniture. Now, released from the pressure of being new, I felt strong enough to ask the all important question.

"Can anyone here fix my bike? My derailleur is broken."

"Bring it over to our garage after tea. I'll get Colin to have a look at it."

Colin was the mission's engineer-cum-nurse and his garage housed every nut, bolt and wrench under the sun and, like Gerrard in Australia, he relished the excuse to show off his mechanical skills. Soon his skills were put to work. Cogs were reversed, chain cleaned and bearings oiled.

"How about the derailleur?"

"The gear's arm is not broken, only the spring. There's no tension.

"What can be done?"

A wonder of improvisation unfolded as a treasure chest of bastardized spare parts spilled on to the floor in front of me. "Let's try this." With no beginning and no end to my knowledge I was soon lost to his lecture and before I had time to ask a question, he was finished. "Just one more thing. Can you press that button, Bernard?" Suddenly, the garage was filled with decibels. "Didn't think we had a compressor, did ya? Got everything here. How else do you think I can maintain a fleet of vehicles?" A final blow dry of all moving parts saw Colin standing back to admire his work. Once the bicycle was repaired I could relax and, while Mikey exercised her fingers on the mission's piano's keyboard, I exercised my belly in their kitchens.

"You're not living decently till you get everything all iced up." America's love affair with ice cooled goodies didn't go untried. Iced water, iced tea and ice cream, all were laid before me. Then, at Mikey's insistence we left before my bike collapsed under the extra weight.

News of our departure spread quickly. Presents came flooding in, plus addresses to stay en route and offers of lifts. "You must take advantage of our 'air ferry' postal service before you leave." In a country where land movement is restricted to a crawl, the invitation to have our letters taken by air to Nairobi couldn't be overlooked. We spent our last day writing letters home and, in the evening, we sat back to watch one of nature's spectacular firework displays. Illuminating our back garden of jungle, Nyirangongo's volcanic eruptions fired the distant night sky in clouds of red and amber.

Chapter 31:
Bernie's Waterloo

RUTUSHURU SAW THE BEGINNINGS OF MY WATERLOO. Since Kampala the cutting edge of my "unplanned trip" had been blunted and all recent attempts to sharpen its value fell on deaf ears. I was beginning to sound as romantic as a car repair manual in Mikey's eyes and, just as useful. Forward thrust had lost its steam and commitment, on both side, was dented. Bumps and blemishes that once delighted now only irritated and, although the mission came as a welcome relief, for once my enthusiasm for the road was dulled. Somewhere the purpose of our trans African Safari had got lost. In the mission we had shadow boxed around the subject. Mikey wanted to go back, not yet, but couldn't see herself going past Beni. All news had been bad news. Colin had told us of numerous roadside villages but, once past Komanda, it could be a problem. For my part, turning back meant breaking with tried and tested rules and, although not admitting it to her, I knew that once they were broken there would be no return. Europe was now more than just a distant possibility.

"Got any water, Mikey?"

Suddenly I fell through the sounds of my own words. My throat was as dry as paper, blood drained from the brain and left tingling sensations all over my body.

"Let's stop for the day. You're as white as a sheet."

Booking into the first hotel we saw in Rutushuru I went straight to the toilet. A gush of warm liquid followed bowel movements. It was dysentery and, following a visit to the local dispensary (a wooden shack) it was made official. I was flattened for twenty-four hours, as fluids entering one end discharged within minutes like a leaky cup at the other end. In my weakened state problems which had seemed small, now looked insurmountable and, once into the market of apologies, the cost for accepting blame for getting us into this mess felt rather permanent.

"If the rains catch us before Beni I'll go back to Nairobi." Once agreed, silent pressure was lifted and that night the rhythms of sex took over from fever. Again, pleasure bathed in sweat and once explored locked us together.

The first shafts of dawn woke me. Today marked my thirty-fifth birthday, my fourth on the road. The night was good and over and under my birthday present still warmed to my sex. Today we would sleep in. Above my head was a sketch. Mikey wanted a truce from early morning rises and today I wasn't complaining.

Still not fully recovered, illness had exposed my soft under-belly of health. Long immune, the illness' suddenness had put the brakes on its unquestioned acceptance and for the next few days I put all food through the microscope of hygiene.

The week's first page opened to a kaleidoscope of wild life. Forced into passing through Virunga National Park, a first class piece of advice found us waiting for a lift at the Park's entry barrier. For two hours we baked. There was nothing, no sounds, no movement. Ahead, the plains shimmered and, behind still smudged with eruptions, Nyirangongo volcano rumbled on. Again inactivity frustrated us and just before a foolish decision could be made, help arrived. Flagged down by the park guards, a Belgian farmer was more than helpful. Out went his African workers and, offering no reisistance, they playfully helped us in with our bikes.

"Is it safe for them to walk through the park?"

The Belgian driver smiled at us. "Don't worry. They know what to expect, you do not. The guards were right to stop you. It is not safe to go through the park on bicycles." His words didn't go unnoticed and, within minutes, we knew our wait had not been in vain. Only yards from the road, two lions lay shading themselves under a tree with their kill. "Want a better look?"

Shielded in our host's Land Rover we could now enjoy Africa's wild life without fear. Soon we were witnessing a river playground of mud bathing hippos. Monkeys laughed at us, antelopes ran away from us and rising on to a treeless plateau, a picture postcard view of grazing wildebeast underlined our first view of the Ruwenzoris. At Bwindi Game Lodge we parted company with our lift only to find ourselves marooned and, with memories of lions lying in wait by the roadside still vivid, we waited the next two days for a lift out of the park.

Once outside, we started our steady climb into the Ruwenzoris. Below and to the west, jungle carpeted our vision and to the east mountains of forest greenery fenced in our view. Every bend released a different breeze and with every scent, a thousand perfumes. Blood red spots marked villages, like so many nickle pieces and roadside markets, like explosions of colour. Everywhere Africa's rhythm was in evidence. Town names jangled in my brain, rolled off the tongue, and tap, tap, tapped in one's toes. Alimbongo, Lubero, Butembo. The bo, bo beat bounced down the road in front of us announcing our arrival at every turn. Mud huts offered shelter, concrete missions, relief and bamboo sheds, that special offering of sleep. Every mile was a different challenge; pot holes, boulders, streams over and rivers under. Steep inclines drained and steep declines threatened and, although our daily progress was umbrellaed in ominous cloud formations we saw little rain.

On reaching Butembo I put up no resistance when Mikey stopped. Clothes needed mending, bicycles oiling and a shower was long overdue so, with the sweet smells of jungle grass still fresh on our clothes, we settled back to the fixed routines of hotel life. Again a town market offered abundant food and within their restaurants, the music to help sooth away the rigours of the road.

In Kenya, restaurant's wall paintings illustrated the freedom of its subjects. Painted in brilliant mixtures of primary colours, buxom ladies, men at work and scenes of Mount Kenya brought life to otherwise squalid surroundings and, unlike their more dustfree western counterparts, a surprising warmth. In Uganda the paintings reflected areas of abundant wild life and here, in Zaire, still heavily influenced by the 60's Congo uprising, bloody scenes of injustice shouted out from every wall.

"Hey, look over here Mikey, the circus has arrived." The travelling road show of western gadgetry - the modern big game hunters - had hit town and everywhere a jungle telegraph of excited children announced its presence. Long extinct, Africa's big game hunters now shoot through the eye of lenses. Gone were the days of hired porters, guides and sore feet. Today's new breed was far more mobile. Pioneers of the modern world, "The Overlanders" were children of curiosity. Armed with their faithful American Express and Nikon, on top of converted army transports, they still, like their counterparts of old, searched out the world's most remote areas. Instant MacDonald's could be prepared in the densest of jungles and fresh fruit eaten in the remotest of deserts. Trapped within their own moveable world, life passed them by at roof top level. Now, in Butembo, they'd touched down with an explosion of goodwill.

"Hi, which direction are you going?" A surprised look greeted my question.

"Hey look over here boys and girls."

"Are they for real?"

It was obvious we weren't an intrusion and soon our time was being rationed out equally between the group.

"We're going west to the Cameroons. How did you get here?"

"By bike."

"You came by bike over that road? It was so bumpy my arse feels like two billiard balls."

"Do you know anything about the road ahead?"

"Better ask Jim, he's our driver."

"Who's he?"

"There, the aging hippy. Better wait till he's had a beer. We've been winding him up and watching his arms go round for days."

Leaving Mikey in the company of our new friends, I joined Jim for a drink.

"Kisangani, you want to go to Kisangani." Jim looked every inch the part of a truck driver and with his "Mack Truck" golf cap, no different from my old friends in Ozz. Better buckle up your seat belt mate. The road's bloody awful at the best of times, not been graded for years. It's not that they haven't got the graders, they do, it's just that they haven't got any petrol to run 'em. When it rains the roads are a sea of mud and, if the mud doesn't swallow you up, the pot holes will. Three months ago on our way down we got stuck for five days outside Mambasa. There were over twenty trucks queueing up just to get stuck in the same mud hole. It was crazy. In the end I got the power saw out and made a detour through the jungle but, by bike, it has been done."

"What about places to stay?"

"Rest houses are spread out pretty thinly, from Beni to Kisangani maybe a dozen; past Kisangani, they're almost non-existent.

"How about villages?"

"If you don't mind roughing it. I'd say every fifteen to twenty miles. Food will be a problem though. Most of the roadside villages are dependent on road traffic for trade and food and, when it rains you could get stuck for days waiting for supplies."

Joining him for another beer we were soon swapping travel stories.

"What's it like chauffeuring tourists around for a living?"

"Driving, I do that just to break up the other routines. On these long distance runs you've got to be driver, mechanic, wet nurse, judge, doctor, you name it, I've got a cap to fit it."

"Ever broken down?"

"What, in this tank? The only thing that could stop us is if someone stole the engine and, I'm not joking, it's been tried I tell you give me a booster rocket and I could pilot this beast to Mars."

"Had any problems from the locals."

"Sometimes, you can't blame them. The truck must look like a veritable treasure chest of goodies. When in cities, I posted guards. We all took it in turns. It wasn't the villagers we were bothered about, it was the soldiers. If it wasn't nailed down they took it. It was that bad."

A soft cushion greeted us in Beni. Beginning on entry and ending on exit, we experienced, for the first and last time, one of Zaire's rare luxuries, a paved surface. Now, north of the equator, seasons had changed. Officially we'd passed into the dry season. Every guide book wrote about it, every person Mikey asked, said it. I even staked our whole trip on it. In fact everyone, except the weather, believed it.

Still chasing, threatening clouds banked up in traffic jams above us. Hadn't anyone told them it was the dry season? To the east Uganda lay tantalizingly close and, to the north, Komanda and my dream of west coast travel. We stayed two days. Every minute I played King Canute. Then, on the third day it cleared. "Camaroons here we come."

En route to Komanda our excitement mounted. Skirting the foothills occasional openings gave way to endless horizons. Green piled upon green and low lying mist hung in lazy 'S' shapes over jungle rivers far below. "Take your last look, Mikey. You won't see another horizon like this for a long time." Two hundred feet below Komanda, the road sank into a green sea. There were no scars, no evidence that roads existed. The new skin of jungle had long ago hidden all trace. "Come on, let's go."

200 -150 -100 -50 -20, Like a big dipper we dropped right into the landscape. Above, trees bridged the road, and their leafy tunnel switched off all colour. Temperatures instantly dropped, scents were accentuated and diffused light played in patterns on our prison wall of trees. Every mile the road dropped, rose, twisted and curved at right angles. Our horizon was now only as far as the next bend and that was never too far ahead. Sudden crashes sent out shock waves and, like returning echoes, set off chain reactions of strange filtered noises. I felt stripped. The constant chatter of unseen neighbours unnerved me. I'd not experienced this kind of exposure before and, for the first few hours, I glued myself to Mikey's progress. By midday, road pools had steamed dry and covering these drier areas in moving carpets of brilliant yellow, millions of butterflies sprayed into the air as we approached. Every few hours the jungle opened into a roadside village and, immediately, bathed us with humidity. On our first day, strength was tapped from new experience but, by the third, jungle monotony had set in.

Big as your fist, the first drop exploded with a loud splash. Above, clouds prickled with electricity and, to the south, a black curtain of rain boomed with thunder, even the jungle knew. Alive with noise on starting, for the last hour we'd cycled like intruders through its stillness. Another drop slapped my head and, within minutes, we were cocooned in a waterfall. Sheets of it. Instantly, the road turned into an ice rink of slippery mud. Visibility dropped, pools boiled and instant rivers filled in every dip.

Washed of body heat we were shivering and by the time we were housed under the corrugated roof of a village shelter, we were shaking uncontrollably. Noises came in deafening waves and, as our hosts ran the gauntlet of water for fire, I began the ritual cigarette hand out. Soon the hut was filled with curious eyes and naked flesh was everywhere. A pineapple was offered and while the men made fire we gave ourselves to the children. Out came our stove, tea was made, gifts were exchanged and by the time sunlight forced its way through shadows, we were dry. As suddenly as it started it stopped and within minutes we were lost in a haze of steam. For thirty minutes we had been imprisoned in water and, for another thirty, we waited for it to dry. The rain repeated itself one hour later and getting caught in no mans land, we called it a day at the next village. This pattern repeated itself for the next two days and, on reaching Epulu, the thought of sleeping on a mattress again, begged more than a day's rest.

Heaven for stranded travellers. We found in this small settlement a veritable encyclopaedia of information. Again the same old stories depressed. Collapsed bridges, road wipe-outs and lack of food. Ahead, one hundred and fifty miles of isolation separated us from Kisangani. Then, an invitation came for Mikey.

"Like to visit a Pigmy village?"

She was interested immediately.

"When are we going?"

"Not we, you. A group of travellers have arranged it. They'll be staying overnight. Still game?"

She didn't need the second invitation and, by afternoon, she had made all the arrangements and had left.

No sooner had Mikey left than Waterloo arrived. It started with a cool swim. A sudden chill gripped me, teeth chattered, my legs wobbled and pains soloed round my head. I'd not taken any malaria tablets since Australia and I feared the worst. Once inside, outlines turned into fluid light and, as night fell, I drifted into a painful imitation of sleep. After India, I had so much looked forward to Africa's physical challenge and now I found it breaking me. Rutushuru was a warning I wouldn't admit. I wasn't ready then to make a decision. I wanted it to end on my terms, reach it at my own pace. I knew it was inevitable some day, but now it was staring me in the face.

All night I was racked with pain and when Mikey returned I felt too weak to greet her. Objects still dropped out of focus and the slightest movement sent my body into spasms of pain. For two days I fought it. Then, on the third, I threw in the towel. Every bone in my body ached, every muscle stung. It was time to retire, leave gracefully, go home before it was too late. Malaria had neatly "Xed" out my trip.

Chapter 32:
Back to Reality

F OR ONCE TECHNOLOGY WAS NEVER AROUND WHEN
needed. We had waited in Epulu for days for a lift. False
alarms and breakdowns hounded us and when we eventually got a lift on a truck, it took us two weeks to cover what had
taken us three months by bike. In Nairobi we had decided to
return separately to Europe. Mikey would go to Amsterdam,
family and much needed rest and, for me, it was to be Madrid and
back to reality.

A mix-up of baggage found me stranded in Madrid's International Airport without warm clothing in unseasonable weather.
Spain's not one of the richest countries in Europe, in fact I'd
chosen it as my port of entry for that very reason, but its lack of
airport heating was making my wait a cold one. Three years of
tropical climates had thinned the blood. Hot coffee made little in-
roads then I downed my first glass of wine in three years and soon
its glow led me into the bar's gourmet selection of labels. I had
arrived still with the sweat of travel on my clothes, but it wasn't
long before its imprint was lost to liquid alcohol. and for the next
few hours, I watched scenes I'd not witnessed in years. Where I
had been, people waved their characters about like flags in the air
and the smooth crust of life had only lasted the length of time it
took to chip its surface. I was used to the sounds of life; roars of
laughter, shouts of anger, whistles, cat calls, but most of all the
background of hum of chatter. The picture of life I saw from the
lounge was not the easy 'B' plot movie I was used to. Here people
were sophisticated, civilized and cool. Fashions had changed.
That worn in travel gave way to designer tears and primary
colours so much a part of my everyday life, now paled to the eye.

On the second day of my wait I took a side trip into the city
and, drawn by shop windows, gave myself to their contents like
a child does to candy floss. It was only the realization that my bike
was unlocked in the airport that forced my early return.

Eventually all was corrected. Mis-directed cycle bags were
returned and soon I was cycling through a freak May snow storm.
All thoughts of a slow journey to Heidelberg and Mikey were now

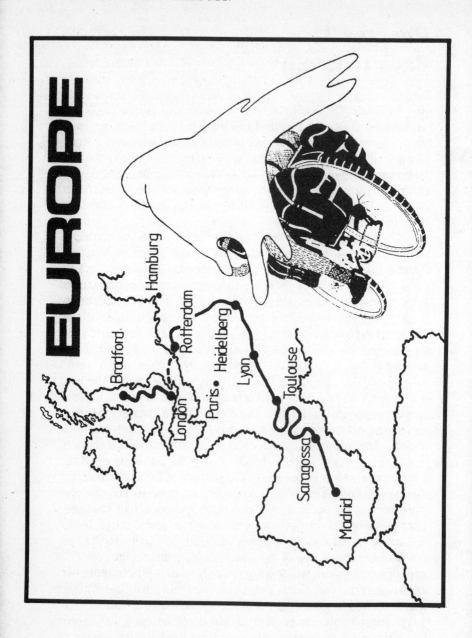

frosted. Deciding on one last burst of energy, I pointed my bike towards the Pyrennes and the quick route to Germany. For three days bad weather forced me into "pensions" then it changed and, under clear skies I found myself sleeping out under the stars. At Barbastro I slept out on a carpet of poppy field and in the Pyrennes I sought out its caves. In France, a wave of euphoria swept me from bar to bedroom, as Liverpool's soccer team beat Madrid on T.V. and, in Germany, breakfast sandwiches, free from an early morning bus passenger, woke me in a village bus shelter. Europe was both in touch and behind its cyclists, as singles, pairs and groups were my constant companions and made for numerous hospitality pit-stops en route to Heidelberg

I was now on a crest of a wave. My return had happened so quickly that, except for the occasional flash back, I did not even think about it. I was still governed by travel's slower pace of life but with few personal contacts so far, could not gauge its difference. To everyone I met, I was a tourist, a visitor to their country and, with the exception of Madrid's airport hustle and bustle, given the same respect and hospitality that I'd experienced in Asia and Africa. Adjustment, I knew, was just around the corner but, for the present, I indulged myself in the last drops of travel experience.

Meeting Mikey in Heidelberg was smashing. Her friends lent us a car and we went sight-seeing. Then a flat above the Necar was offered without payment. Soon I had slipped into the supportive role and while Mikey re-employed herself in nursing, I cooked and cleaned in our new home. For the first weeks I settled myself under Mikey's wing and then inquisitiveness took over and, keen to blood myself in new surroundings, I spent more and more time wandering the streets of Heidelberg. I had to learn new words. "Free range children", "organic food", "the Green People", "muesli" and "market forces". The flavour of the month was changing daily as I spiralled out of four years' of travel and, in the process, tried to condense a new vocabulary into two months.

I now used Heidelberg like a dress rehearsal. For four years I had wiped off the slate of stays within days of moving on. I had made instant relationships, but had lost the art of nourishing them. In Mikey, I now found the parachute needed to touch down on a firm base. I was now saturated with travel experiences and, after three months of readjustment, surrounded by familiar faces, it was a time to reconnect family ties and go home.

My first day in England was lost to nostalgia. Red bricked suburbia soon gave way to hedge bottoms and, rising above lazy hills, church spires overlooked all progress. At dinner time, the smell of fish and chips stained the air. I stopped to buy a milk bottle and a buttered scone and, resting in a village square with the Daily Mirror, followed the pattern of news from back page to front. I passed the time of day with a postman, joked with a baker and, in the evening, reacquainted myself with that uniquely British institution called "the pub". I thirstily downed my first "hand pulled" beer in ten years before booking into a Bed and Breakfast for the night.

The next morning was marked by losing one of my rear bags and when the realization sank in, I was devastated. My whole trip had been ripped out of my hands. If Epulu's illness had broken me physically, then the loss of my rear bag with its four year catalogue of sketches, addresses and cherished gifts had now broken my spirit. Until then I had still harboured thoughts of continuing immediately past my parents back home to Canada, but now those thoughts were gone.

I was now entering Southern Yorkshire's mining country but, strangely, no wheels turned. Large, man made-mountains of slag held no movement. Conveyors frozen in mid air were silenced and dredgers, parked nose to tail, lay idle. Chimneys discharged no smoke, chutes no waste, and my horizon took on an eerie hush. Villages passed through were deserted. Silence had descended where once streets would have been teeming with activity. Shops were shut, pubs closed, then, seeing small pockets of activity, all became clear. Even before I emigrated to Canada I had known that change would have to come. Over-production, high wages and pit head strikes. The pendulum of forces in those days was tilted towards the unions, but now it had swung the other way and, by the look on the miner's faces, with a vengeance. A pit ran through the very vein of a community and that day I witnessed scenes of suicidal fury, not so much against the forces of law, as against its own disintegration. Britain's '84 coal strike was at its peak.

That day I could have made it home, but didn't. I wanted to let the Pit Head scenes mellow but, mostly, I wanted to give my parents time to prepare. My mum would want to make her son some Yorkshire pudding and my dad would never forgive himself if he wasn't at home when I arrived. They had carried me through some rough times without even knowing and demanded the respect of a phone call. On the road, whenever I remembered them, they had seemed like an oasis in my memory. In four years old friends had lapsed and new friends had taken their place, but in the background, always constant and as steady as a rock were my parents.

I got up from the bar stool and went over to the telephone. I didn't know what I'd say, but I knew it didn't matter.

"Hello.........Mum............Dad..........I'm back!"

Chapter 33:
Was It Just a Dream

I WAS BACK IN ENGLAND ALL RIGHT. IT WAS LIKE A BATTLE ground I'd left a long time ago. The rules were still the same but time had altered the goal posts. My friends had welcomed me back and, briefly, I'd basked in their excitement. As long as I was with them I felt like somebody. Alone, I was lost. Outside close friends, communication was almost impossible. I had no hook to hang my cap on. I constantly found myself stepping into other peoples roles just to blend in. With escape cut off, distances crept in, and constant flash backs haunted me.

Four walls melted into brilliant sunsets. Noises of children playing turned into colourful bazaar scenes. A car backfired and, instantly, I was back in Kampala. I sat for hours recounting cities visited. Sydney, Bangkok, Calcutta, Nairobi... This mantra of names had altered my horizons and, with it, my life style. Writing now became my analyst's couch and , through it, my stepping stone back to reality. Now, four years on, the book is published. New friends have been made but old ones, not forgotten.

Janet has exchanged the sedate school life for Auckland's fast lane and Ully, Dar Le Salem for Lamu. Alison is still spreading the word in India but motherhood has tempered its message. Roy and Merlin are resting up on Devil's Island, and Roland could be resting up anywhere. Teddy still enjoys life but sadly Ajit was killed by it. Mikey still visits. Tom is still Tom. And, last but not least, yours truly finally got back home to Toronto.

Did my trip end in England or was it in Canada? For me, it ended when my mother and father burst into tears. I knew, at that moment, I owed them more than just a visit. My trip would have to be put on hold. Maybe the reader feels cheated. After all 'round the world cyclists' should end at the beginning but, then, I didn't plan this trip. It started out as a two month vacation and stretched into an eight year odyssey. For me, it filled a vacuum. I tripped up and fell into it. I still occasionally look over my shoulder at the past, but that's where it is. Yesterday, I was news. Today, only history.

To all friends,
absent but not forgotten.
Take Care,
Love, Bernie

J UST TO PROVE TO MYSELF THAT HISTORY CANNOT BE put away easily. I would like to take this opportunity to bring the reader up to the present. As you may have guessed. My funds ran out in England long before my return to Canada. Then a chance meeting with an old friend rescued me. An invite to my old school followed. A thirty minute slide presentation based on my travels stretched into a full day visit and by the end of the week I had two more bookings. "Bernie the Bike Man's Travelling Road Show" was born.

Fairweather Middle School, Bradford, England

Reprinted below is a review of my presentation to schools published in the TIMES Educational Supplement, England, September 9, 1988, by Angela Neustatter.

The picture projected on the wall of the assembly hall shows a small child having his head examined for nits. Bernard Howgate, conducting this afternoon's slide show and talk, demonstrates by scratching at his bush of unruly hair, how he, too, looked for nits when travelling through Asia. "Suddenly I found this little thing moving. I grabbed it

(top & bottom) Fairweather Middle School — Slide Presentation

wi'me fingers, took a look and popped it in me mouth

There is a gasp of amazement, shrieks of "ugggh" from the children. A broad grin spreads across Bernard's face. "Just joking. I wanted to see if you were still awake!" to grade 6 students"

The picture is replaced with a shot of plates loaded with Indian food: chapatis, rice and vegetables, samosas, spicy snacks and this time there is a cocophany of eating sounds from the audience. "Who knows the name of these foods ? Who knows how they are made ? How many of you have tried them ?" Hands shoot up, answers are fielded, then he's off again.

He is an improbable person to find on the menu in schools. A former design draftsman, has no formal teaching qualifications and admits to having to have "avoided education at school" but he is strikingly informed and informative with the material he delivers to children and his school programs have been constructed around the idea that children should be able to follow up what he shows with work of their own.

His style is more music hall entertainer than pedagogue, an impression added to by the stream of conscious presentation, delivered in his raw northern accent, the immaculate constructed hippie look - shoulder-length hair style circa 1965, a Viva Zapata moustache, careless clothes - and the much-travelled bicycle which he takes with him as a prop. It is a style which keeps some 150 young children rapt for two hours and which has pleased enough schools for him to be invited back, while his engagement book has been more or less full for the past two years.

"My next planned trip. Trans Canada Bicycle Rickshaw Ride. From Vancouver, British Columbia to St John's, Newfoundland. May/October 1990."